Employee
Ownership
in
America

Employee Ownership in America

The Equity Solution

Corey M. Rosen, Katherine J. Klein,
AND
Karen M. Young

Lexington Books

D.C. Heath and Company/Lexington, Massachusetts/Toronto

Library of Congress Cataloging in Publication Data

Rosen, Corey M.
Employee ownership in America.

    (The Issues in organization and management series)
    Includes bibliographies and index.
    1. Employee ownership—United States. I. Klein, Katherine J.
II. Young, Karen M., 1942– III. Title.
HD5660.U5R67   1985   338.6   85–40000
ISBN 0-669-10307-1 (alk. paper)

Published simultaneously in Canada
Printed in the United States of America
International Standard Book Number: 0-669-10307-1
Library of Congress Catalog Card Number: 85-40000

The paper used in this publication meets the minimum requirements of
American National Standard for Information Sciences—Permanence
of Paper for Printed Library Materials, ANSI Z39.48-1984.
∞TM

Contents

Tables and Figure

Tables

Figure

Acknowledgments

W e began this project in 1980 as the first study of the National Center for Employee Ownership. In 1982, we were fortunate to receive a three year grant from the National Institute for Mental Health to carry it out. That grant provided most of the funding for the study, and we are most grateful for their support. In particular, Richard Wakefield and Elliot Liebow were very helpful in guiding us through the grant application process and in helping us focus the scope of our proposal.

Throughout this process, we have benefitted greatly from the support and advice of many people. Joseph Blasi of Harvard University has provided invaluable feedback and encouragement to us since 1978, when he and Corey Rosen met in Washington. Doug Jenkins gave us important assistance in developing our research methodology. William Foote Whyte of Cornell has been an inspiration as a model of a researcher whose work is both scholarly and practical. He has been a much valued source of ideas and useful criticism. Both Professor Blasi and Professor Whyte commented on earlier versions of this manuscript. Professors Michael Conte, Raymond Russell, Art Hochner, and Ramona Ford also gave the manuscript careful and thoughtful readings, and made very useful suggestions. Lisa Gilman, Michael Quarrey, Tod Nugent, and Alan Cohen of the Center's staff provided input into the manuscript, as did Gil Phillips of Phillips Paper Company and Janice Rouiller of the University of Maryland. The comments of all of these people added much to the book. Bruce Katz, Martha Cleary, and Kathryn Geiger of Lexington Books provided valuable editorial assistance and much appreciated encouragement, as did Benjamin Schneider and Arthur P. Brief, editors of this book series.

As this project grew, the National Center grew, and the two were so entwined that we must also thank the many, many people who supported us. They are far too numerous to mention, but we are deeply indebted to them all. Working with the many dedicated, committed people involved in employee ownership has been a great joy.

Several students and faculty members performed case studies included in this book or used in the pre-testing phase. Ramona Ford did four case studies, and was assisted in the Phillips Paper study by Keith Kirkpatrick. Andy Lisak did four case studies. Others doing studies included Megan Campbell, Michael Caudell-Feagan, Jane Delgado, David Mead Fox, Nives Friedman, Ray Kirshak, Doug Kruse, John Lickerman, Shareef Mahdavi, Pamela McCarty, Allison Reed, Scott Sawyer, Sergio Storch, Virginia Simmons, David Toscano, and Bryan Wilson.

Finally, we must thank the people without whom there would be no study—the people who answered all the questions. Each of these case studies required a substantial amount of company time, and we are most grateful for all the cooperation we received.

Researching and writing this book has been a most interesting and rewarding experience, thanks, in large part, to all these people.

1
Introduction
Mr. Smith, Meet Mr. Marx

An interesting thing happened to airline commercials in 1984. Between watching players dunk basketballs, viewers saw a lonely mechanic checking an airplane in the rain and dark. A somber announcer noted that there was a name for people who did what needed to be done, regardless of the weather, time, or job definition. "They're called owners," he said. The ad was for People Express, the fastest-growing airline in history, and a company 33% owned by its "managers" (all employees are called managers).

Not to be outdone, Eastern Airlines aired ads introduced by employees saying "Hi, I'm one of the new owners of Eastern Airline." Western countered with full page newspaper ads saying that its employees owned more (one-third) of the company than employees at any other major airline.

What was going on here? Had Karl Marx infiltrated Madison Avenue? Hardly. The airline industry was undergoing a transformation that over 8,000 other firms in the United States, with 7–8% of the workforce, had, in the last decade, undergone as well. For a variety of reasons, these companies decided to share ownership with employees. In some cases, probably 10–15%, employees actually own a majority of the stock; in some, they own very little; in most they own somewhere between 15% and 40%. While many plans provide only several hundred dollars of stock to employees, a number of firms are spreading around a great deal of wealth. One company, Lowe's Inc., has already created 50 millionaires.

While employee ownership has not yet revolutionized the economy, it has, in a relatively short time, gained a secure legitimacy as a good way to do business. It has been endorsed by everyone from Paul Volcker to Tom Hayden, from the New York Stock Exchange to the Teamsters, from Ted Kennedy to Ronald Reagan, and from the Pope to the Chamber of Commerce. Since 1974, Congress has passed 16 laws to encourage employee ownership, while 13 states have passed 16 laws to do the same.

At the same time, employee ownership has been demonstrating that it deserves these endorsements. A 1978 study by Michael Conte and Arnold Tannenbaum of the University of Michigan's Survey Research Center, for instance, found that employee ownership companies were 1.5 times as profitable as comparable conventional firms.[1] A 1980 study reported in the *Journal of Corporation Law* found that employee-owned companies with employee stock ownership plans (ESOPs) had twice the average annual productivity growth rate of comparable conventional firms.[2] A 1983 study by the National Center for Employee Ownership (NCEO) reported that firms in which a majority of the employees owned a majority of the stock generated three times more net new jobs per year than comparable conventional firms.[3] Another NCEO study, performed in 1984 for the New York Stock Exchange, found that publicly traded companies at least 10% owned by their employees outperformed 62–75% of their competitors on various measures of company performance.[4] A 1983 McKinsey and Company study found that one of the characteristics of the fastest-growing mid-sized companies was a relatively broad distribution of ownership,[5] while a 1984 book entitled *The 100 Best Companies in America to Work For* identified employee ownership as one of the more common characteristics of these firms.[6]

These studies are only preliminary, of course, and one current study still in progress has found that employee ownership firms are neither more nor less profitable than their conventional counterparts, although it has found that they tend to stay in business longer.[7] Moreover, none of the studies has really established causality: if employee ownership really is positively related to corporate performance, is it because ownership causes companies to do better, or is it because better companies establish employee ownership plans?

There may be no way to disentangle this causal link. Nonetheless, the studies have fueled the belief that employee ownership does enhance corporate competitiveness, a belief supported by what seems the common sense notion that employee owners will be better employees. It is, after all, more interesting to mow your own lawn than your neighbor's lawn.

This reputation (deserved or not) for performance has been coupled with generous tax incentives for companies to share ownership. Companies can print new issues of their own stock and contribute it to ownership plans, deducting the value of the contribution. Business owners can sell to employee ownership plans and defer taxes on the capital gains they make in the process. Companies can borrow money through ESOPs and repay the loan in pre-tax dollars. Because banks can deduct 50% of the interest income they receive from such loans, companies borrowing through ESOPs thus can often negotiate lower rates of interest. These and other tax incentives (the most important of which passed in 1984) have made employee ownership very financially attractive, aside from any employee motivation benefits it may have. Although the specifics of these laws may change, Congress is likely to encourage employee ownership plans.

All of this has helped the idea make inroads into hundreds of leading U.S. firms, as well as thousands of smaller ones. For instance:

Publix Supermarkets, Florida's largest chain, is 100% employee owned.

Much of the airline industry is now significantly employee owned, including Eastern (25%), Western (15%), People Express (33%), America West (20%), Southwest (13%), PSA (15%), Republic (15%), Pan Am (13%) and many other smaller carriers.

The Parsons Company, one of the nation's largest and most successful construction and engineering firms, is 100% employee owned.

U.S. Sugar, the nation's largest sugar processor, is 43% employee owned.

Several major trucking companies, including Roadway (16%), Transcon (57%), and CL Motor Freight (51%), are significantly employee owned.

Workers own 100% of Davey Tree, one of the nation's largest tree service companies.

Employees have majority ownership in dozens of high-tech firms, including Science Applications (4,000 employees) and W.L. Gore Associates (3,000).

In retail, Pamida, a 5,000-employee discount chain, is 100% employee owned, as is Otasco, an auto parts hardware chain with 3,300 employees, while Lowe's Inc., the largest retailer of lumber and home-improvement supplies, is 30% employee owned and plans to be 51% or more.

In manufacturing, Weirton Steel (8,000 employees), the nation's most profitable integrated steel maker, and Hyatt-Clark Industries, a 1,500-employee bearing manufacturer, are both 100% employee owned.

These and other employee ownership companies have set up their plans for many reasons. Most of them are ESOPs. Chapter 2 will explain ESOPs and other employee ownership plans in detail. Essentially, in an ESOP, a company sets up a trust fund and contributes cash to it so that it can buy company stock, or simply contributes stock. The shares are allocated to accounts for individual employees, who acquire an increasing right to these allocations through a process known as vesting. They receive their vested shares when they leave the company or retire. Employees rarely buy the stock themselves, or take wage concessions in return for it. ESOPs allow for varying degrees of employee input into job and management level decisions, and provide widely varying degrees of ownership. Our research suggests that about 40% of the ESOP companies put in their plans solely for the tax benefits they provide; most of the rest have a mixture of tax, philosophical, and employee-relations motivations. Almost all the plans are set up in profitable companies. Although employee ownership can be and is used to save failing companies, this is, in fact, a rare use.

There are other forms of employee ownership as well. In worker cooperatives, 100% worker-owned companies, only workers can be owners and all owners have an equal vote. Coops tend to be smaller and more ideologically motivated than other employee ownership companies. Some firms choose neither the coop nor the ESOP route, but instead require all employees to buy a minimum number of shares at a discounted price. Still other firms have more idiosyncratic arrangements, such as one firm where the owner simply gave half his stock to employees, or others where all employees have stock options (options to buy shares of stock at a fixed price even if the stock goes up in value).

Employee ownership has significance beyond what it does or why it is instituted at individual companies, however. To its advocates, it also provides a mechanism to tie social justice to the free enterprise system. For most of our history, indeed most of the history of industrialized nations, a central policy dilemma has been the apparent conflict between promoting equity and stimulating economic growth. On the one hand, growth demands greater investment by those who have the capital to invest. In capitalist countries, this means making the already rich richer. Murray Weidenbaum, former chairman of the Council of Economic Advisors under Ronald Reagan, said on a 1984 National Public Radio "All Things Considered" program that the Reagan Administration consciously chose "growth over equity." Democrats, he said, choose equity, but this means taking capital away from the wealthy, thus depressing investment and economic recovery. As Winston Churchill put the dilemma, "the problem with capitalism is that not everyone shares in its beneficence; the problem with socialism is that everyone shares in its misery."

The same debate resurfaces in labor-management relations. Except in cases of extreme distress, labor generally sees its goal as getting as big a share as it can for its workers, regardless of the long-term costs that may be imposed on their companies. After all, they reason, management has a short-term perspective as well, and there are no guarantees that labor savings will be used to enhance competitiveness. Indeed, they might just be used to add to shareholder dividends, increase management bonuses, or acquire other companies. Management, for its part, often sees labor demands for equity as almost inherently short-sighted and selfish, and thus to be resisted per se. They see their principal obligation as increasing the wealth of their shareholders, shareholders who often are more concerned with short-term returns than long-range competitiveness.

But, we would contend, there is another way. By making employees owners, programs that enhance capital investment automatically enrich workers. At the same time, employee owners need not think of their income solely in terms of short-term wages. If they defer short-term income in *their* company, and the company's value and profits increase, then *they* are the shareholders being enriched. When they leave the company, their shareholdings can be used to start their own businesses, educate their children, invest in other companies, or otherwise stimulate the economy. That broader distribution of wealth can help create a much more dynamic economy, one that is a far cry from today's distribution. The last time such figures were calculated, 50% of the privately owned wealth in the U.S. belonged to just 1% of the population.[8] Lester Thurow highlighted this situation recently when he pointed out that the *Forbes* magazine list of the wealthiest 400 families in the U.S. could, if they just borrowed an amount equal to their wealth, control 40% of U.S. business capital.[9] Aside from how one might feel about the equity of this, such concentration of capital means that there are relatively few people with the resources to create or invest in the new and growing businesses that keep the economy vibrant. As Russell Long, the chief promoter of employee ownership in Congress, has put it, "the problem with capitalism is that there aren't enough capitalists."[10] Or, to quote Ronald Reagan, "Our Founding Fathers well understood that concentrated power is the enemy of liberty . . . Since in any society social and political power flow from economic power, they saw that wealth and property would have to be widely distributed."[11] Reagan went on to endorse the work of Russell Long to promote employee ownership.

In this book, we examine the employee ownership phenomenon, and whether it is living up to the high expectations of its promoters. In the first two chapters, we will review how employee ownership plans operate, the different ways in which they are used, and what previous research tells us about their impact on company performance and employee attitudes. From there, we will move to the central focus of this book, an in-depth analysis of how employee ownership has worked in the over 50 companies in which we have performed case studies over the last three years. While we would unabashedly make the case that employee ownership has the potential to create a much more successful workplace and ecomomic system, we are all too well aware that employee ownership often falls short of the potential. Employees do not always act or think like owners, nor do managers always treat them that way. Employee ownership companies are not always more satisfying or rewarding places to work, nor are they always more economically successful. By contrast, many companies, and their workers, thrive under employee ownership.

What distinguishes the winners from the losers? It is an intriguing question to us, in two senses. First, it is intriguing from an academic point of view. What sorts of workplace reforms really work? Is it money, recognition, the ability to participate in decisions, or something else that really motivates people? While our analysis focuses on employee ownership companies, its implications are broader, for employee ownership can encompass a variety of workplace reform issues.

There is, however, a very practical element to our inquiry as well. Employee ownership is growing very rapidly, perhaps even too rapidly. There are few guidelines to tell managers and workers how to get the most out of their efforts. There is a danger here that a lot of well-meaning effort will be wasted, and that a promising idea will be scrapped because it was misused. Our findings, we believe, can help avoid these problems.

Methodology

Our study has been designed to meet rigorous academic standards, yet provide practical information as well. It was largely funded by a grant from the National Institute of Mental Health's Center for Work and Mental Health. The data are now being shared with independent scholars, who will further explore this phenomenon. Although we frankly want to see employee ownership grow, our firm commitment was to produce a very objective study, for only such a study can provide the reliable guidelines that will make employee ownership work.

Our strategy was straightforward. A detailed explanation of the methodology can be found in chapter 4. Basically, however, we designed a detailed survey for employees, covering everything from job satisfaction to perceived levels of participation in the firm, to attitudes towards being an owner. A copy of the survey is in the appendices. Our assumption was that if ownership is to improve corporate performance at any level—productivity, profits, company longevity— it must first work at the employee-attitude level. Moreover, a positive change in these attitudes is itself an important outcome, especially for the employees. We also addressed the issue of how successful ownership is in building capital estates for workers. Our data here are necessarily preliminary, however, since we did not have access to the detailed records needed for such an analysis. Fortunately, the U.S. General Accounting Office will soon report a thorough study of this question.

We also conducted a lengthy interview with a company official, generally the chief executive officer, at each of the companies studied. The interview was designed to determine how the company has performed, how much stock employees own, and the like. We did not do an analysis of productivity or profitability, however. There were two major reasons for this. First, especially in closely held businesses (companies not traded on a stock exchange), companies are often reluctant to divulge these data or, in the case of productivity, do not gather it. Even where we have usable numbers, however, differences in accounting systems (and changes within companies) make "profits" a very slippery term. Many executives, in fact, warned us that their "profits" were inaccurate indicators, and that many closely held companies work hard *not* to report a profit. Second, the General Accounting Office is now engaged in a study of the financial issues surrounding employee ownership, and has access to corporate tax returns to do the study. That will uniquely give them the kind of data required to do a proper analysis.

We have looked, however, at other performance measures, especially employment and sales growth, as useful indicators of economic success. From the public's standpoint, in fact, we believe employment growth is the most basic performance measure. After all, the ultimate social benefit of profits and productivity is the creation of good jobs.

Our studies were based on a distinctly non-random sample, technically called a "quota" sample. Our goal was not to get a representative group of firms, but to include enough different kinds of companies so that we could assess how varying ownership approaches work. We wanted companies that allow employees a great deal of say in management and companies that offer very little; companies in which employees own most of the stock or only a small percentage; companies where there appears to be a "culture of ownership" and companies where employee ownership is just a benefit plan.

We wanted firms of varying sizes, industries, and regions; firms whose plans were initiated by retiring owners, by existing mangers, and even in response to plant closings (contrary to popular impression, just 1% of all employee ownership cases).

Of the companies we approached, almost half agreed to be studied. Since we suspect more troubled firms were more likely to say "no," we cannot say our firms represent employee ownership generally, but we can say that the relationships we find within our sample between companies (for example, that companies that contribute more stock each year do better than those which contribute less) should hold for all employee ownership cases.

Most of the studies were performed by Katherine Klein. Others were done by other Center staffers, graduate students, and faculty members. Altogether, over 3,700 employees were surveyed. All of the studies were completed between 1982 and 1984. It should be remembered that there was a recession in the United States for most of this time, a factor that will be important in certain aspects of the study, but which we do not believe in any way alters our basic findings.

Results

To understand fully the results we report in this book, it is necessary first to understand how employee ownership plans work, a task addressed in the next chapter. Our basic findings, however, can be outlined here. By far the most important factor in explaining differences in employee attitudes towards ownership is how much stock they receive each year. Employees seem to react to ownership primarily in financial terms. The more their ownership accounts grow each year, the more they like being owners and the more committed they are as employees. In part, this may be a purely financial linkage but, we suspect, it is also an affirmation of the entrepeneurial instinct in many people. They like being owners, and the more stock they have, the more they feel like owners. It is satisfying, in other words, to be able to say, "I have a big stake in this company."

This finding contradicts some of the earlier work in this area which suggested that the ability of employees to control management-level decisions was the key factor in explaining the success or failure of employee ownership. These early studies, however, looked exclusively at companies which employees bought to keep from closing. Moreover, only a handful of companies were studied. In our work, we have looked at more typical employee ownership plans, in which ownership is almost always a contribution from management to employees in addition to their other compensation. Most of these companies are financially healthy, and many of the plans have the potential to provide significant monetary benefits. It seems reasonable that employees in companies in which things are going well financially would place less value on the need to participate in company decision-making than employees in more threatened firms.

There are, however, some cases in which employees do place a high value on control. In cooperatives, for instance, employees explicitly join for that reason. As suggested, it may be that in buyouts or concession arrangements employees want to be sure to protect their investment, or may be more than normally suspicious of management, although we do not have enough buyout cases to prove this point. Moreover, participation opportunities at the job level do seem important in most firms, albeit not as important as financial rewards. Finally, regardless of the impact of allowing employees a say in management on their attitudes towards being owners or towards their company, such a policy can open an important line of communication between workers and managers. Managers of more democratic firms, in fact, are unanimous in saying this input contributes to the company's bottom line.

Company culture also seems to matter. In many of the cases here, managers believe employees *deserve* to be owners. They do not see ownership as a benevolent bestowal on the part of enlightened leaders, but rather as a logical component of good management. This attitude manifests itself in many ways. The company president who walks the floor sincerely seeking employee ideas, the abolition of special management perquisites such as closer parking and separate lunchrooms, and the practice of calling all employees "associates" or "managers" are among the many ways management conveys a feeling that employees are more equals and less hired help.

In fact, overall, it is fair to say that the best plans are the ones that provide constant reinforcement of the ownership idea. Employees receive regular, substantial stock contributions, have participation opportunities on the job, are treated as owners by managers and supervisors, understand how their plans work, and are frequently and effectively reminded of their ownership stake in the firm. Ownership becomes a constantly renewed process, rather than a discrete event that happens once a year when employees receive an account update.

2

How Employee
Ownership Plans Work

The task of the employee ownership writer, and the reader, would be be far simpler if all employee ownership plans followed the intuitive notion that employees just bought stock in their own company. Unfortunately, that almost always isn't the way it works. There are a number of different approaches, each of which has its own complications. The most common form of employee ownership, the ESOP, is the most complicated of all. It is complicated because Congress, in providing special incentives for ESOPs, had to balance public, employee, and employer interests. Understanding these plans, however, is essential to understanding employee ownership.

This chapter will explore how employee ownership plans work, who uses them, why they are used, and how they are structured.

A Definition

At first blush, it seems obvious what employee ownership is and is not. But the term is more ambiguous than it may seem. While everyone would acknowledge that a company in which every employee owns stock and votes for the members of the board of directors is employee owned, agreement is harder to find on other situations. What about a company where only white-collar employees own stock? Or one where most employees only own a few hundred dollars' worth each? Or one where most employees own some stock, but cannot vote their stock or sell it until they retire or leave the company?

In fact, various people have called all these situations employee ownership; others have insisted only the pure case qualifies. There is no obviously right universal definition. At the National Center for Employee Ownership, we define employee ownership as a plan in which most of a company's employees own at least some stock in their company, even if they cannot vote it, and even if they cannot sell it till they leave the company or retire. This definition excludes companies where only managers own stock (as is common in stock option arrangements) or only a minority of employees buy stock (as is common in thrift plans). Its breadth, however, lets us cover a broad range of cases, creating subcategories of different kinds of employee ownership firms.

A Brief History

Broad as our definition is, however, it does not trivialize the issue. The notion that most of a company's employees are at least part-owners of their firms is, if not exactly new, certainly outside the mainstream of U.S. economic thinking. While there have been periodic waves of interest in employee ownership, except for a brief period in the 1920s, it is only in the last decade that the idea has received wide credibility, attention, research, and use.[1]

The current wave of interest can be traced back to the work of Louis Kelso in the 1950s.[2] Kelso, a San Francisco investment banker, argued that everyone should own productive capital, ultimately building a personal capital estate. Not only would this be more equitable, he contended, but it would build support for a capitalist system. Growth and equity could become mutually supportive policies, not, as they generally have been, opposite ends of a partisan seesaw. The best way to accomplish this goal, he wrote, was to create a mechanism whereby corporate finance would automatically make workers into owners. Kelso called his plan to do this an "ESOP" (employee stock ownership plan), something we will explain later.

For over a decade, Kelso tried to convince companies to use his plan, arguing that they could improve productivity and get tax breaks to boot. While Kelso did win a few converts, even companies who knew of and liked the idea were concerned that the courts would rule it improper and void the tax benefits Kelso claimed for it. In 1973, therefore, Kelso arranged a meeting with Senator Russell Long, chairman of the Senate's tax-writing committee. Long was convinced. After all, his father, Huey Long, had become governor of Louisiana and a U.S. Senator proclaiming "every man a king"— and proposing an income redistribution plan to make that slogan a reality. Kelso's plan, however, didn't simply redistribute current wealth. Instead, it sought also to expand the economic pie by providing greater incentives to workers, while financing newly created wealth through employee ownership plans. Employees would thus own the new wealth they created. It was, Long would say later, "Huey Long without the Robin Hood."

Long was arguably the most powerful member of Congress, and he used that power to create a series of tax incentives for employee ownership that have been the primary catalyst for the concept's growth. Long essentially made it clear that the ESOP did qualify for the tax benefits Kelso touted, then added several more to it. In 1974, when Long started, there were only about 300 ESOPs. As of 1984, there were over 7,000, plus a couple of thousand other plans. Over 10,000,000 employees were covered. Put simply, Long made it in the economic self-interest of owners to share ownership.

But tax breaks are not the only explanation for the growth of employee ownership. By the late 1970s, it had become increasingly apparent that U.S. firms needed to be as productive and efficient as possible if they were to survive in a much more competitive world marketplace. At the same time, a more educated workforce was demanding more from work than just a paycheck. Companies were finding that if they could integrate employees more effectively into the firm, they could both improve productivity and meet the demands of their workers. This effort took several forms—quality of worklife programs, employee involvement teams, and gainsharing among them. Similarly, the adversarial relationship between labor and management was increasingly sending both to unemployment lines. New ways were needed to join the two interests together in a manner both fair and effective. The studies described earlier indicated that employee ownership could be one of the best ways to do this.

At the same time, a number of companies or plants were closing, while others needed major employee concessions to stay in business. In a number of cases, employees were able to buy their firms outright and keep them open, or were willing to make concessions in return for an ownership position in the firm. Although these cases, contrary to popular impression, account for only about 2% of all employee ownership companies, they have attracted wide attention to the idea. Since they have also generally been successful, they have increased the credibility of the claim that employee ownership counts on the bottom line.

Finally, the late 1960s and early 1970s produced a number of people not content with traditional values. Some of these people were eager to explore ways to make a living that would be consistent with their beliefs. The notion of a worker cooperative was naturally appealing. Here all employees could share in decision-making and profits, creating a kind of alternative work community. While worker coops tend to be very different from the mainstream businesses that set up ESOPs, they are linked in a common belief that broader ownership is a good idea.

The Employee Ownership Landscape

To say the least, the phenomenon that has resulted from these various motives is a diverse one. It is also one for which descriptive data are spotty. To the best of our knowledge, however, there are about 7,000 ESOPs, about 10–15% of which are majority employee owned.[3] The average ESOP firm is larger than the average U.S. company, since few ESOP firms have under 10–15 employees (due to high ESOP legal costs): 10–20% of ESOPs appear to be in very large firms and typically transfer only small amounts of stock to employees; the rest average about 15–40% of stock owned by the ESOP. In a typical ESOP employees receive an amount equivalent to 5–15% of their payroll in stock. How much this will ultimately mean will obviously depend on how well the stock does, how much stock is "forfeited" (returned to the trust because it is not vested), how much the employee makes, and how long the employee stays with the company. If an employee receives 10% per year in stock, makes $20,000 per year, works for 20 years, and the stock increases at 10% per year, the employee would leave with $114,500. Employees vote their stock on all issues in 25–30% of all ESOPs; in most of the remainder they vote only on certain limited issues required by law. Where employees do not vote their stock, it is voted by a management-appointed trustee. In majority employee-owned ESOPs, however, almost half the plans do provide full voting rights.[4]

There also appear to be about 800 worker cooperatives, although estimates here are necessarily shaky. Most are very small and often are in "alternative" businesses, such as health food stores, bookstores, natural food restaurants, and the like. An unknown number of companies have other ownership arrangements, ranging from requiring everyone to buy stock at a discount (such as at People Express) to profit-sharing plans that use earnings to buy company stock as well as other investments (such as at Hallmark Cards).

How ESOPs Work

ESOPs are the most common form of employee ownership. ESOPs are found only in incorporated businesses (not partnerships or proprietorships). These businesses all have stock representing a paper equivalent of the value of the company. In publicly held firms—those listed on a stock exchange—anyone can buy the company's stock. In "closely held" firms (most companies), stock ownership is restricted, often to an individual, family, or a few key managers. What we describe here applies to ESOP law as of the fall of 1985. Tax reform proposals could change how ESOPs work and the benefits they receive, but the basic concept will remain.

In an ESOP, the company sets up a special trust, somewhat like an internal bank. It then either contributes cash to buy stock from existing owners, or contributes shares of its own stock. That stock can either be stock it simply prints (this is like the government printing more money —it means people with existing shares suffer a "dilution" in their ownership, much like inflation dilutes the value of a dollar) or stock it has issued before, but which has not been purchased by anyone.

Within limits, the value of these contributions are tax-deductible from the company's income. Since most companies pay 46% of their profits in federal taxes on profits over $100,000, every dollar deducted from taxable income is worth 46 cents to the company (although this could be lower if tax reform is enacted). Stock held in the trust is allocated to accounts for individual employees, either on the basis of relative compensation (if you make $40,000 and I make

$20,000, you get twice as much) or some formula more favorable to lower-paid employees. Many companies, for instance, give some credit for seniority. Generally, all full-time employees over 21 with one year's service or more must be eligible to participate in the plan. There are some exceptions, however. The most significant of these is that employees covered by a collective bargaining agreement (union workers) can be excluded, provided that employers agree to bargain in good faith on the issue if the union desires.

The stock stays in the trust until the employee leaves the company or retires. Workers acquire a gradually increasing right to the stock in their accounts as they accumulate seniority, a process known as "vesting." Generally, vesting starts after two to three years at 20–30% and increases gradually to 100% over ten years. In other words, a worker could leave with 30% of whatever is in the account after three years; 100% after ten. Non-vested stock is returned to the trust and reallocated to everyone else. In publicly traded companies, employees must be able to vote the shares allocated to them; in privately held companies, they must be allowed to vote on a limited number of major issues, although about 15% of the privately held firms pass through full voting rights anyway. On issues where employees do not vote their stock, it is voted by a management-appointed ESOP trustee.

When employees receive their shares, they can hold onto them, sell them to another buyer (but the company has a right of first refusal), or require the company to repurchase them at the fair market price. While the shares are in the trust, the employees pay no tax on them; when they are distributed, the employee has a number of ways to minimize the tax. In closely held companies, the value of the stock is determined by an outside appraiser; in publicly traded firms, it is determined by the stock market.

How Companies Use ESOPs

ESOPs have several uses. They can be used as an employee benefit plan, as a means to buy stock from an existing owner, as a technique for borrowing money less expensively, as part of an effort to integrate employees into the company, as a way to save failing firms, and as a tax-favored approach to acquiring or divesting subsidiaries or whole companies. Each is explored below.

As an Employee Benefit Plan

Many companies want to provide employees with an additional benefit, but are not in a position to spend cash to provide it. Others may be in a better cash position, but simply would like employees to share in ownership. An ESOP provides a tax-favored means to do this.

Normally, a company would issue new shares of its own stock to an ESOP; they would then be allocated to individual employees. These contributions are tax-deductible for the full market value of the stock for up to 25% of the payroll of ESOP participants. The contribution, therefore, generates a tax deduction for the company, even though no cash has been spent. There are two drawbacks, though. First, in closely held companies, the firm must buy back the shares of departing employees, thus creating a cash liability later on. This "repurchase liability" exists for all ESOPs in closely held companies and requires careful planning to avoid sudden runs on corporate cash. Second, the ESOP causes a dilution in the holdings of existing owners. Presumably, the financial benefits of an ESOP should outweigh the costs to shareholders, although this may not always be the case. To the extent that participants in the ESOP receive voting rights, however, the ability of shareholders to control their company may be weakened, especially in publicly traded companies where even relatively small blocks of stock can, if voted as a block, exert significant influence. Of course, in closely held companies where employees own less than a majority of the shares, the voting issue is mostly symbolic.

While these considerations can be important, the ability to use an ESOP as a very tax-favored means to provide a meaningful employee benefit plan has made it very attractive to an increasing number of companies. The Lowe's Companies is a good example. Lowe's is a 235-store chain of building-supply and home-improvement stores with over 7,000 full-time employees in 19 central and southeastern states. Sales are over $1 billion per year. In 1961, Lowe's had just 50 employees in 7 stores. That was the same year, however, that Lowe's set up a profit-sharing plan (later converted to an ESOP) that contributed company stock to employee accounts. Today, Lowe's employees own 30% of the company. Sales per employee are two to three times those of competitors, while "shrinkage" (loss due to breakage, theft, and so on) is one-sixth as great.

Lowe's achieved a good deal of notoriety when, in 1975, *Newsweek* told the story of Charles Valentine, a warehouse worker who earned $125 per week. After 17 years at Lowe's, Valentine left with $660,000 in stock. Many management people have left with $1,000,000 or more. These extraordinary amounts resulted from a fairly high level of company contributions to the ESOP and a very rapid appreciation in Lowe's stock.

Lowe's represents one of the great success stories in employee ownership. It is committed to the concept, and hopes employees will eventually own 51% or more of the firm. Employees have full voting rights on their stock (which they have always used to support management), and regular opportunities at store meetings for input into decisions affecting their jobs. Lowe's also makes a concerted effort to make sure employees understand how the ESOP works. Lowe's efforts to integrate employees into the company, however, are not extraordinary. In practice, employees do not have a lot more say in how the company is run than do employees in conventional firms, although their voting rights will one day give them the potential for far greater control. Lowe's success with employee ownership seems mostly to stem from the fact that it has demonstrated that it can provide employees with substantial capital estates, something few employees in this kind of work could ever hope to accumulate otherwise.

Quad/Graphics is another good example of a company that set up its ESOP as a means to provide employees with a meaningful additional benefit. Quad/Graphics is one of the country's most successful printing firms, printing several major magazines. It was started just 13 years ago, and has grown to employ 1,000 workers. Employees work 3-day, 36-hour weeks. They receive an ESOP contribution equal to 12% of their pay, and their stock value has increased almost 12 times since 1976. The company does a number of innovative things to involve employees in the affairs of the company, including one day a year when the managers simply leave. For Quad/Graphics employees, the ESOP appears to be both financially lucrative and an important part of a successful system of labor relations.

Lowe's and Quad/Graphics were both named among the best 100 companies in America to work for.[5] Their success is obviously more than could be expected in most ESOP firms. Hundreds of other companies have set up ESOPs for similar reasons, however. Although few have had such spectacular stock growth, many are likely to provide six-figure or greater accounts for employees who choose to stay with the company for 10 to 20 years or more. Many other companies, however, have much more modest plans. A southwest aviation firm, for instance, provides employees with about 9% of the total company stock. The company set up the plan primarily for the tax break and many of the employees, according to our survey, did not even know the company had a plan. It is doubtful that many employees will ever accumulate more than several thousand dollars worth of stock through the ESOP. Employees show little interest in being owners, and there is no reason to think the plan will have any impact on corporate performance beyond taxes.

At another company, a small bakery in Mississippi, skilled workers were making just over $5.00 an hour and had no pension. There was a small ESOP. The Bakery, Confectionary, and Tobacco Workers Union succeeded in organizing the company, and workers went on strike for better wages and a pension. The company offered a 4% increase in wages and no pension. As Ray Scannell, an official with the union put it, "even with 20 years with the ESOP, people would still retire needing welfare."[6]

Most ESOPs set up as employee benefit plans fall somewhere between the Lowe's and Quad/Graphics and the aviation and bakery firms described here. While the potential for considerable accomplishment is there, there is also potential for abuse or indifference.

As a Market for Departing Owners

Many owners of closely held businesses face an unpleasant dilemma when they decide to cash in their shares in the company. Obviously, they need to find a market for the stock if they are to realize any income from the businesses they have helped build. Markets for closely held firms are limited, however. In some cases, an owner can pass a business on to an heir, but often one does not exist who is willing to take over the company. In other cases, another firm may want to buy the company, but may not want to make an offer the owner considers fair. Even if it is, owners are often reluctant to see their businesses's identity and their employees' fates handed over to another company. In still other cases, no buyer can be found, even though the firm is profitable. Buying and running a small business is a high-risk proposition, especially when alternative investments, such as certificates of deposit, are earning high, risk-free returns. In these cases an owner may see no choice but to liquidate (sell the assets to someone else) or have the firm use its earnings to buy back the shares. In fact, given these potential problems, many small-business owners simply do not plan for their retirement at all. A recent Chase Manhattan survey of owners of small manufacturing firms, for instance, found that two-thirds of the respondents nearing retirement age had done no business continuity planning.[7]

An ESOP provides a very practical alternative. A company can set up a plan and make tax-deductible contributions to it. These contributions are then used to buy the shares of the departing owner. Under previous law, the owner was required to pay capital-gains tax on the sale (a maximum of 20%). Although this was better than the tax treatment for selling the stock directly back to the company (which carried a maximum of 50%), it was worse than the tax deferral which allowed for sales of 80% or more of a business to another business in return for the stock of the acquiring company. If Bill's Carpets sold to Sam's Furniture, for instance, and Bill received stock in Sam's in return, he would pay no tax on the sale until he sold stock in Sam's later, and then would pay only capital gains. Thus, there was a perverse encouragement towards conglomeration rather than sales to employees.

In 1984, however, Congress passed a new law allowing an owner selling to an ESOP to obtain the same tax deferral by reinvesting the proceeds of the sale in the stock of other companies. The ESOP must own 30% of the company after the sale, not 80%, as required in a sale to a larger firm. The law makes an ESOP sale the most tax-favored way to sell a business.

This technique is not just available to principal owners of a firm. Any owner, including outside investors or venture capitalists, can take advantage of the provision. The major requirement is simply that the ESOP must own at least 30% of the company's stock before or immediately after the transaction.

The law was first suggested in 1979 by Ed Sanders who, along with his wife Phyllis, had founded Allied Plywood Company some 20 years earlier. The Sanders' firm was gradually built into a very successful wholesaler of plywood to the building industry. When the Sanders wanted to retire, they first considered having the employees buy the stock directly. That presented a financial burden for most of the workers, however, who would have had to buy the stock out of their after-tax earnings. The Sanders then started having the company buy their stock. The IRS said that was a "redemption," however, and subject to "ordinary income tax," meaning (at the time) that the Sanders would have to pay a 70% tax (now it would be 50%). At about this time, Sanders read a letter to the editor in the *Washington Post* describing how ESOPs could be used to solve this dilemma.

At that time, the company could contribute tax-deductible earnings to the ESOP, which the ESOP then used to buy the Sanders shares. "The check just went from one folder to another," Ed Sanders recalled. The IRS required only capital-gains treatment of the sale, meaning a maximum tax of 28% (now it is 20%). So the plan benefitted Allied and the Sanders in two ways. The company could deduct what it put into the ESOP, saving 46% of the cost (their tax bracket), while the Sanders cut their personal taxes 60%. Still, the Sanders could have done even better by selling to one of the many companies that offered to buy their firm for an exchange of stock. Then the Sanders could have deferred taxes altogether. But they didn't want to do this. "All they care about is profits," Ed Sanders told us. "They'd hire somebody with a whip to come in, and I could see the whole thing going down the drain in a hurry." So, out of loyalty to their valued employees, and a desire to keep the company's identity intact, they sold to the ESOP.

For several years, the company made contributions. Then, in 1982, the ESOP was used to borrow enough money to buy the remaining shares. To its customers, bankers, and employees, the Sanders were Allied Plywood. One employee feared that "the place is going to fall apart" after the Sanders left. In fact, however, the firm has done even better. As when the Sanders were there, the employees receive a relatively low base pay, but also receive a substantial monthly bonus based on the excess of sales over costs. Between pay, bonuses, and stock, the employees earn one-third more than the comparable workers in other firms. Sales have increased another 20% and new president Bob Shaw expects continued growth. Moreover, the employees now play a greater role in the company, with five of the seven members of the board and more of a say in day-to-day company decisions. The Sanders were understandably reluctant to give employees full voting rights while they were still there. They had, after all, founded and built the company. They did, however, run a very open company, with frequent employee meetings. But, as one employee noted, people respected the Sanders almost too much, and were reluctant to speak up or disagree in these meetings.

At the other extreme is Eberhard Foods in Michigan. A medium-sized, locally based, family-owned supermarket chain, Eberhard has had a history of labor problems. Employees have gone on strike three times in an effort to secure a pension plan, never succeeding. Instead, they were given an ESOP, which eventually was used to buy a majority of the company's shares. While the employees saw potential in this, their low wages and lack of a secure retirement plan, as well as generally bad feeling between management and labor, made them very suspicious of it. In 1983, the daughter of the 82-year-old principal owner started a program to try to improve labor relations. Her father disapproved of her efforts and fired her. While he was on vacation, she organized a board meeting at which he was fired. When he returned, he directed the trustee of the ESOP (he controlled the ESOP, which did not pass through voting rights), to vote the ESOP stock to replace the board, then disinherited his daughter.[8] The obvious moral of this tale is that an ESOP, in itself, is not going to solve labor-relations problems. Allied's ESOP works so well in part because it was instituted in a company in which managers and employees already had a great deal of respect for one another.

Generally, however, the use of an ESOP to provide for business continuity appears to be one of its most positive applications for everyone involved. In many cases, employees end up with both ownership and control of the firm; in others they end up with just ownership. In some of these cases, had ownership not been transferred, some or all of the employees would have lost their jobs. At the same time, former owners can ease out of their businesses gradually, and save tax dollars in the process. The community keeps independent, tax-paying businesses alive. Since owners who are motivated to look into ESOPs to allow their employees to continue the firm are often owners like the Sanders—people who care about their workers—these plans have a head start in accomplishing many of the goals ESOP proponents claim employee ownership can create.

To Raise Capital

Say that ABC Baking wanted to buy new pie-making machinery. Normally, ABC would borrow funds and, as it repaid them, deduct its interest payments from its taxable income. If ABC decided to borrow the money through an ESOP, however, it could come out better. ABC would have its ESOP borrow the needed funds, with ABC guaranteeing the lender that it would contribute enough cash to the ESOP to repay the loan. Within certain liberal limits, these contributions are tax-deductible, meaning that ABC could deduct both the interest and the principal on the loan, not just the interest. The ESOP would use the loan to buy new issues of ABC stock, giving ABC the proceeds of the loan and the ESOP ABC stock.

The result of all this is that ABC gets better tax treatment in its repayment of the loan, while the same dollars used to repay the loan are creating an employee benefit plan. ABC employees end up not just with a piece of the pie, but a piece of the pie-making machinery as well.

This same approach can be used to buy existing shares, such as those from a retiring owner or from public shareholders. In 1984, Congress made this approach even more attractive when it passed a law allowing banks to deduct 50% of the interest income they receive from loans to ESOPs. This will at least make loans to ESOPs more available, and often may lower the interest rate banks are willing to offer. This provision may eventually be dropped, however.

Antioch Publishing is an example of a company that has used this "leveraging" approach. Antioch is the largest U.S. printer of bookmarks and other bookstore supplies. It was founded by Ernest Morgan, whose father had been the first chairman of the TVA. The Morgan family had a long history of commitment to social goals, and the ESOP fit in well with their philosophy. In 1983, the company decided to expand by borrowing through an ESOP. The ESOP will borrow cash to buy new Antioch stock, thus increasing the employees' shares and saving Antioch tax costs and possibly interest costs.

There are disadvantages to this approach, however. The issuance of new shares dilutes the holdings of other shareholders. The theory is that the ESOP will create enough benefits to offset this, but this may not always happen. For all the upfront tax benefits of a leveraged plan, closely held companies face an eventual liability when employees start to leave and ask the company to buy their shares. The ESOP loan is treated as a loan on the company's books, but the ESOP stock purchase is not treated as equity, an accounting problem that can be troublesome for some publicly traded companies.

Nonetheless, there are enough advantages to this approach that it is surprising that more companies do not use it to raise capital. Instead, leveraged ESOPs are used primarily to buy existing shares or in an employee buyout of a troubled firm, as discussed below.

As Part of a Participatory Management Philosophy

An ESOP can also be part of a larger corporate philosophy designed to involve employees in the company. According to a 1983 NCEO survey, only about 7% of all ESOP firms believe in employee ownership so much that they would set up plans even in the absence of any tax benefits, but these 7% often provide very visible examples of employee ownership's potential.

W.L. Gore Associates is a good example. Gore is a 3,000-employee high-tech manufacturer known for its "Gore-Tex" fabric coating. It has been growing at almost 40% per year in recent years. All of its "associates," as employees are called, are considered "nonmanagers." According to the Gore credo, no one is a manager at Gore. There are no formal job titles or defined hierarchies, but rather a "lattice" structure in which any employee or group of employees can communicate with any other. This approach might be considered anarchy by some, but it is a very profitable anarchy. Gore limits plant size to 200–400, although the manufacturing economies of scale would be larger, because the company believes larger plants lose human economies of scale.

Gore employees, including the Gore family, own 95% of the company. It has an ESOP which owns a substantial (they will not say how much) and increasing share of this stock. Gore is regularly cited as one of the best places in the country to work. Although it is best to take the company's description of itself with some caution, by all accounts it is a most unusual and successful example of employee ownership and involvement.

To Save Companies

The most publicized uses of an ESOP, although one of the least common, is to buy out companies that would otherwise close. Although other employee ownership techniques can be used, the tax advantages of the ESOP makes it the vehicle of choice.

We estimate that there have been 65 buyouts since 1971. About 90% appear still to be in business (two of the firms are coming out of chapter 11 bankruptcy proceedings, four have been sold profitably to conventional businesses, and five have closed). There are a number of reasons for this success. First, many companies close divisions or subsidiaries, even though they are profitable, because they are not profitable enough or do not fit into the company's plans. Other companies could make a profit if they were better managed, had a more motivated workforce, or were freed from the overhead charges and business restraints of conglomerate control.

To organize a buyout, employees must first arrange for a feasibility study. If this proves positive, sources of funding must be found. Several industrial states now provide assistance in paying for feasibility studies and providing partial loans for the buyout. Limited federal funds have been available as well, but two-thirds of the buyouts have been privately financed. Once all this is arranged, employees form a new shell company. The shell arranges for loans through the ESOP, as described above, to buy the assets of the closing firm. The ESOP then exchanges these assets for the stock of the acquired company. Employees do not actually purchase shares out of their savings (on which they have already paid taxes), nor do they assume personal liability for any bad debts of the company. In some cases, however, employees make a contribution by agreeing to wage concessions.

Weirton Steel is the largest and most publicized of the buyouts. In 1982, National Intergroup announced it would reduce Weirton to a small finishing mill, destroying over 7,000 jobs and probably the small community of Weirton, West Virginia—unless, that is, the employees wanted to buy the mill. National was not adverse to that idea, since its reduction plans would trigger over $700 million in pension and severance-pay costs.

Weirton workers and managers formed a joint study committee and contracted for a feasibility study, which proved positive provided workers took a 19% pay cut. The town held bake sales, parades, and telethons to help pay for the the initial costs, and in January 1984 the buyout was completed. Weirton raised over $300 million to buy the assets, and will raise $700 million more over the next several years to finish plant modernization.

In the year since the buyout, Weirton has become the most profitable integrated steel mill in the country, and has rehired 1,000 employees. An extensive system of shopfloor participation is being instituted, and employees have full voting rights on their shares. The original board was appointed by the firm's financial advisors, and includes three employee representatives. The banks involved in the deal insisted that the initial board have outside directors. Within the next five to seven years, however, Weirton employees will elect the majority of the board. While Weirton will face the same problems as the rest of the steel industry, its early performance is encouraging.

Not all buyouts have had such a record of success. Many of the early buyouts, such as South Bend Lathe, were initiated by local management, and provided employees with little role in the new company. That may not be a crucial factor in healthy companies where the ESOP is a gift to employees, but in buyouts, where employees may have made sacrifices to save their firm, it is probably much more important. At South Bend, in 1979, the employees went on strike against their own company over the issue. By 1984, South Bend was producing much of its product overseas.

Other buyouts have faced financial difficulties. Employees at Rath Packing Company, for instance, saved their company from imminent bankruptcy in 1979 by taking wage cuts in return for 60% of the company's stock. At first, things went well. Rath set up a system of worker participation from the shopfloor to the boardroom that has been widely praised. Productivity rose significantly, leading to a 20% reduction in labor costs per unit of production by 1983.[9] But labor costs were only 15% of Rath's total costs. High interest rates and the cost of inventory made up much of the rest. Unfortunately, Rath is a pork packer, and hog prices were rising while pork consumption and prices were falling. Caught in this squeeze, many packers closed. At the same time, non-union competition was undercutting Rath, which already had to deal with an outdated plant and marketing system. By 1983, Rath could not pay its bills, and sought protection under chapter 11 of the bankruptcy laws. It is now reorganized as a much smaller regional packer. Some Rath employees are bitter about the outcome, but it is difficult, in retrospect, to see what else could have been done to save Rath.

Fortunately, Rath and South Bend are more the exceptions than the norm. Most of the buyouts have at least succeeded financially and many have created systems of labor-management relations that are innovative and successful.

In a Leveraged Buyout
For a variety of reasons, more and more companies are undergoing leveraged buyouts, buyouts in which management and/or investors borrow enough money to buy a controlling interest in their firm. Often, these "LBOs" are used to prevent a hostile takeover. The debt taken on to acquire this controlling interest is then repaid out of the earnings of the firm. Obviously, this puts a strain on the company, since this is a debt it did not have before. Anything that can lower this debt service is, of course, most welcome. Since borrowing through an ESOP lowers the company's taxable income and may lower the interest rate on the loan, the ESOP approach can be very appealling. The ESOP normally gets anywhere from 25% to 100% of the stock this way. Any remaining shares are usually purchased by management or investors. Blue Bell (25%), Raymond International (about 70%), Parsons (100%), Dan River (70%), U.S. Sugar (43%), and Harper and Row (33%) are all examples of major U.S. corporations that have recently used this technique.

These ESOP LBOs are controversial, partly because pension plans have often been frozen or terminated to help finance them, and partly because employees normally cannot vote their shares for at least several years, if at all (Parsons and U.S. Sugar are exceptions). Proponents point out, however, that if an ESOP were not used, the LBOs probably would have proceeded anyway, and pension plans would have been cut back or terminated with no replacement. Moreover, employees can bargain to replace the pension plans, although the law places limits on the percent of pay any employee can receive from benefit plans. In leveraged ESOPs, where large contributions are normally made in the first years after the buyout, adding a pension plan can bring employees over these limits. Reinstating a pension plan thus often must wait for five to seven years, the normal term of the loans.

When pension plans are terminated, employees receive an annuity contract for whatever is in their account, which is fully vested automatically, no matter how many years of service they have. Since pension plans typically provide a percentage of an employee's highest pay, and most employees will not have achieved their potentially highest pay yet, these contracts typically are worth less than what the pension eventually would have been worth. Still, the employees do get this annuity value, and get the ESOP contribution. These ESOP contributions, at least in most of the LBOs so far, have been larger than the pension contributions.

The Parsons Company provides a good example of a positive use of an LBO. The 8,000-employee construction and engineering firm has been consistently profitable. As a publicly traded company, however, Parsons had to respond to the often short-term concerns of its shareholders, and spend both time and money on a variety of reports, meetings, and so on. Since Parsons was generating a surplus, chairman William Leonhard told *Business Week,* there was "no need for a public market for funds."[10] Parsons was already 29% employee-owned through an ESOP, and Leonhard wanted to complete a process of making all employees "partners."

By contrast, Harper and Row used its leveraged ESOP to buy out the shares of a major owner who it was feared might sell to a potentially hostile acquirer. The ESOP paid the owner twice the market value of the stock, a transaction a court later ruled was improper, since ESOPs are supposed to make transactions at fair market value. The pension plan was terminated to help pay for the buyout, although the company's union opposed the move. The company narrowly avoided a strike over the issue, and the union has taken the company to court. Employee relations have soured.

ESOP LBOs are too new to allow thorough assessments of their effects. It is clear, however, that the new tax law will have, as First Boston investment banker Robert Cotter put it, "a dramatic economic impact."[11] A number of very large employee-owned companies are going to be created, and how these companies fare will have a profound effect on how employee ownership develops in this country.

To Acquire and Divest Subsidiaries

Many companies find the ESOP approach attractive when they want to spin off successful subsidiaries or acquire new units. Again, the leveraging technique is used. Control Data, for instance, wanted to divest its profitable Kerotest Valve division, as it no longer wanted to be in that field. By selling to an ESOP, it obtained a fair market price and avoided the costs of seeking another buyer. Moreover, when a subsidiary is put on the block, managers at the company may become insecure and demoralized—or leave altogether—resulting in losses for the subsidiary until it is sold, and possibly a lower sale price as a result. Managers at other divisions may be demoralized as well, since they might fear the same fate. Sale through an ESOP avoids these problems by giving managers an even larger role in the new, independent company.

In the reverse case, where an ESOP is used to acquire a subsidiary, the tax benefits of leveraging are again paramount. An ESOP borrows the needed funds, making it much easier for the company to repay the loans needed for the purchase.

In Return for Worker Concessions.

Although this approach only accounts for a small percentage of all employee ownership plans, it has become increasingly common in the last two years, and has resulted in employees gaining a major ownership position in a number of large companies, especially in the airline and trucking industries. Normally, a company seeking concessions simply says "take them or we will close." In the ESOP approach, the workers often demand, or the employer offers, to match at least part of the concessions with stock, giving the workers a chance to make up their losses and, frequently, to have representation on the board of directors.

Employees have acquired 9% of Continental, 13% of Pan Am, 15% of Republic, 15% of PSA, 25% of Eastern (but not through an ESOP), and 33% of Western through this approach, as well as over 40% of several trucking firms. A few of the trucking firms offered their plans when they were very close to bankruptcy, and employee ownership did not save them. Others, such as Transcon, with over 3,000 employees, are now doing very well. Employees have also used this approach at a few steel firms, at United Press International, at Chrysler (by government mandate) and at a handful of other firms.

Although the number of firms doing this is small, the number of employees and the visibility of the companies are large. The idea of exchanging stock for wages did not surface till 1980 at Chrysler, but has grown quickly since then. As with LBOs, the size and visibility of these firms will make the success or failure of their plans very important to the future of employee ownership.

Worker Cooperatives

Worker cooperatives are the other major form of employee ownership. They are both far simpler and much less common. By definition, a worker cooperative is owned by its members only, and only workers can be members. Each member is limited to one vote on company matters. Cooperatives can, and often do, hire non-owning workers, especially on a part-time or seasonal basis.

Each cooperative sets a membership fee. This may reflect the individual worker's share of the company's total equity, or it may be set at an arbitrary, fixed value. If it does represent the worker's share of the cooperative's equity, it will change in value with the company's fortunes, and must be sold back to the company or to a new worker when the member leaves. Since share prices can rise to significant levels, new members often purchase shares out of gradual payroll deductions. If member fees do not reflect company equity, they are generally set at a lower level ($100 to $2,000 is typical). This fee goes into an account, and each year the member's share of the net profits or losses is added to or subtracted from this account, until the member departs.

Whatever the membership fee system, cooperatives return a share of net earnings to workers, often on the basis of the relative pay and/or hours worked. Any such returned earnings are non-taxable to the corporation, but are taxable to the member. Most of these member earnings can be kept in the employee's account, and can be used by the cooperative until the member leaves and receives his or her money.

Generally, cooperatives are very democratically organized, with employees constituting most of the board of directors. Employees are also usually involved in many corporate decisions. Most cooperatives are quite small, and started as cooperatives, although there are a few large cooperatives, especially in the taxicab industry.

Some of the best known examples of worker cooperatives are the plywood industries of the Pacific Northwest. Started mostly in the 1940s, there were once 30 cooperatives, each with several hundred workers. The cooperatives pay all employees equally, but hire a non-owning general manager. Workers elect other workers to serve on the board of directors. The cooperatives have hired a number of non-owning workers, especially on a seasonal basis. The pressure to hire non-owners, however, is great, since bringing in new owners means further diluting the wealth. It can also be difficult to find people who want to become owners, since workers must purchase a share in the company to become a member. In some of the successful coops, these shares can cost over $100,000. Cooperatives have tried to deal with this problem by allowing new members to pay for the shares out of gradual wage deductions.

The plywood cooperatives have generally been very successful. One study, for instance, found that they were 30% more productive than comparable non-cooperative firms.[12] Some were so successful, in fact, that departing workers could not find buyers for their expensive shares; other cooperatives were sold profitably to other firms. A few have not succeeded, especially in the recent hard times in the industry. Twelve, however, have continued in business. Since the average life expectancy of a U.S. firm is only about six years, this is a fairly good record.

Still, the problem the cooperatives had with shares becoming too expensive for new workers and the related tendency to hire non-owners prompted people interested in this area, especially the Industrial Cooperative Association (ICA, a consulting group), to develop an alternative system based on internal accounts, as explained briefly above. These accounts are very similar to profit-sharing trusts, except that losses are subtracted as well as gains being added. Since the membership fee is reasonable, and does not change with the value of the company, there is no problem in adding new workers and no incentive to avoid hiring them.

At the Workers Owned Sewing Company in North Carolina, for instance, each of the 50 employees (all but one of whom are low-income women) pays a small membership fee. The fee goes into an account. This has been used to provide working capital for the firm, but as it has become more established, the hope is now that some of the profits can be returned directly to the employees. Should there be losses, however, these would be subtracted from worker accounts. Funds in the account earn interest and will be given to workers when they leave.

Another cooperative effort at economic development is underway in New York, where the Community Service Society (CSS) of New York has begun a program to start worker coops. Using some of its own funds (it is the city's largest charitable organization) as well as funds from private lenders and a revolving loan fund established by the ICA, CSS has set up two coops, a construction firm and a home health services company. The construction firm employs about 10 low-income workers, while the health-care cooperative will eventually employ 200. The coops are being set up in fields in which much of the work is normally performed on a contract basis. Employees of these contractors generally receive low pay, few benefits, and no job security. By contrast, in the CSS model, the companies have full-time employees, do their own contracting, and pay better wages and benefits. They can do this in part because intermediary contractors are eliminated and in part because workers, being owners, should be more productive.

Perhaps the most common field for coops is the taxicab industry. There are dozens of taxicab coops, although it is difficult to know whether all should be considered worker owned. In the typical arrangement, drivers organize a cooperative to provide them with dispatching services, insurance, mechanical work, and common colors. Drivers own their own cabs and frequently rent them out to others. Some drivers own several cabs. Since these drivers are not employees of the cab company, but independent contractors, the coops are more like marketing or service cooperatives. Some cab companies, such as Denver Yellow Cab and the new Yellow Cab Cooperative of San Francisco, both the largest firms in their cities, do actually own most of their cabs. Drivers lease the cabs from the company, and all of their income comes from fares and tips. They pay a fee to the coop for insurance, mechanical service, dispatching, and so on. Non-driver employees can also join the coop. These companies consider themselves worker owned, although the drivers are still primarily contractors. Interestingly, since Denver Yellow Cab became a coop in 1981, it has compiled the best safety record of any cab company in the country.

Coops are also very common in "alternative" businesses—book stores, health food stores, natural food restaurants, and the like. Some, such as the Moosewood Restaurant in Ithaca and Freewheel Bicycle in Minneapolis, have become stable, successful businesses, but most others place little emphasis on conventionally defined business success. Unfortunately, that has meant that most have short life-spans.

One exception is the Solar Center, a 25-employee solar energy coop in San Francisco. Founded in the late 1970s by Peter Barnes, the Solar Center was dedicated to providing a responsible product in a democratic fashion. As it found a niche in the market, it found that growth and success could put strains on the consensual decision-making style it valued. Over time, responsibility had to be delegated, the goal of relatively equal pay somewhat relaxed in order to compete for talented people, and an ownership form created that provided more attractive tax and financial benefits to the company and its workers. The company thus merged its cooperative governance structure with an ESOP financial structure and created a committee system to handle more decisions. Still, employees retained clear control of the company, and its most basic values remained intact. At the same time, it has successfully competed in a difficult market.

The combination of an ESOP and cooperative, as at the Solar Center, has become more common, and some leading cooperative specialists, such as the Industrial Cooperative Association, have created practical models of how it can be done. This combination has helped make the cooperative governance structure more financially practical. Moreover, coops have low transaction costs, especially compared to ESOPs: that is, they are not expensive to install or maintain. Nonetheless, coops have not gained a strong foothold in the United States. Existing businesses are obviously more than reluctant to convert to worker cooperative status, so coops are limited to start-ups, buyouts of firms that would otherwise fail, or companies where retiring owners are willing to sell to a coop of their employees. Even in these cases, it is often difficult to find people who are willing to share ownership and control equally.

In Europe, however, worker coops have penetrated mainstream economic sectors, especially in Italy, with 500,000 worker-cooperative members, and in France, with 145,000.[13] In Spain's Basque region, 18,000 workers in over 80 affiliated coops have their own bank, pension system, and research institute, and operate some of the country's most successful and technologically advanced companies. The French and Italian governments provide financial and technical support for the coops, most of which are started from scratch, often in the construction industry. These experiences suggest that the obstacles to coops suggested above are not insurmountable, provided the right kind of support is available.

Some efforts to do this are underway. In Philadelphia, the United Food and Commercial Workers, in response to the closing of A&P stores there, has set up three "O&O" ("owned and operated") worker cooperatives, using worker contributions and government and foundation loans to help finance the efforts. In North Carolina and Boston, local coop support groups have set up small loan funds of their own to help coops get started.

Other Ownership Forms

ESOPs and cooperatives account for almost all the employee ownership plans in the United States, but there are other approaches. In some companies, such as People Express, all employees are required to buy stock in the firm, usually at a significant discount. In a large number of companies, employees can buy stock if they wish, but usually only at a 15% discount (more than this is taxable). While this approach results in some employees owning stock in many companies, it is rare that a large percentage of workers will make this investment. The Tandy Corporation, which owns Radio Shack, is one notable exception: 75% of its workers own 25% of the company's stock. Still other companies, especially in the high-tech area, offer most or all of their employees stock options. Options allow an employee to buy stock at a set price at any time up to a specified date. If an option is granted at $5.00 per share, and the stock goes to $10.00, an employee could still buy it at $5.00, for instance. Options are generally only given to key employees, but, according to Kip Hagopian, president of the National Venture Capital Association, the practice of offering them more widely is apparently spreading in high-tech firms. Finally, some firms use their profit-sharing plans to buy company stock, often along with other investments. These plans end up operating in a manner very similar to ESOPs.

Employee Ownership, Participation, and Control

For many people, all these forms and uses of employee ownership should be evaluated in terms of another objective: do they really provide employees with control rights in their companies, or are they just an elaborate employee benefit? The answer to this question, as with many others about employee ownership, is "it depends."

As noted earlier, employee ownership and control are not the same thing. In ESOPs, employees are only required to be able to vote their shares on all issues in publicly traded companies (about 20% of all ESOPs). In closely held ESOPs, employees only must be able to vote on certain limited issues, such as closings or acquisitions. In majority employee-owned firms, however, 60% pass through full voting rights.[14]

Voting rights are only one indication of participation and control, and probably not the most important one. In closely held companies, shareholder votes are extremely rare. Boards of directors are more overseers (if that) than policy makers, a statement that applies to many publicly traded firms as well. In these firms, employee input at the management level depends more on the availability of specific structures, such as labor-management committees, to provide employee input. Unfortunately, there are no overall data on how common programs such as these are in employee ownership firms.

At the job level, employee participation and ownership would seem a natural mix, but many employee ownership companies provide few opportunities for worker input at this level. Lacking any firm data on this issue, we can say, however, that it does appear that employee ownership companies are at least somewhat more likely to involve employees at the job level than conventional companies. That is more an impression drawn from our general knowledge of employee ownership companies, however, than an empirical conclusion.

To some people, this progress on democratizing work is too slow. Still, while only about 400 companies with ten or more employees are both owned and controlled by their employees, that is 400 more than are controlled by workers but not owned by them. Moreover, a growing number of major firms provide employees with a substantial minority interest and representation on their boards. We know of only a few conventionally owned companies that allow this kind of worker participation. In this country, it is fair to say, employee ownership has been the only legitimate method for involving employees in the decision-making process at the management level. It has accomplished this goal not just in smaller cooperatives, but in hundreds of mainstream and often quite large companies. It can do this, it seems, because employees as owners are seen as much less threatening than employees as non-owning workers. In a number of cases, this process has been gradual, with companies first sharing ownership, and then later sharing control. The second step is made much easier by the first.

To say that the absence of control or participation in a company means that employee ownership is a failure is, we believe, unfair. A case can be made that these elements may enhance corporate performance or make work more satisfying (arguments we address, in part, here), and some would make a moral case that owners should have control rights. Our work here, however, suggests that while control and participation are very important to some workers in some companies, they are not so important to others. Instead, it is the financial part of employee ownership that matters most. Broadening the ownership of wealth opens up all sorts of opportunities for people and for their children that simply are not available otherwise. This is hardly an insignificant achievement.

Unions and Employee Ownership

Prior to 1980, unions were basically opposed to employee ownership. Some feared that ESOPs would be substituted for pension plans, workers would be forced to use their savings to buy doomed companies, and employees would become coopted by management. On the one hand, they called ESOPs that did not provide worker control a sham; on the other, they worried that unions would have no role in companies where workers did have control. Much of this is changing. Some unions, such as the Communications Workers, Teamsters, Steelworkers, and National Maritime Union, have specifically endorsed and bargained for the idea; others, such as the Autoworkers, and the Machinists have provided support for efforts by their locals to gain ownership.

Part of this change is due to a better understanding of the subject. ESOPs are not usually substituted for pensions, although that occasionally happens,[15] nor are most employee ownership plans in distress situations. Even where they are, most buyouts have succeeded. Only three companies have decertified their unions after instituting an employee ownership plan, and in two of those cases it was because the international union opposed the employee ownership effort of the local. In democratic firms, unions have not withered away, but have taken on new responsibility in organizing the workers as voters. Even the most democratic firms still have management and workers, and still need to negotiate wages and working conditions. These negotiations may be less adversarial, but we have not detected any decrease in unionized workers' perceptions that they need a union to bargain for them.

Still, most unions are cautious about employee ownership, and few have sought an active role outside the kinds of distress situations that often demand innovative responses. An active union role could have a very significant impact on employee ownership, and is by no means unthinkable.[16] With union strength declining, new ways are needed to attract workers. As competition increases, new ways are needed to keep union firms competitive. Finally, as employee ownership grows, unions might become more actively involved in working to shape ESOPs and other plans to the needs of their members.

Conclusion

If nothing else, this chapter should suggest that employee ownership is a diverse phenomenon, one with both successes and failures. It is this very diversity that makes it so interesting to study, by offering the opportunity to identify just what mix of factors make it work best. The rest of the book is devoted to that task.

3
In Search of Equity
Research on Employee Ownership

For a phenomenon as recent as employee ownership, there is no lack of research interest in the subject. When we first became involved in employee ownership it often seemed that more people were studying the idea than doing it. The concept, after all, is intellectually intriguing. Employees, once just rented labor, now get a new role as owners. Managers, once simply bosses, now may literally be employees of their workers. Successful companies are suddenly being overwhelmed by an urge to give some of their success away. Failing companies are transformed not only into profitable ones, but social experiments at the same time. Unions may now be negotiating with people appointed by a board elected by the unions' members. Higher productivity, profits, and employee morale are all claimed to be lurking offstage, awaiting only the drop of an ESOP to make their appearance.

It's great fun for theorists too. After all these years of worshipping at the altar of Smith, Marx, or Keynes, here is a whole new paradigm. Neither the market nor the state, nor even some combination, must assume the mythic dimensions and capabilities they often do in conventional theories. Instead, the firm becomes the vehicle for *both* economic growth and social justice. It's not too much of an exaggeration to say that employee ownership may be the shift that launches a thousand dissertations.

Yet for all the interest, the newness of the phenomenon and the built-in difficulties in studying it have, in the felicitous phrase of Harvard's Joseph Blasi, resulted mostly in "advanced storytelling." There are now numerous chronicles of individual companies, but relatively few solid, empirical investigations into just how well employee ownership works in meeting its various goals. Similarly, there is a large body of theory on what an idealized employee-owned or "self-managed" firm or economy should or might look like, but precious little on what they really are like.

There are a number of reasons for this. First, the phenomenon has only established a meaningful foothold in the economy within the last several years, and good research takes time. Second, until very recently, no comprehensive list of employee ownership firms has been available. A list of ESOP firms is now available through the IRS, but only through a freedom of information request. All of the empirical work so far, therefore, has been forced to rely on very spotty lists drawn from newspapers, word of mouth, or a 1976 Department of Labor list of 1,400 firms expressing an interest in setting up an ESOP. The result has been disproportionate attention to those firms easily identified as employee owned. Buyouts of failing companies get more than their share of publicity, and thus have had more than their share of research interest. Finally, the subject is not easy to study. Employee ownership may be a kind of social experiment, but it hardly qualifies as a scientific one. In a scientific experiment, the subject of the study is isolated from other confusing factors. Ideally, we would study companies that had an infusion of ownership sharing, and nothing else at the same time, and then compare them with perfectly comparable non-employee ownership firms. Real life is a good deal messier. If researchers find that employee ownership firms are more profitable than comparable conventional firms, is it because of ownership or is it because the establishment of an ownership plan is simply an indicator of innovative management practices at the company? If employee buyouts succeed in motivating workers, is it because of ownership or the fact that they have saved their jobs? If managers say their companies work better because of ownership, do they say it because it's true or because they had a hand in setting up the plan in the first place? These and similar problems complicate the researcher's task.

Despite all this, a picture of employee ownership is beginning to emerge. In this chapter, we will review what we do know about employee ownership—how it has worked, and what can make it work better. We will review the research on the relationship between employee ownership and corporate performance, and between employee ownership and work satisfaction. We will evaluate what this tells us—and what it leaves us wondering about. We know that employee ownership is a very diverse phenomenon, encompassing all types and sizes of businesses. It has grown very rapidly, largely because of tax and perceived productivity benefits. Although occasionally used in distress situations, it is most common in profitable firms. The actual impact of employee ownership on corporate performance has not been finally established, but there is at least some very suggestive research indicating this effect may be very positive. There is also some preliminary evidence that it can, under the right circumstances, make work more rewarding, and some spotty evidence that it can and sometimes does increase worker participation at various levels.

Researchers have tended to argue that participation makes employee ownership effective, but this seems more an article of faith than an artifact of evidence. In fact, we know very little about why and when employee ownership is an effective work reform. If, as we argued earlier, employee ownership is to be much more than an economic hoola hoop, it is vital that we learn a great deal more about just how the idea can and should be used if it is to benefit employees, companies, and society. Used well, the concept can revolutionize American business and society; used poorly, it will quickly lose the crucial political and economic support that has helped it grow. Providing guideposts on how to use it well is thus the core concern of this book.

What We Have Learned: Who Does What and Why

Thanks to a few good surveys, we now have a fairly clear idea of the broad characteristics of ESOPs, although we know far less about coops and other plans. The first two chapters reviewed much of this material. As noted, there are about 7,000 ESOPs and perhaps 2,000 more cooperatives and other plans, encompassing 7–8% of the workforce. In the typical ESOP, employees own about a third of the stock, while employees own 51% or more in 10–15% of the plans.[1] But this figure is misleading because it takes snapshots of companies. The nature of ESOPs, however, is generally to increase the percentage owned over time. Since so many ESOPs are new, the current percentage owned is not reflective of how much employees *will* own in these firms. A more dynamic picture is presented by the percentage of annual pay contributed by companies: 32% contribute 5% or less, 37% contribute 6–14%, and 31% contribute 15–25%.[2] Thus, in a typical ESOP company, an employee making $20,000 a year gets about $2,000 more in stock. These figures applied to 1980. In 1981, contribution deductions limits were raised for ESOPs that borrow money, so at least some companies will now contribute more than 25%. Generally, smaller companies contribute more. Most plans in very large companies are "PAYSOPs," special versions of ESOPs that provide tax credits for very small contributions. This kind of ownership plan has been attractive to these companies, but results in only nominal amounts of ownership for employees.[3]

Two-thirds of all ESOP firms are "mid-sized" (100–1,000 employees); 16% have under 50 employees and 12% have over 1,000; 20% are publicly traded.[4] There are no particular patterns by industry, but employee ownership generally is more common on the East and West coasts than in between. While some might attribute this to tides and lunar cycles, it is actually a result of the fact that most consultants who have pushed the idea live in California or the Boston–Washington corridor.

Companies set up their plans for a variety of reasons. Various surveys seem to concur that about a third of all these plans are set up to provide a market for a retiring owner, a percentage that will increase with the generous provisions of the new tax law.[5] About a quarter are used to borrow money, a percentage that will also rise as bankers learn about the 50% interest income deduction they can get on ESOP loans.[6] Perhaps another third are set up simply as an employee benefit, although it is difficult to separate this out from other uses. The remaining 10% or so include such uses as distress buyouts, divestitures, leveraged buyouts, and stock-for-concessions deals.

There is another way of looking at motivations for setting up plans. In 1983, we asked employee ownership consultants (for all kinds of plans) why their clients set up their plans. They were asked what percentage of their clients would agree with the following statements:

a. Employee ownership is so important our company would set up a plan even if there were no tax benefits.
b. Making employees owners makes sense, but we would not do it if there were no tax or other financial benefits.
c. If we could get the tax or financial benefits of employee ownership without making employees owners, we would prefer that arrangement.

According to the consultants, 7% of their clients were described by statement a, 50% by statement b, and 43% by statement c. Most of the consultants are lawyers, however, and their view of their clients may be somewhat biased because they deal more with tax and financial concerns than broader issues of employee relations. Still, the results suggest two clear conclusions:

1. If it were not for the tax breaks, we probably would not have written and you probably would not be reading this book, because employee ownership would be little more than a curiosity.

2. Despite what we just said, a majority of employee ownership firms have been persuaded, one way or another, to go beyond tax breaks. At least 57% of the companies agree that making employees owners makes sense, even though most needed the tax breaks to push them over the edge to actually set up a plan. This is important, for it is these firms that are likely to be most innovative in their use of employee ownership. Congress's willingness to continue to provide tax breaks for employee ownership is in large part motivated by the belief that the employee ownership companies will make a greater contribution to the economy. Firms that see employee ownership only as a financial tool are, almost by definition, less likely to produce the kind of effort that can maximize the motivational and productivity benefits of the concept. Having a substantial percentage of companies willing to go beyond finding ways to avoid taxes, therefore, is critical to the future of employee ownership. Finally, we know at least a little about the relationship between ownership and participation. On the face of it, it is clear that employee ownership has opened up management decisions to worker input in more companies than any other corporate reform ever. At least 400 companies, we estimate, have a majority of their stock voted by employees; perhaps 50 or more medium-to-large firms have employee owners

electing a minority of board directors.[7] Most publicly traded employee ownership companies pass through full voting rights (most have to). About 10–15% of closely held companies pass through full voting rights.

Beyond this, general descriptions of employee ownership companies are much harder to come by. One recent study found that employee ownership companies provide employees more financial information, but are not notably more participative at the job level.[8] The study had a sophisticated measure of participation based on the number of meetings a company holds between various levels of employees but, as the authors would readily admit, this measure may miss other more important and informal kinds of employee participation. Moreover, the degree to which employees have an impact on these meetings is only open to conjecture. Our impression (and that is all it is) from working with employee ownership companies, however, is that there is at least a very common interest in some kind of worker participation, and that a substantial minority of firms have joined ownership to thoroughgoing work reform. Chapter 7 will explore this subject in detail.

Employee Ownership and Corporate Performance

For most people, the bottom line on employee ownership is the bottom line. It's really an unfair burden. The original proponents of employee ownership argued that creating a more equitable distribution of wealth was the primary purpose of the concept. But the pursuit of equity doesn't get many employee ownership plans underway. The pursuit of profit does, so unless employee ownership makes that pursuit easier, it isn't likely to grow. The tax breaks take one long step in this direction; company performance needs to be the other.

The most obvious way in which ownership might affect performance is through employee motivation—employee owners may work harder, smarter, or more productively, while using resources more carefully. Others would contend, however, that ownership will only have an impact if linked with participation programs. A number of studies suggest that participation programs increase productivity, communications, and innovation,[9] but others are more skeptical.[10] Even if the participation advocates are correct, however, it remains true that many jobs will still be boring, no matter how participative. Many others are not very amenable to participation reforms. Ownership can provide a kind of residual motivation for these jobs after all the work reforms have done what they can.

Ownership can also help attract and keep high quality, experienced employees, a factor of considerable importance in some industries. Perhaps most importantly, ownership plans may provide an essential synergy without which other factors won't work. Participation, for instance, may be a key to productivity, but 75% of all participation programs last less than four years, in part because they are often not linked to financial rewards.[11] Ownership can provide the link. Alternatively, a company's success may depend on the introduction of new technologies, new work rules or routines, a willingness to forego short-run earnings for long-run investment, or any number of other efforts which non-owning workers may resist entirely, or make less effective once in place, but which employee owners may accept or even embrace. These changes may not make employees like their work any better, but many nonetheless show up in company performance.

Some theorists have gone a step further and argued that an economic system in which all firms are worker owned and managed will be more productive than a traditional system.[12] Workers, in this view, are more likely to encourage their firms to maximize long-term competitiveness and efficiency, rather than short-term profits and dividends, leading to a better use and allocation of capital. The arguments are couched in complex econometric equations well beyond the scope of this book, but add an interesting fillip to a discussion of employee ownership in the United States.

Does all this theory work? The studies to date suggest it may. The first was a study of the Northwest worker plywood coops that found that these firms were 30% more productive than comparable conventional plywood companies.[13] These coops are organized differently from most employee ownership firms, and are all in one industry, however, so the results can only be generalized with caution.

The second test of the theory, a 1978 study by Michael Conte and Arnold Tannenbaum of the University of Michigan's Survey Research Center, studied 98 employee ownership companies.[14] The sample was heavily biased towards buyouts and non-ESOP firms, as the authors did not, at the time, have access to good lists of firms. Thirty of the companies provided data on profitability. Conte and Tannenbaum found that these companies were 50% more profitable than the companies in their industries, and that the more of the company the employees owned, the higher was the ratio. No other variable explained why some companies did better than others, including the presence or absence of voting rights. As Conte and Tannenbaum pointed out, however, their sample was too small to say that the results were more than suggestive (they were not statistically significant). No matter—the results were seized on by advocates and have been quoted in virtually every major article on employee ownership. The study almost singlehandedly created the belief that employee ownership companies make more money, and has been a major factor in the passage of employee ownership legislation.

Next came Thomas Marsh and Dale McAllister, two law students at the University of Iowa. Using a list compiled by the Department of Labor of 1,400 companies interested in establishing ESOPs, the authors performed a detailed survey of the characteristics and performance of these firms. Although this was a better sample of employee ownership firms, it included only ESOPs, and at that time, only early ESOPs. Our own data, as we will see later, indicate that the later ESOP companies have more substantial and participative plans. Moreover, Marsh and McAllister only received productivity data from 128 firms and overall data from 229 (out of 1,400 surveyed).

Nonetheless, the study suggested that ESOP firms were more productive than non-ESOP firms and that, perhaps as important, their management overwhelmingly *believed* that the plans improved company performance. The most significant finding was that ESOP companies had an average annual productivity growth rate of + .78%, compared to a rate of − .74% for comparable conventional firms.[15] A productivity growth rate of 3% per year is considered a sign of prosperity, so this 1.52% per year difference is impressive. As in Conte and Tannenbaum's study, voting rights were not correlated with enhanced corporate performance. Company size did seem to matter, with mid-sized firms doing best and the largest and smallest firms doing the worst. Unfortunately, the study did not further probe why this might be true, nor did it reveal other factors which could explain the differentials in performance.

The managers at these companies were almost all enthusiastic about employee ownership: 32% reported a measured improvement in work quality, while 36% saw a measured improvement in turnover, 59% thought the ESOP improved morale and 79% thought it boosted employee interest in the company.[16] On all these scales, almost no one said the ESOP made things worse. Of course, if you have a hand in setting up a plan, as many of the respondents no doubt did, it is only natural to pat yourself on the back when evaluating your good judgement in setting it up.

A third study emerged in 1983, when the National Center for Employee Ownership completed a survey of 130 firms we had positively identified as majority employee owned. Our primary purpose was to see if these companies grew faster, as measured by net new jobs added per year. Of the 130, 98 firms provided some data, but only 43 provided enough data, or had had their plans for at least two years. We took the annual employment growth rates of these firms and compared them to those for their broadly defined industry. We found that the employee ownership firms grew at about 3.87% per year compared to a weighted rate of about 1.14% for firms in general.[17] That may seem to be a small difference, but it means a growth rate three times as fast, and one that would produce 300 more new jobs for every 1,000 existing jobs every ten years. Due to the limited sample size, the study could not address why this growth occurred. As in the Marsh and McAllister study, we also found that managers were almost universally enthusiastic about their plans.

In a related 1984 study, we looked at a sample of over 350 fast-growing, high-tech companies and found that there was a strong positive correlation between employment growth and the degree to which these firms, through various plans, shared ownership with employees.[18] In that study, companies that shared ownership with more, most, or all of their employees had median sales and employment-growth rates over twice those of companies that had no employee ownership. Moreover, their growth rates were over three times those of companies that shared ownership only with key employees. This gives more of a suggestion that there may be a causal relationship between employee ownership and corporate performance. If the explanation of enhanced performance among employee-owned companies were simply that these companies had more enlightened management (and it was the presence of such management that accounted for growth), then how can these results be explained? Is management at the firms that share ownership only with key employees the least enlightened, with those who share it with none doing better, and those sharing it broadly doing best? That does not seem a plausible progression.

This study does have limits, however. The 364 companies represented only a 5% response rate to our survey of approximately 7,500 companies. The survey was called an "employment growth study," and we do not believe that companies that disperse ownership more broadly, and that grow faster, would be more likely to respond than other companies, so there may be no "response bias." Still, a better response would be much more conforting. Moreover, although this study makes the argument that employee ownership does really have an impact on performance more plausible, it cannot, in itself, prove the point.

In that same year, we completed a study of publicly traded firms that were at least 10% employee owned. Could employee ownership work even in large firms with widely dispersed ownership? Would sharing ownership scare away investors? We were able to identify 13 firms that met the 10% test, had had their plan for at least two years, and were in industries where comparisons with other public firms were possible. Each of the 13 firms was matched with its public non-employee ownership competitors and ranked amongst them in terms of various financial measures. In terms of overall return to investors, the companies did about the same as their competitors, but on our other four measures (net operating margin, sales growth, book value per share and return to equity) they outperformed 62–75% of their rivals, depending on the measure.[19] In other words, these companies performed better, but the stock market has not yet caught up with that fact.

Perhaps the toughest crucible for employee ownership, however, is where employees buy a failing firm. Here is a clear, if unusually demanding, test of the concept's mettle. There is less confusion here about a plan just being a sign of good management. These were fail-ing firms that were not employee owned before and were after.

Studying these companies is not easy, however. There is no gov-ernment list of buyouts, nor even an obvious definition (does a com-pany that is marginally profitable and might have been closed ex-cept for the buyout qualify?). Nonetheless, relying on newspaper accounts from a clipping service of all U.S. dailies, we have esti-mated that there have been about 60–70 buyouts since 1971, most of which occurred in the last five years. Two declared chapter 11 in 1984 (chapter 11 provides protection from creditors under the fed-eral bankruptcy code); one of these has reorganized as a smaller firm, the other has been sold. Four have been sold at a profit to out-siders, and we know of five firms that have closed. Given all the publicity these firms receive, we are reasonably sure that the rest are still in business. Moreover, according to our 1983 survey of major-ity employee owned firms, the 13 buyout companies in our sample had an employment growth rate twice that of comparable conven-tional firms. In other words, these companies are doing very well, especially considering the odds against them.

Finally, there is some research on the performance of worker ownership abroad. France, Italy, and Spain all have significant worker cooperative sectors, and there are isolated cases elsewhere. Yugoslavia's businesses are worker controlled, although not owned. There is some evidence that these sectors are more economically ef-fective than their conventional counterparts, although the evidence on Yugoslavia is, at best, mixed.[20]

Most of these studies have one major problem. Is the fact that employee ownership firms perform better a causal result of owner-ship sharing, or is simply an artifact of management innovative enough to set up a plan? What is needed are studies which track firms for several years before they set up a plan and several years after. A few such studies are now underway.

One recent study, however, somewhat clouds this sunny assess-ment. Arnold Tannenbaum and his colleagues at the University of Michigan recently did a follow-up to their 1978 study, this time looking at 55 of the firms they studied before, and 60 additional employee ownership companies. These were matched to 99 conven-tional companies.[21] They then looked at how ownership affected profits, productivity, and technological adaptiveness. They found that the employee ownership firms were little different from the conventional firms, with one significant exception—they were 10% less likely to go out of business over the 1976–82 study period, half of which was a recession. This was intriguing. Could it be that the employee ownership firms accepted lower earnings in bad times, while competitors closed their doors? Since some poorly performed conventional firms would have gone out of business before the study was started, there would be fewer poor performers in the conventional company sample, thus improving the numbers for those included. It would also mean lower productivity figures for the employee ownership companies, since their workers would be being paid more to produce less. In our work, we had seen numerous examples of companies who at least said it was their policy to accept lower profits, or even absorb losses, in order to keep people employed. Tannenbaum and Conte speculated that this might be the case, which could partly explain why the employee ownership companies could be more profitable than their competitors in good times (such as the 1976–78 period of the first study), but about the same in poorer ones. The study's sample also included a high percentage of distress buyouts, and these firms could be pulling down the numbers. Nonetheless, these results do indicate that the issue of the impact of employee ownership on corporate performance requires further research.

Fortunately, the General Accounting Office is now working on a comprehensive study on this issue, using tax returns of employee ownership companies. A report is due in late 1986. In the meantime, the studies described above have already created a very favorable impression of employee ownership in countless news stories, in the minds of legislators, and in an increasing number of company managers who believe the results. These management impressions may be especially important, for if these managers believe employee ownership will work, they may well act to make sure it does.

Employees and Ownership

What happens to the company's bottom line may be important to the spread of employee ownership but, after all, the ultimate point of the idea is to benefit employees. Does it?

Theorists and practitioners in the field have focused on three partially overlapping ways in which ownership can work for workers: increasing their participation in the company, making work more satisfying, and increasing their personal wealth. The research on the participation question was discussed earlier: employee ownership may well create more participation opportunities at all levels, but research on this point is lacking. Many academic observers of employee ownership have, however, contended that participation, especially at the management level, is the most important factor in determining how well employee ownership works for workers.[22] Unfortunately, there are few studies on this issue, and those there are focus on buyouts, where employees might well want more control than they would where, as is usually the case, employee ownership is essentially just a gift. Even so, the research from these cases presents a mixed picture of how much employees value management-level participation suggesting that while they do want more input, they only sometimes want a great deal of responsibility beyond the job level. Like members of most democratic organizations, it seems, they very rationally hope that their organizations will run well without their having to get too involved, although they may want the power in reserve to change things if needed. How many of us, if given the chance, would want to participate regularly in the management of our companies, cities, or voluntary organizations? Most of us, however, would like to be able to choose the people who will represent us in these matters. At the job level, however, employees do seem to want more input. Here, employees are already involved anyway, and may feel much more competent about their ability to make decisions. Our own data will address in much greater detail the question of how important participation is to employees.

A second issue is job satisfaction. Aside from any increase in wealth or participation, does just being an owner make work better? There is some reason to think it might. Imagine the typical non-owning worker's day. A machine is run repeatedly, customers are served the same products over and over again, someone's else letters are typed for eight hours, the same problems are serviced every day. Not all work, of course, is boring and repetitive, but much of it is, and few people really enjoy their work so much they would do it without pay, or even for less pay if they could make more elsewhere. Worse yet, machines run, products served, letters typed, and problems serviced all ultimately help build a business that belongs to other people. Would it make a difference to how employees feel about work if that work were for themselves? Don't we all feel different about cleaning our own house, fixing our own car, typing our own letters, or countless other routine things? Indeed, don't some things that are work for others even become hobbies for us when they are, literally, *for* us?

Obviously, the answer is yes, but we simply do not know if this same notion carries over to being a part-owner at work, and sometimes only a very small part at that. Existing research has only scratched the surface of this question. One study of San Francisco's employee-owned garbage collection companies compared the attitudes of these worker-owners with those of municipal garbage collectors, and found some support for the idea that ownership per se makes work more satisfying.[23] But the study was limited by the fact that these companies are unique social systems as well, with strong ethnic and family ties. They were formed in the 1920s by Italian immigrants and over the years came to dominate the Bay Area's garbage collection contracting. They were very democratically structured and provided equal pay for everyone, although over time they have tended to take on more and more non-owning employees. Because of the uniqueness of these companies, the authors caution against overinterpreting the results.

Two other studies compared workers at Pacific Northwest plywood cooperatives with workers at conventional plywood companies.[24] The plywood coops are also quite unusual, and also provide equal pay for all employees, a strong social system at work, and democratic management. Both of the studies of these coops found that the worker-owners were more satisfied with their jobs than the non-owners, although both found that participation was important in enhancing these feelings. Here too, however, it is hard to generalize these findings to all employee ownership companies.

A third study looked at three different companies, and found that the larger the share of the company owned by employees the more satisfied they were.[25] Again, participation enhanced these feelings.

The study was intriguing, but three companies do not, of course, suggest more than a fruitful line of inquiry.

Finally, there is the question of how much money employees will get from owning stock. Other studies, such as the one just mentioned, looked at the percentage of a company owned by workers, but this may or may not translate into dollars: 10% of a profitable, capital intensive company, for instance, will probably be worth more than 100% of a marginally profitable, labor intensive one. There are really two questions here: (1) how much do employee owners get out of this? and (2) does how much they get matter to how they feel about work? Other than this, however, only one study addresses either issue, and then only as a sidelight. In this study the authors disappointedly concluded that workers at an early employee buyout seemed to view their stock more as an investment than as a vehicle to gain more control of their companies, indicating that money matters more than control.[26] Otherwise, alas, the research is silent on these questions. The reason for this, in itself, is an interesting question. Why is it that most of the existing research on employee ownership focuses on how much money the company makes or how such employee ownership increases employee participation, both side benefits of a concept principally designed to broaden the ownership of wealth?

Partly, the answer is that data are hard to obtain. Companies are reluctant to reveal to outsiders how much employees own. Moreover, the nature of employee ownership is that the amounts grow over time and vest over time. Since the phenomenon is so new, it is difficult (but not impossible) to estimate just how much employees are getting. Fortunately, the General Accounting Office study, with access to detailed records, will be answering this question. We will address it as well. Part of the explanation, however, seems to be a reluctance to admit how important the issue may be to employees. Are researchers, who themselves probably can and do look to intrinsic factors at work for satisfaction more than would other workers, projecting their own values onto the subjects of their research? Whatever the reason, this oversight has been very important, for the major finding of our project is that money matters very much to employee owners, and is the key factor in determining how they react to being owners.

Workers and Work: Lessons from Other Research

If the research on employee ownership is still in its infancy, research on work generally, of which there is an abundance, may shed additional light. What is it that makes work rewarding? First and foremost, work offers important monetary rewards. Research finds that the more money an employee earns, the more satisfied he or she is likely to be, even after taking into account (controlling for) the worker's managerial level.[27] Nonetheless, the bulk of recent psychological research and theory points to intrinsic factors at work— especially job challenge, autonomy, and influence—as the primary determinants of work satisfaction. This emphasis is apparent in research on job characteristics, leadership, quality of work life, and related topics. By contrast, researchers and theorists devote relatively little attention to compensation and its effects. It is almost as if researchers take pay for granted and prefer to look elsewhere for research targets.

Research and theory on what makes work rewarding is a book—or even a library—in itself. Here, we can only just barely skim the surface in order to provide some general sense of current psychological thinking about work and motivation. We very briefly review several prominent theories in organizational psychology.

The job characteristics model of job satisfaction and motivation suggests that five key job characteristics are most important for motivating employees.[28] The five characteristics are:

1. Skill Variety (the degree to which a job involves a variety of different activities that require different skills and talents of the worker).
2. Task Identity (the degree to which a job requires completion of a "whole" and identifiable piece of work, i.e., doing a job from beginning to end with a visible outcome).
3. Task Significance (the degree to which the job has a substantial impact on the lives of other people, inside or outside the organization).

4. Autonomy (the degree to which the job provides substantial freedom, independence, and discretion to the individual in carrying out the work).
5. Feedback (the degree to which carrying out the work activities provides the employee with information about the effectiveness of his or her performance).

Clearly, the job characteristics approach shares the common emphasis on the intrinsic satisfactions of work. According to a strict interpretation of the job characteristics model, employee ownership would make work more satisfying if, for example, employee ownership increased workers' *skill variety* (as owners, perhaps workers get to do more highly skilled and varied work), *task identity* (as owners, perhaps workers perform more complete tasks, or perhaps they acquire a better understanding of the whole company operation), or *autonomy* (as owners, perhaps workers gain more freedom and influence on the job).

Research on leadership also highlights, from the opposite side of the coin, the importance of leaders providing their subordinates as much respect, courtesy, and freedom as possible. This style of leadership is typically associated with high employee morale, though not always with high employee productivity.[29] When it is important that subordinates understand, accept, and commit themselves to implementing a decision, researchers suggest that the leader involve subordinates in the decision-making as much as possible.[30] In this way, subordinates may be active participants in adopting, planning for, and implementing the decision, instead of bystanders or even victims of the decision-making. Again, the implications of this area of research for employee ownership are fairly obvious: Employee ownership will improve morale and employee commitment if employee ownership makes leaders treat employees more supportively and participatively.

In recent years, quality of work life (QWL) has become the latest bandwagon in both the popular and academic work-related press. QWL innovations—quality circles, autonomous work groups, and the like—are designed to increase employees' job satisfaction and organizational commitment while maintaining or enhancing employees' productivity. QWL programs typically increase employees' influence in job-related decision-making. Most of these innovations derive from several basic principles of work design that emphasize worker autonomy and dignity.[31] For example, the principle of "minimal critical specification" says that only very important ("critical") job tasks and procedures should be required by ("specified in") established rules and procedures. Beyond the most important and basic requirements, workers should have as much freedom as possible in carrying out their tasks. In this way, workers will be more satisfied, committed, creative, and, ultimately, productive in their work. Proponents of QWL principles and innovations would argue that employee ownership will have positive effects on employee morale and productivity if employee ownership also leads to increased autonomy and responsibility on the job.

Obviously, the three areas of research just described have much in common. They come to the same basic conclusion: Give workers respect, autonomy, and as much power and influence as possible, and workers will respond with high morale, longevity, and performance. Still, it is important to recognize that other areas of research highlight somewhat different aspects of the job, including compensation (as suggested above), promotions, physical working conditions, and the employee's work group. These areas of research might suggest alternative hypotheses about the effects of employee ownership.

What We Need to Learn

So where does all this leave us? What do we know, and what do we still need to learn, about employee ownership?

We have a pretty good grasp of what employee ownership is—how it works, who does it, and why companies and employees do it. We have some preliminary evidence that employee ownership can improve company performance, and much more detailed studies are underway. We have some evidence that ownership increases participation and job satisfaction, but it is very preliminary and limited to a few atypical cases. We have no evidence on what employee ownership does for workers' bank accounts, or how much workers care about that.

We also know very little about what makes employee ownership work, either in terms of company performance or worker attitudes and behaviors. Why do some companies do better than others? Why do some end up with motivated employees, lots of cooperation, lower turnover, and more employee input—all the things that can lead to more money and better work for everyone—than do others? We have a lot of theorizing that it is participation or control that makes the difference, and some that it is how much of the company is owned by the employees. The participation theory even has some evidence behind it, although it is limited and based on idiosyncratic firms or samples. But there is also contradictory evidence that at least one measure of participation, voting rights, does not make a difference. We have no evidence on whether such things as company size or industry, profitability, stock performance, communications programs, age of the plan, size of the individual employee accounts, plan structure, workforce composition, or other factors make any difference.

This leaves us in something of an academic and practical quandry. If this idea of sharing ownership with employees makes any difference, just how does it do it? As researchers interested in the theory of work, what do we learn from employee ownership efforts about how work works? As consultants, company or union officials, policymakers, or employees, what should we look for, or insist on, to make sure employee ownership succeeds?

These are the questions with which the rest of this book will deal.

4

The Mystery and the Method

Tracking the Causes of Employee Ownership Success

A t this point in a book, authors often describe their "method-ology." They treat this chapter like a plate of boiled spinach in a meal of cheeseburgers, french fries, and ice cream. "Go ahead and skip this chapter," they indulgently tell their readers. "No one will notice."

For us, however, this would mean skipping one of the best parts. To risk another analogy, we think this chapter is a lot like the last chapter of a mystery novel, the one where the detective tells you how he figured out who did it. In mysteries, the results come first; methods are only revealed in the end. Here, we won't make you wait.

To push our analogy a little further, the mystery at hand is this: What makes employee ownership work best? In this chapter, we won't tell you the solution to the mystery (though we have left plenty of clues in the preceding chapters). The solution comes in the next chapters. Here, we tell you how we solved the mystery—how we set about to isolate the apparent causes of employee ownership success. And we'll discuss the likely "culprits"—our educated guesses, or hypotheses, about the possible causes of employee ownership success. While ours is a "what-did-it," rather than a "whodunit," we think the process is equally interesting.

The Case of the Withering Ownership Plan
Or
What's Employee Ownership Success?

Even before we started our research, we'd heard tales of withering employee ownership plans—tales of companies that had set up employee ownership plans and then watched nothing happen. From management's point of view, workers weren't more motivated, didn't stay with the company any longer, and still complained about their work. Employees, on the other hand, saw employee ownership as little more than a tax gimmick for the company. Yet managers at other companies regaled us with fabulous accounts of eager employee owners watching every penny, working harder and smarter, and enriching both themselves and the company. Why were some companies so successful with employee ownership while others plodded along or even faltered? This was the mystery we wanted to solve.

The first step was to define the "crime"—in our case, really no crime at all, but the feat of employee ownership success. What is employee ownership success? Is it company profitability or productivity? One can define employee ownership success in this way; many people have. But as we discussed in the previous chapter, focusing on the profitability or productivity of employee ownership companies can be very tricky. Isolating the causes of a company's financial success is extremely difficult. And even if we could do that, we would still have problems measuring company financial success. Profitability and productivity seem like good measures, but most closely held companies use widely varying accounting systems. This makes profitability comparisons of little value. Productivity is even less useful, as relatively few firms keep productivity records and those that do measure productivity in different ways.

Ultimately, we opted for a more immediate and certain definition of employee ownership success: employee attitudes. What do employees think of owning stock? Are employees committed to the company? Are they satisfied in their work? Do they value being owners? Do they have plans to leave the company? Interestingly, almost every other definition of employee ownership success (even profitability and productivity) implicitly or explicitly encompasses this definition. Employee ownership observers often assume that any positive effects of employee ownership are caused by changes in employee attitudes. For example, the belief that employee ownership leads to company financial success is based on the assumption that employee owners work harder and better than conventional workers.

Thus, we decided to go after "the thing itself," the key to almost any kind of employee ownership success—employee attitudes. Below, we discuss in greater detail just how we measured these attitudes, but first we discuss our hypotheses about the factors that might lead to positive employee attitudes about employee ownership.

Likely Culprits
Or
What Causes Employee Ownership Success?

As employee ownership is a new phenomenon on the American scene, there is relatively little research on the subject. What's more, as we discussed in the preceding chapter, most of the existing research on employee ownership has examined only one or a handful of companies, not enough to establish a sound, generalizable pattern of results. Finally, there is no single, well-established theory of employee ownership success. In initially plotting out our research, then, we were on our own.

Ultimately, we turned to previous research on employee ownership, to research on work satisfaction in general, and to common sense in developing our research hypotheses. The most obvious starting place was the employee ownership plan itself. Maybe something about how the plan was set up influenced employees' feelings about owning stock and about the company as a whole.

The first likely culprit was the percentage of the company owned by the employees. Wouldn't employees who owned, say, 60% of their company be more satisfied than employees who only owned 3%? This seemed an obvious point, and one that previous research had suggested as well.[1]

A second suspect was employee stock voting rights. Voting rights are at the heart of what many people think it means to be an owner. If you can't even vote the stock that you own, isn't stock ownership a hollow victory, a false promise? This too seemed an obvious point and we incorporated it into our arsenal of potential causes of employee ownership success.

Along somewhat similar lines, we wondered about the reason the company had established an employee ownership plan. If the company had established the plan primarily for the plan's tax benefits, wouldn't employees smell a rat? Wouldn't they see through management's vain promises and resist employee ownership as one more management trick? Conversely, if the company put in an employee ownership plan because of management's deep-seated belief in sharing control and profits with employees, wouldn't employees respond quite differently, and much more positively, to employee ownership? While these two extreme points (tax reasons and philosophical reasons) were rather clear, it was more difficult to predict the outcomes of intermediate reasons (on our implied continuum) for installing an ownership plan. How would employees respond to a plan set up to buy the company during a corporate divestiture? How would employees respond to a plan established because the company wanted to provide employees with a retirement benefit? Because we couldn't answer these questions as well as we would have liked, we considered a fourth variable, management's philosophical commitment to the concept of employee ownership, all the while keeping the primary reason for employee ownership in the hypothesis arsenal.

Management's commitment to the concept of employee ownership is itself a rather slippery concept. What we were trying to capture was the strength of management's belief in the importance of sharing ownership with employees. Did management view the employee ownership plan as an isolated, purely pragmatic tax-saving plan? Or did management see employee ownership as more than that—as a part of the company's overall culture, human relations policy, and/or commitment to employees?

We reasoned that management's commitment to the concept of employee ownership might be related to the primary reason management installed an ownership plan, but that the two were not the same thing. Take, for example, two companies that are both using an ESOP to cash out the founder and transfer ownership to employees. For both companies, the primary reason for employee ownership is, crudely speaking, to put cash in the founder's pocket. For one company, that may be all there is to employee ownership. But for the second company, employee ownership represents the embodiment of the company's longstanding emphasis on "the company family" and sharing with employees. This is a difference we thought employees would feel and to which they would respond.

Our fifth suspect was management communication to employees about the employee ownership plan. Most employee ownership plans are complicated legal instruments. Unless the plans are well explained to employees, employees won't understand or appreciate them. Just how much does management do to explain and publicize their plans to employees? Is there an employee ownership seminar series, an employee ownership newsletter, an annual meeting for employee stockholders? In theory, too much communication might unrealistically raise employee expectations about the benefits of employee ownership. But we didn't think this would happen very often. In fact, communication programs about employee ownership should educate employees and reshape their unrealistic expectations.

The first five suspects, or independent variables, that we have just reviewed emphasize both the intrinsic and instrumental benefits of employee ownership; employees will feel more like owners and/or will have more ownership power when (a) employees own more company stock; (b) employees have voting rights; (c) management installed the plan for philosophical reasons rather than tax purposes; (d) management is committed to the concept of employee ownership (regardless of the exact reason for establishing the ownership plan); and (e) there are a number of programs to educate employees about employee ownership.

Still, we thought something was missing from this conception of the dynamics and rewards of ownership: Money. When people buy stock on the stock market, they do so in order to make money, and they are excited when they do make a profit. Was employee ownership really so different? We thought not. Hence, the next two suspects in our line-up describe the financial benefits of employee ownership.

In a typical employee ownership plan (an ESOP), four factors determine the financial benefits of employee ownership to individual employees: (1) the employee's salary (because stock is typically allocated according to wages or salary); (2) the employee's tenure with the company (the longer s/he has been with the company, the more stock s/he will have acquired and the more vested his/her stock will be); (3) the size of the company's contribution to the employee ownership plan; and (4) the performance of company stock. The first two of these four factors are individual characteristics. Because we are primarily interested in what companies can do with their plans in order to change employee attitudes, we emphasize the second two factors.

The size of a company's contribution to the employee ownership plan tells us how much stock the employee receives annually. Recall that in almost all ESOPs, stock is allocated according to employee salary. Thus, the size of a company's contribution to the employee ownership plan can be measured as a percentage of the covered payroll. This number tells us whether employees of a given company all receive an amount equal to 1%, 5%, 10%, 13.37%, or whatever of their pay in the ESOP each year. This figure may vary from year to year, depending on the company's financial performance, legal commitment to the plan, and a variety of other factors. The larger the company's contribution to the ESOP (again, as a percentage of the covered payroll), the more money any given employee's ESOP account is worth.

A brief ESOP example may clarify this point. If a company contributes 1% of the covered payroll to the ESOP each year, a $20,000-a-year employee will receive $200 in his/her ESOP account each year. If the company contributes 10% of the covered payroll, the same employee will receive $2,000.

The other key factor that determines the financial benefits of employee ownership is our seventh suspect: the performance of company stock. If stock values climb, the ESOP benefit is much larger. Surely employees would rather own stock in a profitable, growing company than a declining one.

We had thus identified seven suspects, seven ESOP characteristics that seemed to capture the essential nature of employee ownership. Each hypothesis seemed "obvious," but still we had no idea which "obvious" hypothesis was correct. Our actual study would identify the key culprits, the real ring leaders, from these seven.

Before closing the door on this stage of our research, however, we identified one last suspect, not a characteristic of the ESOP, but of the company as a whole: worker participation. Much of the existing employee ownership literature argues that employees will only respond positively to employee ownership when they have a relatively high degree of influence in company decision-making. While the evidence linking worker participation to employee ownership per se or even linking worker participation to employee satisfaction with stock ownership is quite weak, the hypothesis is very common. One more suspect to include in the research. Our measure of participation looks at the influence employees have over everything from social events to company financial decisions.

In sum, we identified eight possible determinants of employee satisfaction with stock ownership:

1. The percent of company stock owned by the employees;
2. Employee stock voting rights;
3. The primary reason the company established an employee ownership plan;
4. Management's commitment to employee ownership;
5. The employee ownership communications program;
6. The size of the company contribution to the ownership plan (as a percent of the covered payroll);
7. The performance of company stock; and
8. Worker participation.

These eight variables would, we believed, allow us to differentiate between "successful" and "unsuccessful" employee ownership companies. Remember that our definition of employee ownership success focuses on employee morale—employee satisfaction with stock ownership and with the company in general.

We should note, parenthetically, that we also identified (and measured) a variety of basic company characteristics, such as company size, industrial sector, company financial status, unionization, and the age of the employee ownership plan. On the basis of previous research and our own conceptualization of the effects of employee ownership, we did not believe, however, that these variables would be signficantly related to our outcome measures.

Tracking the Suspects: A Description of Our Research Strategy

The mystery was obvious. The key suspects were all identified. The problem now was that the solution of the mystery was all conjectural.

To make our case, we needed to gather hard evidence for each alternative hypothesis. Our research model dictated certain research directions and constraints. Our focus was on *company* success, our independent variables were *company* characteristics. This dictated that we use the company, rather than the individual employee, as our primary unit of analysis. Thus, we would need to study a relatively large number of companies in order to validly test our hypotheses and generalize our results.

At the same time, our research emphasized employee perceptions. Thus, a simple mail survey to company presidents would not suffice. We needed not only to study a relatively large number of companies, we needed to study them in depth. This combination of extensive research (studying a relatively large number of companies) and intensive research (conducting employee surveys) would let us bridge the gap between the existing large-scale mail surveys of employee ownership companies and in-depth case studies of one or a handful of employee ownership firms.

In order to achieve this goal within the limits of time and funding, we gave up other aspects of the ideal study of employee ownership. Ideally, one would compare employee-owned companies with conventionally owned companies. For a variety of reasons, we opted to study only employee ownership firms. First, it would have been practically infeasible to find matched controls for the employee ownership companies. Second, comparing employee-owned and conventionally owned "comparison" (not matched) companies can be very misleading; unless companies are carefully matched, there may be important differences between the employee-owned and conventionally owned firms in addition to employee ownership. Third, the variability in employee ownership characteristics across our sample of companies allowed us to use statistical controls as a partial substitute for the ideal matched controls research design.

Other compromises were less significant, though still unfortunate. We would, for example, have liked to interview employee owners at the firms we studied. That would have been very time consuming, however, both for ourselves and the companies. Many companies would not have agreed to such a study. Thus, we relied instead on a carefully designed and quite thorough employee survey. Further, we collected the necessary financial background information on each firm, but no more than that. While a pure economics study might have gathered more financial and technical data than we did, this was beyond the focus and scope of our research. All of these compromises were, we believe, well justified in terms of the data we were able to gather.

At the end of our study, we had collected data in more than 45 employee ownership companies: 37 ESOPs, five coops, and three hybrid forms of employee ownership. In each company, we interviewed a management official of the company (usually the company president, a vice-president, or the head of personnel) and surveyed all or a random sample of employees. In all, more than 3,700 employees completed our survey, making our study by far the largest study of employee perceptions of stock ownership to date.

Having provided this general introduction, we must turn to a somewhat more technical discussion of our research methodology. To use the mystery metaphor once again, this is the time to describe our sleuthing paraphenalia, the color of the mackintosh, and the shape of the magnifying glass.

Subjects

Most of our data analyses are based on the responses of 2,804 ESOP participants in 37 ESOP companies. Though we surveyed both ESOP participants and non-participants in most of the study companies, we only included ESOP participants in our data analyses. The full sample of ESOP participants and non-participants has 3,459 subjects. We excluded non-participants because the opinions of non-participants about the company ESOP would be difficult to interpret. Also, we wanted to insure comparability across the company sample.

(All employees automatically participate in the company ESOP unless the company ESOP rules exclude certain employee groups from ESOP participation. A company may exclude one or more of the following groups from ESOP participation: employees under 21 or 25 years of age; employees who have not yet reached a full year of company service; part-time employees; and employees who are union members.)

Our non-ESOP companies (mostly cooperatives) are analyzed separately in chapter 8. We analyzed these separately because the structure of these firms, as well as the motivation of employees in these firms, are too different from ESOP firms to group them together.

Table 4–1 summarizes the demographic characteristics of the 2,804 subjects in the 37 ESOP firms. Approximately 69% of the respondents were men. Approximately 91% were white. The vast majority of the respondents had completed high school, and approximately 29% had completed college. Average employee tenure was seven years and the average respondent was 37 years old; 34% of the respondents earned between $10,000 and $20,000 a year; 29% earned between $20,000 and $30,000 a year; about 13% earned more than $40,000 a year. Thus, our prototypical ESOP participant was a fairly well educated, rather well paid, 37-year-old white male who had worked for his employer for seven years.

Sampling
Sampling of ESOP companies is always difficult. Until very recently, no comprehensive lists of ESOP companies were available, even from the federal government. In our research, we relied on several fairly thorough but still incomplete lists of ESOP firms. We received a partial list of ESOP companies from the U.S. Department of Labor, and then supplemented this list with company names from newspaper clips, professional ESOP specialists, and other researchers. From these lists we identified conveniently located ESOP firms near the two major study sites, Arlington, Virginia, and San Francisco.

We asked at least 75 ESOP companies to participate in our research; 37 agreed, for a company response rate of approximately 49%, quite respectable for this kind of research. Of the 38 companies that refused to participate, approximately 10% said they would not participate because the company was undergoing serious financial troubles and they either did not want to be bothered at the time or did not want to survey employees when morale was low. The other companies refused to participate because company management did not approve of the research, did not think the timing was right for an employee survey, did not think the research was appropriate for their company, or had a policy of refusing all research requests.

The 37 ESOP companies provide a good mix. Twenty-two companies are located on the West Coast, nine on the East Coast,

Table 4–1
Background Characteristics of the Survey Respondents:
Frequencies and Percentages for Categorical Variables,
Average and Standard Deviation for Continuous Variables

Background Characteristics	Frequency[a]	Percentage
Sex		
Males	1894	68.6
Females	867	31.4
Ethnicity		
Black American	82	3.0
Asian American	42	1.5
American Indian	13	.5
Spanish-surnamed American	64	2.3
White	2471	90.7
Other	51	1.9
Education		
Some elementary school	18	.6
Completed elementary school	42	1.5
Some high school	144	5.2
High school diploma	680	24.5
Some college	1089	39.3
College degree	389	14.0
Some graduate school	186	6.7
Graduate degree	225	8.1
Present Pay (per year)		
Less than $10,000	230	8.5
$10,000 to $19,999	920	33.9
$20,000 to $29,999	788	29.0
$30,000 to $39,999	418	15.4
$40,000 to $49,999	208	7.7
$50,000 or more	149	5.5
Average Age	37.10	
Standard deviation	11.75	
Average Years with the Company	7.04	
Standard deviation	7.53	

[a]Due to incomplete data on some responses, item totals are not equal.

and six in other parts of the United States. The average ESOP owns 42.33% of company stock, with the smallest ESOP owning 1% of company stock and five ESOPs owning 100% of company stock.

Twenty-one companies are primarily manufacturing firms, seven are professional service companies, and nine are retail and/or wholesale outfits. The companies have an average of 514 employees.

The company sample appears to be quite representative of ESOP companies. The sample may, however, be biased insofar as (1) some less profitable companies declined to participate; (2) approximately 38% of the companies are majority employee owned; and (3) the sample is made up of companies that thought enough of their ESOP to want to participate in our research.

We describe the study companies and their ESOPs in more detail in the subsequent chapter. In addition, several of the most successful ESOP firms are profiled in chapter 7.

Design

The study is correlational. This means that we cannot actually prove that there is a causal relationship between any of the study variables. If we could study employee ownership using a perfectly controlled laboratory study, we might be able to show proof of causality with our results. But, as is often the case in the social sciences, the most stringent research tools are not applicable to the most interesting real-life research issues. Throughout our research, we have tried to uphold the twin goals of good research (in the methodological sense) and important research (in the substantive sense), for surely these goals are inextricably related.

Procedures

In contacting a company for study, we first approached an appropriate company official (the company president, vice-president, treasurer, or personnel director) with a brief introductory letter that explained the purposes of our research and requested a meeting. We found that if the company official agreed to a meeting, chances were good that the company would participate in the study; those managers who had no interest in the study would not even consent to a preliminary meeting.

At the preliminary meeting, we used a structured interview to gather background information on the business of the firm, the firm's history, its management practices, and its employee ownership plan.

We also asked the management official for his or her appraisal of the employee ownership plan. We typically concluded the meeting with a discussion of how the employee survey would take place.

The surveys were administered in one of four ways. They were either: (1) distributed to employees and collected at a central company site, usually the personnel office, with employees given up to two weeks to complete the surveys; (2) mailed to employees' homes and mailed back to the researcher; (3) distributed and collected at a single hour-long meeting at the company; or (4) distributed and collected in a manner that combines the first three methods.

The average survey response rate, by company, was 55.13%. Not surprisingly, the response rate was highest in those companies that held a meeting for employees to complete the survey (option #3). Only two companies chose this option, however.

In addition to the actual survey, employees received a cover letter that explained the purpose of the research and assured employees that their answers were anonymous and their participation voluntary. Employees also typically received a letter from a company management official encouraging them to participate in the study. In return for participation, we gave each company a feedback report on the results of the survey at that company.

Measures of the Independent Variables
The measures of ESOP and company characteristics were based on the interview data gathered from the managerial respondent.

Percent of Stock Owned by the ESOP measured the number of shares owned by the ESOP relative to the total number of company shares at the time of the employee survey.

Voting Rights measured whether employees were allowed to vote their ESOP shares on all issues (0 = no, 1 = yes).

To measure *The Reason the Company Established the ESOP*, we asked the managerial respondent to pick from a list of seven reasons: (1) Employee Benefit (to provide a retirement benefit for employees); (2) Incentive (to provide an incentive for employees to work harder); (3) Financial (to gain a tax advantage or raise capital); (4) Philosophical (to give employees an opportunity to own part of the company they work for); (5) Avoiding a Shutdown (to finance employee purchase of a plant that would otherwise close); (6) Business Transfer (to provide a private market for stock of existing shareholders who want to sell their stock, especially to purchase all or part of the founder's stock); and (7) Corporate Divestiture (to finance employee purchase of a division that the corporate owner is offering for sale).

To measure *Management's Philosophical Commitment to Employee Ownership*, we asked the management official to respond to three items and then averaged the respondent's answers. The items were:

1. Employee ownership is a central part of our management philosophy.
2. For our company, the employee ownership plan is primarily a tax-saving or financing mechanism. (Reverse scoring)
3. Employee ownership plays a major role in our corporate culture and identity.

Respondents answered by using a seven-point response scale ranging from Strongly Disagree (1) to Strongly Agree (7). Chronbach's alpha, a measure of the internal consistency and statistical reliability of survey scales, is .49.

Employee Ownership Communications is a measure of the number of different ways in which management attempts to inform and educate employees about employee ownership. The managerial respondent simply checked the relevant items on a checklist of strategies (for example, employee ownership mentioned in company letterhead, employee ownership discussed in initial orientation for employees, annual meeting for employee stockholders). The maximum score for Communications is 12.

The Size of the Last Annual Company Contribution to the ESOP was the amount of cash or stock the company contributed to the ESOP trust in the year preceding the employee survey. The Company Contribution was calculated as a percent of the covered employee payroll. A company's contribution to its ESOP could range from 0% (no contribution that year) to 25% of salary of participating employees.

Change in the Market or Appraised Value of Company Stock measured the percentage change in the value of company stock during the two-year period preceding the employee survey. These data were available for 33 companies.

Management-Perceived Worker Influence measured the managerial respondent's assessment of the average level of employee influence over seven areas ranging from social events to company financial policy. The questions used a five-point scale ranging from "Workers have no say" (1) to "Workers decide alone" (5).[2] This scale measures both formal and informal worker influence insofar as it does not specify the mechanisms by which workers assert their influence. Chronbach's alpha is .86.

Formal Worker Participation Groups is a second measure of employee influence. In contrast to the above measure, this measure examines the formal, established mechanisms for company decision-making and policy formation. The scale asks whether the company has "any active working groups or committees" pertaining to seven substantive areas (for example, quality control, strategic planning, budget and financial control). The measure is scored to reflect whether each committee includes the chief executive officer and his/her immediate subordinates (1 point); other managerial or supervisory person(s) (2 additional points); and/or non-supervisory person(s) (3 additional points). Thus, the lowest possible score is 0 points (no formal committees at all). The highest possible score is 42, indicating formal committees in all areas that all involve all three levels of employees (7 committees $\times$ (1 + 2 + 3) = 7 $\times$ 6 = 42).[3]

These nine measures were the most important ESOP and company characteristics for our statistical analyses. We measured several additional ESOP and company characteristics for background information analyses. These include the *Age of the ESOP* (the number of years the company had had its ESOP, up to the time of our company survey), the *Number of Years Until ESOP Vesting Begins* (the number of years of ESOP participation required before an employee's ESOP account begins to vest), the *Number of Years From Initial to Full ESOP Vesting* (the number of years it takes for an employee's ESOP account to become fully vested), and also more basic company characteristics. For example, we measured *Company Size* (the number of full-time employees in the company at the time of the employee survey, regardless of the number of actual ESOP participants in the company), the company's *Primary Industrial Sector* (coded as manufacturing, sales, or professional services), *Annual Sales, Unionization* (yes or no), *Public/Private Status,* and also *Shared Financial Information,* (whether management shares company financial information with non-managerial employees).

Measures of the Dependent Variables
We used several different measures to quantify employee work attitudes. We considered strong positive scores on these measures to be indicative of employee ownership success.

Wherever possible, we used pre-existing, validated measures of employee outcomes. These measures were available for Organizational Commitment, Job Satisfaction, and Turnover Intention. No such measures existed for employee satisfaction with stock ownership, however. Hence, we created our own measure of this variable. We began by writing 15 scale items to assess employee views of stock ownership. On the basis of statistical and analytical techniques (factor analyses, reliability tests, and conceptual analyses), we dropped seven of the 15 items from our statistical analyses and created an eight-item measure of *General ESOP Satisfaction.* We dropped these items in order to be sure that our final measure of ESOP Satisfaction really measured just that, and that it did not also measure other employee opinions about the ESOP (for example, employee beliefs about the relationship of employee ownership and worker influence). We did, however, keep all 15 items for our descriptive analyses, presented in the next chapter.

General ESOP Satisfaction measures employees' general attitude about the employee ownership plan. Chronbach's alpha is .91. The eight items in the scale are:

1. Because of employee ownership, my work is more satisfying.
2. I really don't care about the employee ownership plan in this company. (Reverse scoring)
3. I'm proud to own stock in this company.
4. Employee ownership at this company makes my day-to-day work more enjoyable.
5. Owning stock in this company makes me want to stay with this company longer than I would if I did not own stock.

6. It is very important to me that this company has an employee stock ownership plan.
7. Owning stock in this company makes me more interested in the company's financial success.
8. Employee ownership at this company gives me a greater share in company profits.

In addition to this measure of ownership satisfaction, we included three common measures of employee work satisfaction. *Organizational Commitment* measures the employee's sense of involvement and identification with his or her company.[4] The scale has nine items (for example, "This organization really inspires the very best in me in the way of job performance"). Alpha for the scale is .90 in this research.

Turnover Intention is a three-item scale measuring whether employees are thinking of leaving the company (for example, "I will probably look for a new job in the next year"). Alpha for the scale is .91 in this research.

Job Satisfaction is a three-item scale that measures employees' overall assessment of their job (for example, "In general, I like working here").[6] Alpha is .84.

For supplementary data analyses, we included a second set of independent variables describing employees' perceptions of worker influence and supervisory relations. We used these measures to better assess the relationship of employee ownership and worker participation, and of worker participation and employee satisfaction. Though somewhat tangential to our primary focus, the study of the relationship of employee ownership and employee satisfaction is (as discussed in chapter 3) at the heart of several previous studies of employee ownership.

To assess *Employee-Perceived Worker Influence*, we asked employees to complete the same seven-item scale that we used, in the management interview, to assess Management-Perceived Worker Influence.[7] Again, this scale asks how much influence non-managerial employees have over seven specific subject areas. Alpha for the scale is .77.

Desired Worker Influence measures how much influence employees think that non-managerial employees *should* have in company decision-making. This scale parallels Employee-Perceived Worker Influence, but asks "How much say or influence do you think that non-managerial workers in your company should have over the following areas?" (Employee-Perceived Worker Influence simply asks, "How much say or influence do non-managerial workers in your company actually have over the following areas?") Alpha for the scale is .80.

The scale items for all of the employee survey items are listed in appendix A.

Statistical Analyses

The company was the unit of analysis for all tests of the relationships between ESOP characteristics and employee attitudes. In other words, the dependent variable was the average company score on each outcome measure; our N was 37 companies, not 2,804 ESOP participants. This means that our research really addresses the question, "How is a given company or ESOP value related to the general or average employee attitude in each company?" and *not*, "How does a given company or ESOP characteristic affect the individual employee?" Aggregation of data is a complicated statistical issue that baffles many researchers. The important point to remember is that we are describing company averages, not individual employees.

The company level of analysis is appropriate for several reasons: (1) the ESOP is a company-wide intervention that is intended to influence employees as a group; (2) the ESOP is not a matter of individual choice—employees are usually automatically included in the ESOP; (3) individuals are nested within companies and thus individual scores cannot be considered random, independent observations; and (4) the unit of analysis must be the company in order to treat ESOP characteristics as random, rather than fixed, variables and permit generalization to other ESOP companies.[8]

An analogy to research on another subject may be helpful. In research on leader effectiveness, for example, it is important to aggregate subordinates' perceptions of the leader to the level of the leader.[9] In this way, the focus is on the leader, not on the subordinates. We aggregate to the ESOP because we are studying ESOP effectiveness.

Summary

This chapter has described our primary research questions, our hypotheses, and research methods. In a nutshell, we want to solve a simple mystery: What causes employee ownership success? What makes employees most satisfied with employee ownership and most committed to their companies?

In the following chapters, we present our research results. Chapter 5 describes our study companies and then examines employee perceptions of stock ownership. It answers the question, "What do employees think about owning stock?" Chapter 6 describes the relationship of the key ESOP characteristics and employees' ESOP and work satisfaction. It answers the question, "Under what conditions are employees most satisfied with ESOP employee ownership and with their companies in general?" Chapter 6 also discusses the relationship of employee ownership and worker participation. Chapter 7 provides an in-depth examination of some of our most successful study companies and chapter 8 focuses on the worker cooperatives and other non-ESOP companies that we studied.

5
Company Characteristics and Employee Reactions to Ownership

Imagine that your boss comes to you one day and says, "I'm going to make you an owner. I'm going to set up a special trust fund and contribute money or stock to it. You don't have to pay anything. If you stay here long enough, you can take the stock with you when you leave. If the company does well—and you can help make sure that it does—you will leave this company with a lot of money."

How would you react? Would this make a difference to your life at work? Would you work harder? Would you enjoy your work more? Would being an owner give you more influence in the company? Would you even want more influence? Would you really get richer through stock ownership?

And just what kind of company would do such a thing? It must be, many people would think, an unusual company—maybe a high-tech firm that needed incentives to attract good people, or a basic industry that was offering stock in lieu of wages. Perhaps only small companies would do this, for there it might be easier to get the employees to pull together as owners.

In this chapter, we answer these questions by looking at data from our 37 ESOP companies and 2,804 survey respondents. Our answers, it turns out, are very clear. The companies that set up employee ownership plans are remarkable only in how unremarkable they are. If you didn't know these firms had employee ownership plans, you might well think they were just a typical cross-section of U.S. companies.

The employees in these companies are pretty typical too, except that they are owners. And they like being owners. What they like most about ownership is the potential for economic gain, a potential these companies seem to be realizing. The median stock performance for our study firms was +9% per year, during a time (1981–1983) when stock prices were declining sharply on major indices. While employees are enthusiastic about the financial benefits of ownership, they are less convinced of its ability to increase their influence in their companies.

Our results provide a general picture of employee reactions to ownership. On the basis of the data we present here, we cannot tell what makes some companies' ESOPs great motivators and others little more than an obscure employee benefit. That is the burden of the next chapter.

Basic Company Characteristics

The material presented below is drawn from our interviews with a key management official in each company we studied. The material provides an idea of just what kinds of companies participated in our study.

Company Size. Our 37 companies average 514 employees (standard deviation = 1167.12). The companies range in size from 15 to 7,080 employees. Twelve companies have fewer than 100 employees. Twenty have more than 100, but fewer than 1,000 employees. Five companies have over 1,000 employees.

Industrial Sector. Twenty of the 37 companies are manufacturing firms. For example, four companies print and publish books, magazines, and annual reports, two companies manufacture scientific equipment, one firm makes picture frames, another makes combustion burners, another manufactures computer parts, and another makes camping gear and clothing. Nine of the firms are in wholesale or retail sales. For example, one company is a wholesale seller of infant toys and supplies, another is a wholesale and retail seller of hardwoods, one firm operates a chain of 32 retail record and tape stores, and another operates a chain of 22 bowling alleys. Finally, eight firms are professional service firms, including two engineering and defense contractors, one social science research firm, and a bank.

Annual Sales. The companies' annual sales range from $830,000 to one billion dollars. Average annual sales are $56 million (standard deviation = $165,387,374.34), though the median in company sales is only $16 million.

Public/Private. Thirty of the companies are privately held. Seven are publicly traded.

Unionization. In nine of the 37 companies, some or all of the non-professional or non-managerial workforce belongs to a union. The percentage of company employees in the union(s) varies in these firms from 7.5% to 87.5% (average = 54%, standard deviation = 31.44). In five of the nine firms, union members are included in the ESOP.

ESOP Characteristics

In their basic company characteristics, our ESOP firms are similar to mainstream companies in general. So too, in their ESOP characteristics, our 37 study companies are similar to ESOPs in general.

Percent of Company Stock Owned by the ESOP. The average company is 42.33% employee owned (standard deviation = 33.11). Five companies are 100% employee owned. Eleven are less than 20% employee owned. Our average ESOP owns somewhat more stock than do ESOPs in general, but not a great deal more.

Voting Rights. Thirteen of the companies offer employees full ESOP stock voting rights. Of these, seven are publicly held and thus legally required to pass through full voting rights. The remaining 24 companies do not pass through full voting rights. These percentages are close to the norm for all ESOPs.

Reason the Company Established Its ESOP. The 37 companies established their ESOPs for a variety of reasons. Nine companies said they were motivated by *philosophical* reasons to establish their ESOPs. Eight companies established their ESOPs in order to provide an additional *employee benefit*. Seven used an ESOP as a mechanism for *business transfer,* that is, to provide a market for the stock of company founders and shareholders who wanted to sell their shares. Four used an ESOP as an *incentive* for improved employee performance. Another four companies used an ESOP to purchase the company during a *corporate divestiture.* Still another four companies used an ESOP as a *financing or tax-saving mechanism.* Finally, one company used an ESOP to *buy out a plant and thereby avoid a plant shutdown.*

In listing these reasons for establishing an ESOP, we caution that we asked companies to describe their primary reason for establishing an ESOP. But, in fact, most companies establish an ESOP for several reasons—for example, because management believes in sharing ownership with employees, wants to cash out a founder's shares, *and* needs the tax savings an ESOP offers.

Employee Ownership Philosophy. Management's philosophical commitment to employee ownership is difficult to measure. As we described in the preceding chapter, we asked a key managerial official in each company to respond to three items designed to capture management's general views of employee ownership. As table 5–1 shows, 82% of managerial respondents agreed with the statement, "Employee Ownership is a central part of our management philosophy"; 67% agreed that "Employee ownership plays a major role in our corporate culture and identity." Finally, 62% disagreed with the statement, "For our company, the employee ownership plan is primarily a tax-saving or financing mechanism."

For our statistical analyses, we averaged the management officials' answers to the three items. The gross percentages reported above underestimate the differences among managers' views. On the seven-point response scale, Employee Ownership Philosophy varied from 1.53 to 7 (average = 5.14, standard deviation = 1.48).

ESOP Communications. To describe their ESOP communications efforts, managerial respondents completed the simple checklist shown in table 5–2. Thirty-three of the 37 ESOP firms completed

Table 5–1

Frequency of Responses on Employee Ownership Philosophy Items
(percent)

Item	Strongly Disagree	Disagree	Slightly Disagree	Neither Agree Nor Disagree	Slightly Agree	Agree	Strongly Agree
Employee ownership is a central part of our management philosophy.	2.9	11.7	—	2.9	14.7	35.3	32.3
Employee ownership plays a major role in our corporate culture and identity.	—	9.1	9.1	15.1	6.1	42.4	18.2
For our company, the employee owner-ship plan is primarily a tax-saving or financing mechanism.	11.8	44.1	5.9	11.8	17.6	5.9	2.9

the form. To promote the employee ownership plan to its employees, every company provides ESOP participants with annual account balance statements. Almost all the companies (87.87%) discuss the ESOP during the company's initial orientation for new employees. Similarly, approximately 82% of the companies describe the employee ownership plan in the employee handbook and hold informal conversations with employees about the ESOP. Almost half of the firms (45.45%) hold an annual meeting for employee shareholders. And 18% of the companies mention employee ownership in the company letterhead (for example, The Such-and-Such Company, An Employee-Owned Corporation). On the average, the companies used five or six of the ESOP communications mechanisms listed in table 5–2 (average = 5.58, standard deviation = 1.99).

Annual Company Contribution to the ESOP. Company Contribution to the ESOP is at once a confusing and very important variable. Each year, a company contributes a certain amount of stock or cash

Table 5–2

Company Communications about the ESOP

Percentage of ESOP Companies That Use Each Mechanism

Communication Mechanism	Percentage
Annual account balance statements for each ESOP participant	100.00
Employee ownership plan discussed in initial orientation for new employees	87.87
Employee ownership plan described in employee handbook	81.81
Informal conversations with employees about the employee ownership plan	81.81
Employee ownership plan regularly mentioned in company newsletter or company letter to employees	54.54
Annual meeting for employee stockholders	45.45
Small group meetings about employee ownership	39.39
Employee ownership plan described in slide show or film for employees	21.21
Employee ownership posters around the company	21.21
Employee ownership mentioned in company letterhead	18.18
Employee ownership payroll stuffers	6.06

to its ESOP. Because this company contribution to the ESOP is allocated to employees' accounts on the basis of each employee's base pay, the easiest way to measure the company contribution to the ESOP is as a percentage of the covered payroll. If a company contributes stock or cash equal to 5% of the covered payroll to the ESOP, this means that each employee covered by the plan receives stock or cash equal to 5% of his or her salary in his or her ESOP account. The important point to remember is that the ESOP Contribution is *above and beyond* base pay. In other words, the employee receives 100% of normal pay, plus an *additional* 5% of normal pay in company stock in his or her ESOP account.

On the average, our companies contribute stock or cash equal to 8.17% of the covered payroll to the ESOP each year. This means that employees in the average company received a "bonus" of 8.17% of their salary *in addition to their pay* in their ESOP account in the year preceding our employee survey. Five of the companies gave no contribution to the ESOP in the year preceding our survey. Eight companies contributed between 1% and 5% of payroll. Thirteen contributed 5.1–10% of payroll to the ESOP. Six contributed 10.1–15% of payroll to the ESOP. Finally, three companies contributed 25% of payroll, the maximum amount for which the company may claim a tax deduction. (Only 35 companies provided data on the company contribution to the ESOP.)

Change in Company Stock Value. Change in stock value measures the percentage increase or decrease in the value of company stock in the *two-year* period preceding the employee survey in each company. In our sample, stock change varies from a low of − 35% to an incredible high of 429.63% in a company whose stock split seven for one when the company went public. The average two-year stock change is 37.05%, though the median stock change is a more modest 17.92%. In five companies, stock prices fell in the two years preceding our survey. In three companies, there was no change in stock value. Seven companies showed two-year stock increases of over 50%. In three of these seven firms, the two-year increase in stock values was over 100%. As we noted above, these are impressive figures, especially considering that stocks in general declined sharply during the study period of 1981–1983.

Of the 33 firms for which we have stock value data, five are publicly held. The average two-year stock performance of these five firms is 124.48% (standard deviation = 182.40), with a low of − 31%, and a high of 429.63%. The latter company's stock performance may be deceptive, however, because much of the stock gain may reflect a normal increase in price associated with a successful public offering.

In each of the 28 privately held firms, stock value was determined by an outside, independent evaluator. This is required by ESOP law. The evaluator assigns a dollar value to company stock on the basis of the company's overall financial performance (sales, inventory, and so on), relative to other firms in the same industry. Thus, stock value provides a superb proxy variable to assess a company's financial status. The average two-year stock increase in the privately held firms was 21.44% (standard deviation = 35.10). Stock change ranged from −35% to 140%.

ESOP Vesting Schedule. Unfortunately, it is difficult to describe concisely the typical ESOP stock-vesting schedule. Vesting schedules vary from company to company in terms of at least three dimensions: (1) when the employees enter the ESOP; (2) when ESOP stock begins to vest; and (3) how long it takes to become fully vested. In 35 (94.59%) of the ESOP firms, employees are automatically included in the ESOP after one year of company service (average = 1.03, standard deviation = .37). After employees have entered the plan, their stock typically begins to vest within one to four years (average = 2.58, standard deviation = 1.76). Employees' ESOP accounts are typically fully vested by the time the employee has been in the ESOP for ten years (average = 9.13, standard deviation = 3.49).

These numbers have important implications for employees in each ESOP company. For example, if an employee leaves his or her company within three or four years of joining the company, he or she is likely to forfeit his or her ESOP account balance (it often takes one year to be admitted to the plan, and two or three years after that for ESOP stock to begin to vest). The employee in a typical ESOP firm must stay with the company for 11 years for his or her ESOP account to be fully vested.

ESOP Stock Distribution. Twenty-nine of the companies give an employee the vested portion of his or her ESOP account when the employee leaves the company. At that time, the employee typically sells his or her stock back to the company or, if the company is publicly traded, sells the stock on the public market. Our discussion of vesting, above, assumed that the ESOP company did cash out employees at a break in service as do the vast majority of ESOP firms.

Four of the 37 companies, however, do not distribute employees' vested ESOP shares until the employees reach retirement age (50 in one company, 60 in the other companies), regardless of when the employee leaves the company. Thus, a departing 35-year-old employee who is fully vested will receive no stock until he or she reaches retirement age. He or she will have to wait 15 to 20 years, depending on the company, to receive his or her vested shares. The employee's ESOP shares grow (or shrink) during the interim. That is, when the employee receives his or her shares, they reflect the growth of the company since the employee's departure. (Stock distribution data were unavailable for four of our ESOP companies.)

Age of the ESOP. To be included in our study, a company had to have had its ESOP for at least one year. The average ESOP was 6.05 years old at the time of the employee survey (standard deviation = 2.85).

Employee Attitudes about Owning Stock

Having provided this brief overview of our 37 companies, we move on to discuss employee attitudes about the ESOP.

What do employees think about owning stock? Are they excited or indifferent, motivated or apathetic? Do they think that owning stock makes them work harder? Do they think that they have more influence in company decision-making because they own stock? Do they think that owning stock makes them pay more attention to the company's financial performance—to the bottom line?

Many observers simply assume that they can answer "Yes" to these questions, that employee ownership makes employees excited, motivated, hard-working, powerful, and attentive to the bottom line. But we wanted more certain answers. To find them, we turned to the descriptive results of our survey: Just how much did employees agree or disagree with the 15 original Employee Ownership Attitude items on our questionnaire?

Interestingly, we found a common pattern across all the ESOP companies. Though employees' scores differed from company to company, with some companies scoring very high while others scored very low, the same basic pattern emerged in each company. Regardless of company, employees tended to agree with certain items and to disagree with others.

Table 5–3 lists the average employee score for each of the 15 items, across all 37 ESOP companies and all 2,804 employees. The items are listed in order of employee agreement. Employees agreed

Table 5–3
Averages and Standard Deviations of ESOP Attitude Items

Item	Average	Standard Deviation	% Agreeing
1. Owning stock in this company makes me more interested in the company's financial success.	5.61	1.40	84%
2. I'm proud to own stock in this company.	5.42	1.40	75%
3. It is very important to me that this company has an employee stock ownership plan.	4.95	1.61	65%
4. Owning stock in this company makes me want to stay with this company longer than I would if I did not own stock.	4.87	1.66	65%
5. Employee ownership at this company gives me a greater share in company profits.	4.84	1.69	65%
6. Because of employee ownership, my work is more satisfying.	4.31	1.73	50%
7. I am more careful and conscientious in my work because I own stock in this company.	4.24	1.72	46%
8. Employee ownership at this company makes my day-to-day work more enjoyable.	4.22	1.63	41%
9. Because of employee ownership, people here try to cooperate more.	4.15	1.68	44%
10. I work harder on my job because I own company stock.	4.08	1.74	43%
11. I feel like a real owner in this company.	3.84	1.85	42%
12. Because of employee ownership, managers here treat workers more like equals.	3.57	1.73	31%
13. Employees here have more influence in company decision-making than they would if they did not own company stock.	3.44	1.73	29%
14. Employees have more say in company decisions because they own stock.	3.11	1.58	28%
15. I really don't care about the employee ownership plan in this company.	2.38	1.48	10%

[a]Excludes those who neither agree nor disagree and those who disagree.

most with the first items and disagreed most with the last items. The items were not listed in this order on the employee survey.

As table 5–3 shows, employees usually agreed with the five following survey items:

1. Owning stock in this company makes me more interested in the company's financial success.
2. I'm proud to own stock in this company.
3. It is very important to me that this company has an employee stock ownership plan.
4. Owning stock in this company makes me want to stay with this company longer than I would if I did not own stock.
5. Employee ownership gives me a greater share in company profits.

These five items fall neatly into two categories. Items 1, 4, and 5 describe, or reflect, the financial benefits of employee ownership. Items 2 and 3 describe general positive perceptions of the ESOP. Employee responses to these five items are thus easy to interpret: Employees broadly endorse employee stock ownership and are particularly enthusiastic about employee ownership's potential financial benefits.

Employees are more ambivalent about the next six items in table 5–3:

6. I am more careful and conscientious in my work because I own stock in this company.
7. Because of employee ownership, my work is more satisfying.
8. Employee ownership at this company makes my day-to-day work more enjoyable.
9. Because of employee ownership, people here try to cooperate more.
10. I work harder on my job because I own company stock.
11. I feel like a real owner in this company.

Employee responses to these items indicate that an ESOP may have relatively little impact on employees' day-to-day work experiences and work efforts. Employees say that the ESOP does not make their actual daily work more satisfying, nor does it make them work harder on the job.

Finally, employees tend to disagree with the following items:

12. Because of employee ownership, managers here treat workers more like equals.
13. Employees have more influence in company decision-making than they would if they did not own company stock.
14. Employees have more say in company decisions because they own company stock.
15. I really don't care about the employee ownership plan in this company.

Employees' disagreement with items 12, 13, and 14 makes it clear that—from the employee perspective, at least—an ESOP does little to increase employee influence in the company. However, employees' disagreement with the last item reinforces the point that employees do value and appreciate stock ownership, even if it does not increase worker influence.

Summary and Comments
Though simple and straightforward, the results are revealing and important. Employees' appreciation of the ESOP's financial benefits is a reminder that the ESOP is first and foremost an employee benefit plan. Employees appreciate it as such. Previous employee ownership theory and research have underestimated the power of financial gain, of employees' capitalist and entrepreneurial interests: employees are happy to make money.

Given employees' appreciation of the financial rewards of stock ownership, it is somewhat surprising that employees say they do not work harder or more conscientiously because they own stock. One might expect employees to work harder in order to maximize company profits so that the company can afford a large ESOP contribution and so that stock values rise.

Three reasons may explain employees' reported failure to increase their work efforts in response to stock ownership. First, the relationship between individual effort and stock values, company profits, and the size of the company contribution to the ESOP is quite removed; employee work effort is only one small factor among many that determine profits, stock values, and the size of the company's ESOP contribution. Employees are likely to recognize this. Second, employees do not actually receive the ESOP benefit, in hand, until they leave the company or retire. Thus, unlike other gainsharing programs that provide monthly, quarterly, or yearly cash rewards for increased employee productivity, the ESOP provides few if any immediate rewards to the employee. Finally, employees may be reluctant to *say* they work harder because of stock ownership, even if they do. Saying they work harder, after all, suggests they were not doing their best before.

Employees do not feel that owning stock increases their influence in company decision-making. Given that ESOPs do not necessarily provide stock voting rights, and that ESOPs do not necessarily reflect an egalitarian, participative style of management, this result is not surprising. It is instructive to note, however, that employees are still satisfied with ESOP employee ownership, even though they they recognize that an ESOP does not necessarily give them full ownership rights.

Finally, employees feel that owning stock does not increase their work enjoyment. Our questionnaire items do not, however, query employees about the effects of the ESOP on their general satisfaction with and commitment to the company. Instead, the items ask very specifically about the effects of the ESOP on employees' *day-to-day* satisfaction. Though the ESOP has little bearing on employees' daily work activities and experiences, we suspect that an ESOP can increase employees' overall commitment to the company. We base this conclusion on employees' generally positive endorsement of employee ownership (items 2, 3, 4, and 15, above) and on the statistical results discussed in the next chapter.

Against the background of previous employee ownership research, two of the above findings really stand out: (1) Employees emphasize and value the financial benefits of employee ownership; and (2) Employee ownership does not necessarily increase worker influence. These findings whet the appetite for more. Below, we focus on just these two findings.

The Financial Benefits of Employee Ownership

Just how good are the financial benefits of employee ownership? Have we surveyed a particularly greedy bunch, or are the ESOP's financial rewards really so substantial? We have not surveyed a greedy bunch. In many, though certainly not all, cases, an ESOP provides employees with very substantial capital wealth.

Let's take a few examples. Above, we found that the average company contributed 8.17% of the covered payroll to the ESOP in the year preceding our employee survey. In addition, we found that the average two-year stock change was 37.05%, though the median stock change was 17.92%. Suppose you work for the average company. Your salary is $20,000 a year. How much money will you make through the ESOP?

Let's take the median case first. The company contributes 8% of salary to the ESOP each year. For the sake of this example, let us suppose your salary remains stable at $20,000; 8% of your salary is $1,600. You receive this amount of cash or stock in your ESOP account each year (assuming, again for the sake of this example, that the company contribution to the ESOP remains stable). At the end of five years, you have $8,000 in your ESOP account, and at the end of ten years, you have $16,000, right? Wrong.

We also need to factor in the change in stock values. The median two-year stock change is 17.93%. Thus, with rounding, the median annual increase in stock value is 9%. Taking this into account, your ESOP account is worth $10,437 at the end of five years and $26,497 the end of ten years. If we use the average (not median) annual stock increase (18%) in the example, your ESOP account is worth $11,447 at the end of five years, and worth $37,634 at the end of ten years.

These are impressive numbers, but they reflect the performance of our average companies. Consider some of ESOP firms that give the largest contributions to their ESOPs and show the greatest increases in stock value. For example, one small company in California contributed 25% of employee salary to the ESOP and showed an annual increase in share price of 26%. If you worked for this company, and still earned $20,000 a year in base pay, your ESOP account would be worth $35,542 at the end of five years, and worth

$174,723 at the end of ten years. A small, fast-growing company in Virginia contributed 15% of the employee salary to the ESOP and showed an annual increase in share price of 21%. If you worked for this company (again, maintaining your $20,000 annual salary), your ESOP account would be worth $22,766 at the end of five years and $81,822 at the end of ten years.

Of course, these examples are very inexact. Your salary would change over the years. Your company's annual contribution to the ESOP would fluctuate, as would the annual rate of change in company stock value. Moreover, your ESOP accounts would vest over time. Most ESOPs are not fully vested until the employee has participated in the plan for at least ten years. In addition, the size of your ESOP account might be substantially increased by other employees' forfeitures of their non-vested ESOP shares if they left the company before they were fully vested. Finally, your ESOP company might not be so successful. In two of our study companies, for example, the company made no contribution to the ESOP in the year preceding our employee survey, and stock prices fell at an annual rate of − 5% and − 12% respectively.

Still, the ESOP examples make the potential financial benefits of ESOP employee ownership more concrete. Employees do have a lot to be excited about. We will say more about the links between employee satisfaction and the financial benefits of employee ownership in the next chapter.

Worker Influence

Above we suggested that employees value and appreciate stock ownership, even though they think that owning stock does not increase their influence in company decision-making. Does that mean that employee influence and participation in company decision-making are unimportant to employees? Not by a long shot. Here, we discuss employees' perceptions of and desires for participation in company decision-making. In the next chapter, we discuss the impact of worker participation in company decision-making on employee attitudes.

As we described in the preceding chapter, our employee survey asks employees how much influence *non-managerial* employees at their company have over the following areas:

1. social events;
2. working conditions;
3. the way workers perform their own jobs;
4. pay and other compensation;
5. hiring, firing, and other personnel decisions;
6. selection of supervisors and management; and
7. company policy, for example, investment in new equipment or planning for the company future.

Measuring worker influence is always difficult. The measures are highly subjective. The actual items in the survey measure may be inappropriate (for example, perhaps employees have a lot of influence over hiring, but no influence over firing). And it is difficult to know just who should fill out the questionnaire items. In our research, all the employees who completed the survey answered the above items. This means that both managerial and non-managerial employees completed our measure of non-managerial employees' influence. (Recall that the measure asks the respondent to rate how much influence non-managerial employees have over the various areas.) In spite of these measurement problems, the worker influence measure above, and the comparable one for *desired* worker influence, provide valuable information about company decision-making practices, employee perceptions, and employee desires.

According to our employee survey data, employees feel that they have the most influence over company social events, and the least influence over the selection of supervisors and management. More specifically, the topic areas in order of employee influence (from most to least employee influence) are: (1) social events; (2) the way workers perform their jobs; (3) working conditions; (4) pay and other compensation; (5) company policy; (6) hiring, firing, and other personnel decisions; and (7) selection of supervisors and management.

Employees' desires for worker participation closely mirror the above results. For example, employees feel they should have the most influence over social events, and the least over hiring, firing, and other personnel decisions. More specifically, the topic areas listed in order of desired employee influence (from most to least desired employee influence) are: (1) social events; (2) working conditions; (3) the way workers perform their jobs; (5) company policy;

(6) selection of supervisors and management; and (7) hiring, firing, and other personnel decisions. Table 5–4 summarizes all of the worker influence results.

Desired worker influence is always higher than perceived worker influence. In other words, employees always think they should have more influence, more power and responsibility, than they feel they currently do have. This is a common finding in the research literature. Employees long for a stronger role in shaping company decisions.

Still, it is important to note that employees' desires are rarely extreme. For example, they desire the greatest influence over those matters about which they are most knowledgeable: social events, working conditions, and the way they perform their jobs. As the numbers in table 5–4 show, employees seek only a modest degree of influence over the traditional areas of managerial authority.

Interestingly, the largest discrepancies between current employee influence and desired employee influence pertain not to shopfloor and job-related issues, but to three more far-reaching areas: (1) pay and other compensation; (2) selection of supervisors and management; and (3) company policy. Employees feel they have little influence over these areas and they think they should have more influence. In contrast, they appear to be relatively satisfied with their level of influence over job-related and shopfloor tasks (social events, working conditions, and the way workers perform their jobs). They feel that they have little influence over hiring, firing, and personnel decisions, but they do not desire a great deal of influence over these issues.

In addition to the employee survey data on worker influence, during the management interview we asked the key management official in each company to complete the same measure of worker influence. We used the key management official's answers as a measure of *Management-Perceived Worker Influence*. Contrasting Management-Perceived Worker Influence and Employee-Perceived Worker Influence, we find that management typically overestimates—by employee standards—the level of worker influence. Management thinks employees have more influence than employees think that they have. Table 5–4 provides more data on this point.

This finding has potentially important implications for research and practice. The discrepancy between management's and employees'

Table 5–4
Employee-Perceived Worker Influence,
Employee-Desired Worker Influence,
and Management-Perceived Worker Influence

	Average Employee-Perceived Worker Influence (N = 2804)	Average Employee-Desired Worker Influence (N = 2804)	Discrepancy Between Employee-Desired and Actual Worker Influence (N = 2804)	Average Management-Perceived Worker Influence (N = 37)	Discrepancy Between Employee and Management Perceptions of Worker Influence (N = 37)
Social events	3.01	3.60	.59	4.00	.99
Working conditions	2.75	3.54	.79	3.05	.30
The way workers perform their jobs	2.98	3.50	.52	3.22	.24
Pay and other compensation	1.94	3.07	1.14	2.03	.09
Hiring, firing, and other personnel decisions	1.67	2.47	.80	2.16	.49
Selection of supervisors and management	1.44	2.58	1.14	1.78	.34
Company policy	1.74	2.83	1.09	2.22	.48
Average for all seven topics	2.22	3.09	.87	2.64	.42

Code: 1 = Workers (should) have no say
       2 = Workers (should) receive information
       3 = Workers are (should be) asked their opinion
       4 = Workers (should) decide with management
       5 = Workers (should) decide alone

Note: Items are listed in the order asked.

views of worker influence suggests that researchers should exercise caution in interpreting (and accepting) management's descriptions of worker influence. Much research relies solely on key managerial respondents who, it appears, may have unrealistically positive views.

For practice, the implications of the data are, we think, more complicated. If management significantly and systematically overestimates the level of worker influence (at least by employee standards), management may be hostile to the idea of granting nonmanagerial employees even more influence in decision-making. As we saw above, however, more influence is precisely what employees want.

On the other hand, management's tendency to overestimate the level of worker influence may reflect management's enthusiasm for shared worker control. If this is the case, then the overestimation bias may be helpful; managers may be more likely to spread the word about the benefits of worker participation to other managers in other companies.

Summary

This chapter lays the foundation for a closer and more in-depth look at our data. We have gained a good feel for our ESOP firms—how similar they are to non-ESOP companies in general, and also to the general population of ESOP firms. We have learned a lot about what employees think of stock ownership. We understand that they most appreciate the financial benefits of employee ownership and we have seen that these financial benefits can indeed be substantial. Finally, we know that employees typically desire more influence in company decision-making than they have, but we recognize that employees' desires are rarely extreme; employees seek the most influence over the issues that they know best.

But all this information leaves the real mystery unsolved. Just what causes employee ownership success? Why are employees in some ESOP companies so much more satisfied and committed to their companies than are employees in other ESOP companies? We take on these questions in the next chapter. We leave one final clue: Our findings about employee attitudes about stock ownership already tell us much of what we need to know in order to solve the main mystery. Sherlock Holmes would already have the case locked up.

6
The Mystery's Solution
The Roots of Employee Ownership Success

T his chapter moves us to the heart of our study: our attempt to isolate the causes of employee ownership success. What causes one company to thrive under employee ownership while another one falters? What is it that makes employees most satisfied with employee ownership and most committed to their companies?

In social science research, causality is a misnomer; one can never be absolutely certain about what causes what. Still, we hope to come as close to certainty as possible. In this way, we can provide sound, practical suggestions for employee ownership companies and at the same time refine and extend the theoretical and empirical research on employee ownership.

How do we approach certainty? How do we try to ascertain the causes of employee ownership success? We begin with a sound research design. We learn everything we can about the phenomenon under study. We develop a careful conceptualization of the independent and dependent variables. We use a large sample of subjects and we measure our variables with precision and care. We took these steps in our research and described them in the first four chapters of this book. In the fifth chapter, we presented the descriptive results of our study.

One step remains: statistical analysis of the data. We take this step in the present chapter. For those of you who are not conversant with statistics, it may seem like a very large step indeed. Still, we urge you to bear with us. In a study of this complexity, there is no way to answer our research questions except with statistics. We make every attempt to present the data simply, to explain our statistical procedures, and to accompany the numbers with text that clarifies just what the numbers mean. For those of you who are conversant with statistics, the data presented here will allow you to evaluate our findings and come to your own conclusions.

Before presenting the research results, a brief review of our research hypotheses may be helpful. In chapter 4, we discussed our hypotheses about the causes of employee ownership success and we listed seven key ESOP characteristics:

1. The percent of company stock owned by the employees.
2. Employee stock voting rights.
3. The primary reason the company established the plan.
4. Management's philosophical commitment to employee ownership.
5. The employee ownership communications program.
6. The size of the company contribution to the ownership plan.
7. The performance of company stock.

We wondered how these factors might influence employee attitudes about stock ownership and about work in general. In essence, we sought the answers to seven questions:

1. Do employees respond more favorably to employee ownership when the ESOP owns a large percentage of company stock?
2. Does allowing employees to vote their ESOP stock make them respond more favorably?
3. Does the reason the company established its ESOP make a difference for employee attitudes?
4. Do employees respond more favorably when company management is philosophically committed to employee ownership?
5. Do employees respond more favorably to employee ownership when the company has an extensive employee ownership communications program?

6. Do employees respond more favorably to employee ownership when the company makes a large contribution to the ESOP?
7. Do employees respond more favorably to employee ownership if company stock remains stable or increases in value?

Finally, we added an eighth variable—worker participation—and hence an eighth question. It is listed separately because it is a characteristic of the company, not the ESOP.

8. Do employees respond more favorably to employee ownership when they have considerable opportunities to participate in company decision-making?

The questions seem "obvious." So do the answers. Isn't it obvious that each of the ESOP characteristics makes a difference in how employees feel about stock ownership? Isn't it obvious that employee owners must actively participate in company decision-making or they will be dissatisfied? It may be *obvious,* but it is not necessarily *true.* Our questions seem obvious because the logic behind them is very plausible. We need to go beyond the merely plausible, however, to find which of the alternative explanations are correct.

The data we have analyzed here allow us to draw fairly clear conclusions. Of all the ESOP characteristics, the size of the company contribution to its ESOP is most important. The larger the company's contribution to the ESOP, the more satisfied employees are. In other words, employees are most enthusiastic about employee ownership when they are making a lot of money through the ESOP. It is as if employees examine their annual ESOP stock certificates each year and ask one question, "Is my ESOP account larger than it was last year?" The larger it is, the better.

Financial considerations are not the only important factor, however. Management's commitment to the concept of ownership, the company's ESOP communications program, and the workers' opportunities to influence company decision-making also make a difference. Employees are most satisfied when management is actively committed both to employee ownership and to worker participation. By contrast, the percentage of the company owned by employees, the company's recent financial performance, the size or line of business of the company, the presence or absence of voting rights, and several other factors are not significantly related to employee morale.

Most of this chapter presents the statistical data supporting these conclusions. The results are summarized in the closing sections of the chapter.

A Brief Introduction to Correlation, Analysis of Variance, and Regression

The easiest way to begin to answer our research questions is to examine the statistical relationship between our independent and dependent variables. We use three basic statistical techniques to assess this relationship: correlation, analysis of variance, and multiple regression. Here, we take a moment to explain these techniques. Those of you who are familiar with these statistical procedures may want to skip ahead.

Correlations (or, more formally, Pearson product-moment correlations) indicate the extent of the relationship between two continuous variables. Imagine a simple graph with variable A plotted on one axis and variable B plotted on the other, as in figure 6–1. The correlation coefficient provides a number to describe the resulting pattern. Does the graph show a straight line indicating a perfect relationship between the two variables? If so, the correlation coefficient would be $+1.0$, for a positive relationship, or -1.0, for a negative relationship. Is the resulting pattern more messy and diffuse? In this case, the correlation coefficient would have a smaller absolute value (say, between $-.67$ and $+.67$). Is there no discernible pattern at all? In this case, the correlation coefficient equals zero.

A more concrete example may clarify the discussion. What is the relationship between inches and feet, or between pounds and kilograms? In both cases, the relationship is perfect: $+1.0$. If I know how tall someone is in inches, I can tell you their height in feet. If I know how much somebody weighs in pounds, I can tell you how much they weigh in kilograms.

What about more messy relationships? What is the relationship of height and weight? The variables are closely related, but not per-

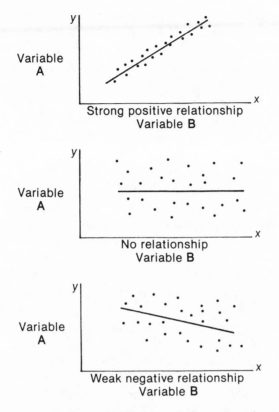

Figure 6–1. *Pearson Product-Moment Correlations*

fectly so. One would expect a fairly strong positive correlation. What is the relationship between age and physical fitness. If one measures through the adult life span, one would expect a fairly strong negative correlation. (Physical fitness declines with increasing age.) But the resulting relationship is clearly far from perfect. Finally, what is the relationship between driving ability and liking broccoli? Unless there's something we don't know about eating broccoli and driving a car, we would expect a zero relationship; liking for broccoli and driving ability are unrelated.

A correlation can never prove that a causal relationship exists. The correlation coefficient simply documents a statistical relationship. Consider a business example. What is the relationship between company size (number of employees) and the company's annual sales? In our sample, at least, the correlation is strong and positive. But having a large number of employees doesn't necessarily *cause* a company to achieve high annual sales. Nor do high annual sales necessarily *cause* a company to employ a large number of people. One must interpret correlational data with caution; the correlation of variable A and variable B may reflect the fact that A causes B, or that B causes A, or that a third variable C causes both A and B, or even that there is spurious random or chance association between variables A and B.

This raises another point about correlations. What is a significant correlation? What is a chance relationship? The scientific convention is to measure statistical significance as a probability statement: What is the probability that I would discover a given correlation (say .59) between two actually unrelated variables by chance? A correlation coefficient is considered *significant* if there is only a 5% chance or less ($p \leq .05$) that I would find this kind of relationship between two actually unrelated variables. If we sampled 10 adults and found a .80 correlation between height and intelligence, this would indeed be statistically significant. But it would be a chance finding that would evaporate with more people in the sample. One determines the statistical significance of a correlation coefficient by comparing the correlation coefficient and sample size with the values in a standard statistical table. The larger one's sample size, the smaller the correlation coefficient has to be to reach statistical significance. Note, however, that statistical significance does not tell us much about conceptual significance. While the correlation of pounds and kilos is highly statistically significant, it is not exactly a scientific breakthrough.

The square of a correlation coefficient tells us how much of the variance in one variable we can explain as a function of the other variable. Pounds and kilos are perfectly correlated. Thus, r (the abbreviation for the correlation coefficient) equals $+1.0$. The square of $+1.0$ is 1.0. This means we can explain 100% of the variance in pounds in terms of kilos (and vice versa). Suppose the correlation of height and weight is $+.80$. This tells us that we can explain 64% of the variance in weight in terms of height ($r = .80$; $r^2 = .64$); 36% of the variance in weight is due to other factors—eating habits, exercise, and so on.

Analysis of variance (ANOVA) is another basic statistical tool. ANOVA is appropriate when the predictor variable is a categorical or nominal variable. We use analysis of variance to examine the relationship between the reason for setting up an ESOP and the employee outcomes. "Reason" is a categorical variable. Establishing an ESOP for financial reasons is not "more" or "less" than establishing an ESOP in order to purchase stock from a retiring company founder. Classic examples of categorical variables are gender, religion, race, and nationality. ANOVA tells us whether there are significant differences between the subjects (companies in our case) in each category. The result of an analysis of variance is an F statistic, which one again compares (with sample size and number of categories) to a standard significance table for ANOVAs. The same rule of thumb exists for ANOVA as for correlation: what is the probability that one would find these differences between groups by chance if there were actually no differences in the total population? Analysis of variance, like correlation, also provides a measure of r^2, the percent of variance in the outcome variable explained by the subject's membership within the categorical variables.

Correlation and ANOVA are our basic tools for statistical analysis. More complicated analytical procedures build on these basics. These more complicated analytical procedures are designed to let the researcher assess the relationship between the independent variable and more than one dependent variable. In this chapter, we will frequently rely on multiple regression for precisely this purpose. Suppose we discover that variable X (Physical Fitness) is significantly related to both variable A (Age) and variable B (Daily Exercise). How well can we predict variable X on the basis of both variables A and B? Multiple regression yields an overall R and R^2 that can tell us the answer. These are interpreted in the same way as the r and r^2 in correlation analyses.

In a multiple regression analysis, one can also assess the significance of each of the dependent variables in the regression equation. To do this, one examines the standardized regression coefficient, or beta weight, for each dependent variable. In a simultaneous regression analysis (one in which all the dependent variables are simultaneously entered into the regression equation), a variable's beta weight shows whether, given all the other dependent variables in the equation, the focal variable is a significant predictor of the independent variable.

Let's consider another practical example. In the regression suggested above, we wanted to predict Physical Fitness on the basis of Age and Daily Exercise. The beta weight for Age tells us whether Age is a significant predictor of Physical Fitness, after one has already considered (or, effectively, "removed") the effects of Daily Exercise. The beta weight for Age thus answers the question, "If a group of people all exercise for the same amount of time every day, are the younger people still likely to be in better physical condition than the older people?" The beta weight for Daily Exercise tells us whether that variable is a significant predictor of Physical Fitness, after one has already considered the effects of Age. The beta weight for Daily Exercise answers the question, "In a group of people who all are the same age, are those who exercise more often likely to be in better physical condition?"

Occasionally, two independent variables in a regression equation effectively cancel each other out. For instance, suppose you know from a correlation analysis that your two independent variables are both significantly related to your outcome variable, but when you do a regression analysis, one or both of your betas is insignificant. What is going on here? The problem is that your two independent variables are highly intercorrelated.

Let's take two final examples (before you think we have switched from studying employee ownership to studying height, weight, and physical fitness). Suppose we now want to predict Body Weight. Our two independent variables are Height and a measure of the individual's Daily Exercise. Both Height and Daily Exercise are significantly related to Weight. Furthermore, Height and Daily Exercise are insignificantly related to each other. By considering both Height and Exercise at the same time, one can significantly improve one's prediction of Weight. Both Height and Exercise have significant beta weights. The overall R^2 for Height and Exercise predicting Weight is appreciably higher than r^2 for either Height or Daily Exercise alone.

Now consider an example when our two independent variables are highly intercorrelated. Suppose we are again predicting Body Weight, but our two independent variables are a measure of Physical

Fitness and Daily Exercise. Both are significantly related to Weight. But if one already knows a person's overall Physical Fitness level, additional information about the person's Daily Exercise is not very useful. The two variables are very highly related: people who get more daily exercise are in better physical condition. The beta weights for Physical Fitness (given Daily Exercise) and for Daily Exercise (given Physical Fitness) might well be insignificant. Further, R^2 for Physical Fitness and Daily Exercise predicting Weight is little higher than r^2 for Physical Fitness or Daily Exercise alone. High intercorrelations among one's independent variables is a common problem in social science research, and one that may distort and mask one's true results. It must be watched closely.

For the statistical novice, this has surely been a whirlwind introduction to correlation, ANOVA, and regression analyses. These analytical techniques will become increasingly familiar and comprehensible as we use them, and explain our results, in the remaining sections of this chapter. Below, we first present our research results and then conclude the chapter by discussing the implications of our research results for employee ownership practice and future employee ownership research.

The Relationship of ESOP Characteristics and Employee Outcomes

Table 6–1 shows the correlations between all of the ESOP characteristics (except Reason for Setting Up an ESOP) and the four outcome variables: ESOP Satisfaction, Organizational Commitment, Job Satisfaction, and Turnover Intention. Because Reason For Setting Up an ESOP is a categorical variable, ANOVA results are presented for this variable.

The results indicate that three of the seven ESOP characteristics are significantly related to at least some of the employee outcomes. Company Contribution to the ESOP shows the strongest correlation with the employee outcomes. The results are in the predicted direction. Contribution is significantly positively related to ESOP Satisfaction, Organizational Commitment, and Job Satisfaction, and significantly negatively related to Turnover Intention (employees are less likely to leave if Contributions are large). Management's

Table 6–1

Correlations between ESOP Characteristics and Employee Attitudes

	ESOP Satisfaction	Organizational Commitment	Job Satisfaction	Turnover Intention
Percent of Company Stock Owned by ESOP	.05	– .13	– .07	– .04
Voting Rights	.16	.15	.08	– .07
Reason Why Company Established Its ESOP	F = 1.20	F = 1.92	F = 1.45	F = .62
Employee Ownership Philosophy	.49**	.49**	.36*	– .37*
ESOP Communications	.40*	.27	.03	– .41*
Company Contribution to ESOP	.54***	.46**	.53**	– .56***
Stock Change	.23	.29	.28	– .29

* $p \leq .05$
** $p \leq .01$
*** $p \leq .001$

Employee Ownership Philosophy shows a similar pattern. It too is significantly positively related to ESOP Satisfaction, Organizational Commitment, and Job Satisfaction and significantly negatively related to Turnover Intention. Finally, ESOP Communications is significantly positively related to ESOP Satisfaction and significantly negatively related to Turnover Intention.

Returning to the eight questions we posed earlier in this chapter, the results in table 6–1 already suggest that our obvious questions—and obvious answers—are not so obvious at all. It looks as if we can answer only three of the questions in the affirmative:

4. Do employees respond more favorably to employee owner-ship when company management is philosophically com-mitted to employee ownership?
5. Do employees respond more favorably to employee owner-ship when the company has an extensive employee ownership communications program?

6. Do employees respond more favorably to employee ownership when the company makes a large contribution to the
ESOP?

We need to examine more statistical analyses to be sure that we
know how to interpret the results for Contribution, Employee Ownership Philosophy, and ESOP Communications. But the results for
the other variables are clear: according to our data, Percent (of Stock
Owned), Voting Rights, ESOP Reason, and Stock Change do not
significantly influence employees' ESOP and general work attitudes.

A Closer Look at Our Principle Findings

In order to come to a complete understanding of our results, we
must unravel the connections between Company Contribution to
the ESOP, Management's Employee Ownership Philosophy, and
ESOP Communications. For example, if Contribution and
Philosophy are highly intercorrelated, then the effects of Contribution may really be due to Philosophy (companies that give large
ESOP contributions are also philosophically committed to employee ownership), or vice versa. In addition, we need to examine
the connections between the three ESOP characteristics and other
company characteristics. Another example: perhaps companies that
give large ESOP contributions are small companies and people just
like to work in small companies. Maybe company size explains the
relationship, not ESOP Contribution.

We first examine possible alternative explanations of the Contribution effects and then explore the Employee Ownership Philosophy and ESOP Communications results.

Company Contribution to the ESOP. The first step in ruling out alternative explanations of the Contribution results is simply to examine the correlations of Contribution and other ESOP and company
characteristics. The results in table 6–2 show that Contribution is
not significantly related to any of the other six key ESOP characteristics (Percent of Company Stock Owned by the ESOP, Voting Rights,
Reason for Setting Up an ESOP, Employee Ownership Philosophy,
ESOP Communications or Stock Change.) Furthermore, Contribu-

Table 6–2
Intercorrelations among ESOP Characteristics

	Percent	Voting	Reason	Philosophy	Communication	Contribution
Percent of Company Stock Owned by ESOP	1.00					
Voting Rights	-.13	1.00				
Reason Why Company Established Its ESOP	F = 4.06**	F = .70	1.00			
Employee Ownership Philosophy ESOP	.02	.47**	F = 3.29*	1.00		
Communications	.15	.33	F = 1.15	.53**	1.00	
Company Contribution to ESOP	.08	.09	F = 1.19	.13	.09	1.00
Stock Change	-.28	.26	F = .96	.27	.24	-.00

* $p \leq .05$
** $p \leq .01$

Voting Rights: 0 = No, 1 = Yes

tion is not significantly related to any of our more ancillary ESOP characteristics, including ESOP Age and Number of Years Until Full Vesting. Thus, we cannot explain the Contribution results by referring to any other ESOP characteristic.

As a brief aside, we call particular attention to the *nonsignificant* relationship of Change in Stock Value and Company Contribution to the ESOP. Many people would argue that companies that make large contributions to the ESOP are companies that have performed well financially. As we noted earlier, we did not attempt to measure company profitability because many of our firms are closely held and either did not want to provide us data or, if they did, cautioned us that different accounting techniques make these numbers misleading. In stock price, however, we have an excellent proxy for company performance.

As we discussed in the preceding chapter, in a closely held company, an annual valuation is performed by an outside, independent appraisal. This appraisal takes into account all of the factors (earnings, asset value, change in the economic environment, and so on) that determine a company's financial position and then assigns a dollar value to company stock accordingly. In other words, the valuation is a very sophisticated analysis of economic performance. As we cannot get comparable data for non-ESOP firms, we cannot use this intriguing measure to compare our companies' performance to that of other firms, but we can test whether it has an independent effect on employee attitudes, or on our other variables.

As the results presented thus far indicate, Change in Stock Value does not have a statistically significant impact on the outcome variables, nor is it significantly related to the size of company contributions to the ESOP. Apparently, companies do not contribute more to the ESOP in years when their performance is better. This makes sense when one realizes that most ESOPs are *not* forms of profit-sharing. They may be set up to buy out an owner, as part of a leveraged transaction, or for some other corporate purpose that requires a fixed level of contribution to the ESOP, regardless of company performance. Even if this is not the case, a company may still contribute new issues of stock, with no cash cost, and hence no reliance on earnings. Thus, the insignificant relationship of Contribution and Stock Change is not so surprising.

Returning to our search for alternative explanations of the Contribution results, we must consider the relationship of Company Contribution to the ESOP and various company characteristics. Is Contribution related to any company characterstic? The results in table 6–3 show that it is not. Contribution is insignificantly related to Company Size, Company Sales, Unionization, Public/Private Status, and Shared Financial Information (whether or not management shares company financial information with non-managerial employees). Further, these variables are insignificantly related to the

Table 6–3

Correlations between ESOP Characteristics and
Company Characteristics

	Size	Sales	Union	Private/ Public	Shared Financial Information
Percent of Company Stock Owned by ESOP	−.14	−.17	−.10	−.41	.20
Voting Rights	.26	.26	−.29	.66***	.35*
Reason Why Company Established Its ESOP	F = .60	F = .61	F = 1.27	F = 2.36	F = .58
Employee Ownership Philosophy	.27	.26	−.33	.33	.49**
ESOP Communications	−.01	.00	−.06	.02	.46**
Company Contribution to ESOP	.13	.11	.05	−.03	−.26
Stock Change	.17	.31	.13	.46**	.10

* $p \le .05$
** $p \le .01$
*** $p \le .001$
Voting Rights: 1 = No, 2 = Yes
Union: 1 = No, 2 = Yes
Private/Public: 1 = Private, 2 = Public
Shared Financial Information: 1 = No, 2 = Yes

outcome measures. (See table 6–4.) Here again, then, the Contribution results do not appear to be a function of any extraneous company characteristic.

Finally, we consider the relationship between Contribution and various measures of formal and informal worker participation in company decision-making. The results are shown in table 6–5. Contribution is not significantly related to any of these measures (Management-Perceived Worker Influence, Employee-Perceived Worker Influence, or Formal Participation Groups). We discuss the relationship of these variables to the outcome measures in a later section of this chapter. Here, the important point is that the Contribution results cannot be explained in terms of worker participation. Companies that give high contributions to the ESOP are not necessarily any more participative than companies that give low ESOP contributions.

So, how do we explain the Contribution results? There appears to be only one plausible explanation: Receiving a large ESOP Contribution makes employees feel good about stock ownership, about their company, and about their work. We will discuss this interpretation

Table 6–4
Correlations between Company Characteristics and Employee Attitudes

	ESOP Satisfaction	Organizational Commitment	Job Satisfaction	Turnover Intention
Company Size	.21	.12	.13	– .10
Annual Sales	.22	.11	.12	– .10
Union	.18	.23	.22	– .34*
Private/ Public	– .02	.03	– .02	.08
Shared Financial Information	– .07	– .09	– .22	.06

* $p \leq .05$
Voting Rights: 1 = No, 2 = Yes
Union: 1 = No, 2 = Yes
Private/Public: 1 = Private, 2 = Public
Shared Financial Information: 1 = No, 2 = Yes

Table 6–5

Correlations between ESOP Characteristics and
Measures of Worker Influence

	Management- Perceived Worker Influence	Employee- Perceived Worker Influence	Formal Participation Groups
Percent of Company Stock Owned by ESOP	.23	.19	.06
Voting Rights	.41*	.23	.15
Reason Why Company Established Its ESOP	F = .36	F = 1.11	F = 1.11
Employee Ownership Philosophy	.41*	.28	.29
ESOP Communications	.33	.35*	.26
Company Contribution to ESOP	.12	− .04	.01
Stock Change	.03	.00	− .17

* $p \leq .05$

in greater depth later in the chapter. But, first we turn to an examination of the Employee Ownership Philosophy and ESOP Communications results. Unfortunately, these results are not as clearcut as the Contribution results.

Management's Employee Ownership Philosophy and ESOP Communications. Once again, the first step in ruling out alternative explanations of the Employee Ownership Philosophy results is to examine the correlations between Philosophy and the other ESOP characteristics, company characteristics, and measures of worker participation. As table 6–2 showed, Employee Ownership Philosophy is significantly and positively related to both Voting Rights and ESOP Communications. These results indicate that if a company's management has a strong, philosophical commitment to the concept of employee ownership, that company is also likely to give employees full ESOP stock voting rights and to utilize a large number of techniques to educate employees about the ESOP.

As we saw in table 6–1, Voting Rights are not significantly related to any of the employee outcomes. Thus, the correlation of Employee Ownership Philosophy and Voting Rights does not suggest an alternative explanation of the Philosophy results, but only a corroboration and validation of our measure of Employee Ownership Philosophy. It makes sense to us that Philosophy and Voting Rights are positively related, but it is also clear that Voting Rights do not account for the Philosophy results. In fact, many companies that are very committed to employee ownership do not pass through voting rights; they are simply more likely to do so than less committed firms. Regression analyses support this conclusion. Regressing the employee outcomes on Employee Ownership Philosophy and Voting Rights shows that Philosophy is a significant predictor of the employee outcomes (even after controlling for the rather high correlation of Philosophy and Voting Rights).

Interpreting the significant relationship between Employee Ownership Philosophy and ESOP Communications is a bit more complex. It makes sense to us that these two variables are highly intercorrelated. Managers that are highly committed to employee ownership go to great lengths to explain and advertise the ESOP to employees. The problem is that, as table 6–1 shows, ESOP Communications is significantly related to two of the employee outcomes. This means that the Philosophy results might actually be due to ESOP Communications. Regression analyses suggest the opposite conclusion, however. After controlling for Employee Ownership Philosophy, ESOP Communications is not a significant predictor of any of the four employee outcomes. We will talk more about the relationship between Employee Ownership Philosophy and ESOP Communications below. For now, the important point to remember is that Management's Employee Ownership Philosophy and ESOP Communications are, logically enough, highly related, but that Employee Ownership Philosophy seems to be the more important variable.

One final note about the correlations between Employee Ownership Philosophy and the other ESOP Communications: Table 6–2 also shows that Philosophy is significantly related to the Reason the Company Established Its ESOP. However, ESOP Reason is not significantly related to the employee outcomes. And as we discuss later, ESOP Reason turns out to be a somewhat ill-conceived variable.

The next step in the search for alternative explanations of the Philosophy results is to examine the relationship of Philosophy and company characteristics. Table 6–3 shows that Philosophy is only significantly related to one of the company characteristics, Shared Financial Information. If a company has a strong philosophical commitment to employee ownership, that company is also more likely to share financial information about the company with employees. However, Shared Financial Information is not significantly related to any of the employee outcomes. (See table 6–4.) Thus, as with Voting Rights, above, the correlation of Philosophy and Shared Financial Information validates our measure of Employee Ownership Philosophy, but does not explain the Philosophy results. The regression analyses support this conclusion. Even after controlling for Shared Financial Information, Philosophy is significantly related to the employee outcomes.

Last but not least, we consider the relationship of Employee Ownership Philosophy and our measures of worker participation. The correlations are shown in table 6–5. Employee Ownership Philosophy is significantly positively related to Management-Perceived Worker Influence. Substantively, these results are consistent with our correlation results above. Together, the results suggest that a company's strong Philosophical Commitment to Employee Ownership is associated with a variety of participative management practices, including Worker Influence, Employee Stock Voting Rights, ESOP Communications, and Shared Financial Information.

The correlation of Employee Ownership Philosophy and Management-Perceived Worker Influence is especially important because (as table 6–6 shows) Management-Perceived Worker Influence is significantly related to the employee outcomes. Given the significant relationship of Management-Perceived Worker Influence and the employee outcomes, could it be that the apparent effects of Employee Ownership Philosophy are actually the result of participative management practices in companies that are high in Employee Ownership Philosophy? In other words, is it the Employee Owner-

Table 6–6

Correlations between Measures of Worker Influence
and Employee Attitudes

	ESOP Satisfaction	Organizational Commitment	Job Satisfaction	Turnover Intention
Management-Perceived Worker Influence	.43**	.39*	.30	− .32
Employee-Perceived Worker Influence	.49**	.42**	.34*	− .26
Formal Participation Groups	.22	.18	.07	.01

* $p \leq .05$
** $p \leq .01$

ship Philosophy or the high Worker Influence that makes the difference in employee attitudes? Recall that we asked the same question about the relationship of Employee Ownership Philosophy and ESOP Communications.

A regression analysis answers our question, or at least begins to do so. The results show that Management-Perceived Worker Influence is not a significant predictor of the employee outcomes if we first control for the effects of Employee Ownership Philosophy. By contrast, if we first control for Management-Perceived Worker Influence, Employee Ownership Philosophy does remain a significant predictor of the employee outcomes. The results suggest that management's Employee Ownership Philosophy is the more important variable and that the amount of Worker Influence in company decision-making does not make a difference in employee attitudes above and beyond the effects of Employee Ownership Philosophy.

Several fairly technical research problems make us wary of accepting this interpretation too quickly, however. First, our measures of Worker Influence are less than perfect. This is hardly surprising; worker participation and worker influence are very difficult to measure. Unlike employee ownership, which can be defined and measured quite easily (for example, percent of stock owned by employees, presence or absence of voting rights), there are no obvious and clearcut ways to quantify worker participation. Rarely do companies have formally established and well-documented worker participation programs. More often, they have a loosely defined policy of involving employees in company decision-making. Thus, Management-Perceived Worker Influence may not provide a truly accurate assessment of the level of worker participation in a company. Indeed, as we saw in chapter 5, Management-Perceived Worker Influence tends to overestimate worker influence, at least relative to employees' own perceptions.

Because of these measurement concerns, we used three different measures of worker influence in our study: Management-Perceived Worker Influence, Employee-Perceived Worker Influence, and Formal Participation Groups. The high intercorrelations among these variables (see table 6–7) gives us confidence that, together, our three measures adequately describe worker influence.

What does all this have to do with our interpretation of the results for Employee Ownership Philosophy? A lot. Given the difficulties of measuring worker influence, we cannot be entirely certain about the implications of the strong correlation of Employee Ownership

Table 6–7
Intercorrelations among Measures of Worker Influence

	Management-Perceived Worker Influence	Employee-Perceived Worker Influence	Formal Participation Groups
Management-Perceived Worker Influence	1.00		
Employee-Perceived Worker Influence	.66***	1.00	
Formal Participation Groups	.32	.52**	1.00

** $p \leq .01$
*** $p \leq .001$

Philosophy and Management-Perceived Worker Influence. Our uncertainty about the meaning of the correlation of Philosophy and Management-Perceived Worker Influence is only compounded by the fact that Employee Ownership Philosophy is *not* significantly related to the other two measures of worker influence (Employee-Perceived Worker Influence and Formal Participation Groups). Perhaps the managers who *tell* us they are most committed to employee ownership are more likely to *perceive* a high level of worker influence, even if it does not exist.

Finally, one last methodological problem makes us yet more hesitant to jump to conclusions about Employee Ownership Philosophy. In our analyses above, we tried to use regression analysis to separate and contrast the effects of Employee Ownership Philosophy and Management-Perceived Worker Influence on the employee outcomes. The problem is that, in this case, this is not really a logical or legitimate tactic. The two variables are so highly correlated that one variable seems to entail the other. As we have shown, companies that are highly committed to employee ownership tend to give employees voting rights. They tend to give employees financial information about the company. And management, at least, perceives that non-managerial employees in these companies have a lot of influence in company decision-making. Thus, we cannot truly analyze Management-Perceived Worker Influence "above and beyond" Employee Ownership Philosophy. Management-Perceived Worker Influence and Employee Ownership Philosophy are not really alternatives in alternative explanations. The two variables are not one and the same, but they are close, much like the relationship of Physical Fitness and Daily Exercise that we mentioned earlier. This is also the case for Employee Ownership Philosophy and ESOP communications. These two variables are even more highly intercorrelated than Employee Ownership Philosophy and Management-Perceived Worker Influence. As above, we cannot really analyze ESOP Communications "above and beyond" Employee Ownership Philosophy (or vice versa).

As a consequence of the statistical and measurement issues we have just outlined, it is difficult for us to arrive at a wholly satisfying and absolute conclusion about the relationship of Employee Ownership Philosophy, Management-Perceived Worker Influence, ESOP Communications, and the employee outcomes. Nonetheless, we'll try. We focus on Employee Ownership Philosophy because it is more strongly and consistently related to the employee outcomes than either Management-Perceived Influence or ESOP Communications. Within the limits of correlational data, it is clear that a company's philosophical commitment to employee ownership has a positive impact on employee work satisfaction. And it is clear (again, within the limits of correlational data) that management's philosophical commitment to employee ownership is associated with a variety of participative practices (Voting Rights, Shared Financial Information, and ESOP Communications, and, to some extent, at least, Worker Influence). Thus, we think that a strong philosophical commitment to employee ownership does make a difference for the employee outcomes, and that this difference is largely attributable to the positive managerial behaviors that are associated with a strong commitment to employee ownership.

Happily, this interpretation is consistent with our original thinking about the effects of management's Employee Ownership Philosophy. In hypothesizing that management's Employee Ownership Philosophy influences employee attitudes, we implicitly assumed that managers who were strongly committed to employee ownership would *act differently* towards their subordinates than would less philosophically committed managers. In other words, we assumed that a set of managerial behaviors would be associated with a strong philosophical commitment to employee ownership and that these behaviors would in turn motivate employees. Now we have research results that lend support to this contention.

One final comment on the results we have just discussed: Are we exercising too much caution? Are we splitting hairs? We don't think so. One of the exigencies of social science research is that the results rarely come in neat little packages. The conclusions that seem obvious to the non-researcher are not at all obvious to the researcher. Instead, they reflect the researcher's careful thought and precise methods (we hope) and (we fear) his or her seemingly endless struggle with knotty tangles of theory and data.

ESOP Characteristics and the Employee Outcomes

To summarize the results we have discussed thus far, we return to the questions we posed at the beginning of this chapter. We have fairly clear answers to at least seven of our eight questions.

1. Do employees respond more favorably to employee ownership when the ESOP owns a large percentage of company stock?

No. There is no relationship between the amount of stock the employees own through the ESOP and employee ESOP Satisfaction, Organizational Commitment, or Turnover Intention. Owning a lot of company stock does not make employees any more satisfied (or dissatisfied) with the ownership plan, their work, or their companies.

This is not as implausible as it seems. What really matters to an employee is how much stock he or she receives each year—how much money he or she is earning through stock ownership. But this has no relationship to the percentage of company stock that the ESOP holds. For example, an employee in a company that is 30% employee owned, but will never be more employee owned than that, will, other things being equal, receive a smaller contribution than one in a company that is now 10% employee owned, but will eventually be 100% employee owned. Similarly, an employee in a 100% employee-owned firm that is very labor intensive might receive a smaller contribution than an employee in a 20% employee-owned firm that is very capital intensive.

2. Does allowing employees to vote their ESOP stock make them respond more favorably to employee ownership?

Again, the answer is no. There is no relationship between Voting Rights and the employee outcomes. Employees of companies that offer full stock voting rights are not significantly more satisfied than employees in companies that do not offer full voting rights. This too is not such a surprising result upon closer inspection. In most companies, voting rights are more symbolic than important. Many companies go for years without a shareholder vote on anything except board elections. Many boards, in turn, simply ratify management decisions. Even where boards do make important decisions, employees may not be interested in getting involved in them, as we saw in chapter 5.

3. Does the reason the company established its ESOP make a difference for the employee attitudes?

No. We have no evidence that employees in ESOPs set up for different reasons differ significantly in their satisfaction with stock ownership, their work, or their companies. Whether a company sets up a plan to buy out an owner, as an employee incentive, as a tax-saving mechanism, or for some other reason is of little consequence for employee attitudes.

4. Do employees respond more favorably when company management is philosophically committed to employee ownership?

This is our first affirmative answer. While we are not certain that management absolutely must be highly committed to employee ownership to motivate employees, our evidence certainly indicates that it helps. The more philosophically committed management is, the higher the company's score for ESOP Satisfaction, Organizational Commitment, and Job Satisfaction, and the lower the company's score for Turnover Intention.

5. Do employees respond more favorably to employee ownership when the company has an extensive employee ownership communications program?

We think so. The more effort the company makes to promote the ESOP to employees, the more satisfied employees are with stock ownership and the less likely they are to want to leave the company. Again, we don't know that companies absolutely must put a great deal of effort into ESOP communications, but it does seem to help. Moreover, it seems to go hand in hand with other beneficial management practices.

6. Do employees respond more favorably to employee ownership when the company makes a large contribution to the ESOP?

Yes. Though we can't be certain that the company absolutely must give a large contribution to the ESOP before employees respond favorably, the data show a strong positive relationship between the size of the company's Contribution to the ESOP and employees' ESOP Satisfaction, Organizational Commitment, Job Satisfaction, and Turnover Intention.

This is a key finding. Employees respond to ownership primarily as a financial incentive, something the data in the previous chapter indicated as well. The central idea behind early ESOP legislation was to broaden the ownership of wealth; employees appear to endorse the idea.

7. Do employees respond more favorably to employee ownership if company stock remains stable or increases in value?

No. Our data show no significant relationship between the change in a company's stock value (over the preceding two-year period) and employee satisfaction. This may seem to contradict the last finding, but the Size of the Company's Contribution to the ESOP each year is a much more important determinant of the size and growth of employees' ESOP accounts than is Stock Value. Moreover, employees may recognize that short-term fluctuations in stock price are relatively unimportant if the employees plan to stay with the company for a long period of time. We suspect, however, that longer term or severe declines in company fortunes will have a strong negative impact.

In sum, we have gained a far better understanding of the dynamics of employee ownership than we had previously. We know that three ESOP factors are most important in shaping employee attitudes: (1) the size of the company's contribution to the ESOP—a measure of how lucrative the plan is for employees; (2) the company's philosophical commitment to employee ownership—a measure of management's attitudes about employee ownership and indirectly, we believe, of management's behavior towards employees, and (3) just one of those important management behaviors—the ESOP communications program.

But, at least one of our questions is still open:

8. Must employees have considerable opportunities to participate in company decision-making before they respond favorably to employee ownership?

We touched upon this subject in our discussion of Employee Ownership Philosophy. Now we take a closer look.

Worker Influence and Employee Outcomes

Table 6–6 showed the correlations between several measures of worker influence and the employee outcomes. As we noted earlier,

Management-Perceived Worker Influence is positively related to ESOP Satisfaction, Organizational Commitment, and Job Satisfaction, and negatively related to Turnover Intention. (Management-Perceived Worker Influence is only *significantly* related to ESOP Satisfaction and Organizational Commitment, however. The other relationships are almost significant.) The presence of Formal Employee Participation Groups is not significantly related to the employee outcomes, though the results are in the predicted direction. Finally, Employee-Perceived Worker Influence is significantly related to the employee outcomes. For the sake of consistency, we calculated the correlations between Employee-Perceived Worker Influence and the employee outcomes at the company level of analysis.[1]

Before giving our interpretation of the results, we need to reiterate an earlier warning: of necessity, we relied on fairly subjective and imperfect measures of worker influence. It is difficult to capture the phenomenon of worker participation or worker influence with one, two, or even three different measures. Hence, we can only comment on the general trend that we see in our data. If we had more precise data and measures, our correlations might be different. We cannot— on the basis of our statistical data—provide precise, practical suggestions about how to structure a worker participation program. In chapter 7, however, we take a closer look at several of our most successful and participative companies.

So, what do we know about the effects of worker participation? The results indicate that there is a strong positive relationship between worker participation and employee attitudes. The more influence employees have in company decision-making, the more satisfied they are. This of course corroborates recent research and theory.

The Relationship of Employee Ownership and Worker Participation

Having established that two of the ESOP characteristics (Contribution and Employee Ownership Philosophy) are associated with positive employee outcomes in ESOP firms and that worker participation (Management-Perceived Worker Influence) is also associated with positive employee outcomes in these same firms, the next question is obvious: What is the relationship of employee ownership and

worker participation? Can we determine why some employee ownership firms are more participative than others?

First things first. We cannot tell from our data whether employee-owned firms are any more participative than non-employee-
owned firms. This is unfortunate, for it means that we cannot tell if
employee ownership itself makes companies more participative. We
can only ascertain whether any of the ESOP characteristics are associated with any of our measures of worker influence.

Look again at table 6–5. From the table, we see that Voting
Rights and Employee Ownership Philosophy are significantly related to one measure of employee participation, Management-Perceived Worker Influence. In addition, ESOP Communications is significantly related to Employee-Perceived Worker Influence. None of
the other ESOP characteristics is significantly related to any of
our measures of worker participation. The Voting Rights results indicate that ESOP companies that offer employees full ESOP voting
rights are likely to be more participative than ESOP companies that
do not offer full voting rights. But even this may be an overstatement. Voting Rights is significantly related only to *Management*-
Perceived Worker Influence, not to *Employee*-Perceived Worker Influence (even though the two measures of worker influence are
highly intercorrelated). Similarly, we note again that Employee
Ownership Philosophy is significantly related to Management-Perceived Worker Influence, but not to Employee-Perceived Worker
Influence. Finally, ESOP Communications is related to only one of
the three measures of worker influence (Employee-Perceived Worker
Influence).

In sum, the most participative ESOP firms are those which offer
full ESOP voting rights, those which have a relatively substantial
ESOP communications program, and those in which management is
firmly committed to employee ownership. These results are not very
elucidating. Not all three measures of worker influence and participation are significantly related to Voting Rights, Philosophy, and
ESOP Communications. Further, Management-Perceived Worker
Influence, Voting Rights, ESOP Communications, and Employee
Ownership Philosophy are, to some degree, just different ways of
measuring the same thing. Given the fervor with which advocates
discuss their pet theories linking employee ownership and worker

participation, our results appear anticlimatic at best, tautological at worst. The results are perhaps most interesting for what they do *not* show. First and foremost, they do not show a significant relationship between the amount of company stock that employees own and worker participation. Second, they do not show a significant relationship between why a company set up a plan and worker participation. Both of these results counter previous research and theory.

Putting It All Together

How strong are our results? How much do we know? A useful way to answer these questions is to refer back to the "R-square" (R^2) statistic, a statistic we mentioned in our explanation of correlation, analysis of variance, and regression. R^2 measures explained variance. It answers the question, "how much of the variance in our outcome variable (average employee satisfaction) can we explain or account for on the basis of our predictor variables (ESOP characteristics and worker participation)?" We can also use R^2 to contrast the effects of Contribution, Employee Ownership Philosophy, ESOP Communications and Management-Perceived Worker Influence on the employee outcomes.[2]

Table 6–8 summarizes the necessary data. Alone, Contribution explains between 19% and 30% of the variance in the outcome measures. Alone, Employee Ownership Philosophy explains between 10% and 21% of the variance in the outcome measures. Alone, ESOP Communications explains between 0% and 4% of the variance. Finally, Management-Perceived Worker Influence explains between 6% and 16% of the variance in the outcome measures. The results thus suggest a hierarchy of importance, with Contribution most important, Philosophy second, Worker Influence third and ESOP Communications fourth. Recall, however, the high correlation of Philosophy, Worker Influence, and ESOP Communications. Again, this means that it makes little sense to compare the relative effects of Philosophy, Management-Perceived Worker Influence, and ESOP Communications; they are that highly intercorrelated.

Finally, we look at the total variance explained by the significant independent variables. Neither Management-Perceived Worker Influence nor ESOP Communications add significantly to the variance in the employee outcomes that is already accounted for by Contribu-

Table 6–8

Percent of Variance (Adjusted R-Square) in the Employee Attitudes Explained by Company Contribution to the ESOP, Employee Ownership Philosophy, and Management-Perceived Worker Influence

	ESOP Satisfaction	Organizational Commitment	Job Satisfaction	Turnover Intention
Company Contribution to the ESOP	27% ***	19% **	25% **	30% ***
Employee Ownership Philosophy	21% **	22% **	10% *	11% *
ESOP Communications	14% *	4%	0%	14% *
Management-Perceived Worker Influence	16% **	13% *	6%	8%
Company Contribution to the ESOP, and Employee Ownership Philsophy	39% ***	32% **	26% **	34% ***

Note: These numbers represent the adjusted R^2 before the other variables listed in the table are held constant. The last line represents the combined R^2 for Company Contribution and Philosophy. Influence and ESOP Communicaitons are left out here because they do not, when added to these other variables, increase R^2 significantly.

* $p \leq .05$

** $p \leq .01$

*** $p \leq .001$

tion and Philosophy. Accordingly, we consider only the percentage of the variance in the employee outcomes that is explained by Contribution and Philosophy. Together, these two variables account for 26% to 39% of the variance in ESOP Satisfaction, Organizational Commitment, Job Satisfaction, and Turnover Intention.

Before we comment on these figures, we should note two statistical issues. First, it is important to recognize that we are describing the amount of variance that we can explain in the *company* average scores. We can explain much less of the variance in *individual* employee outcome scores on the basis of Contribution and Philosophy. Second, and even more technical, we have reported "adjusted

R-square," instead of the standard "R-square." Adjusted R-square reduces R-square if the sample size is small, as ours is. For our data, adjusted R-square is approximately two to five percentage points smaller than R-square.

How strong are our results? Very strong. We can explain 26% to 39% of the variance in the company average scores on the basis of just two of the ESOP characteristics. That's a lot. It suggests that the ESOP characteristics are very powerful determinants of the overall level of employee satisfaction in the study companies. For a standard of comparison, contrast the effects of Contribution and Philosophy with the effects of Company Size and Company Sales. Size and Sales account for an insignificant proportion of the variance—between 1% and 5%—in the employee outcomes. "Adjusted R-square" turns these figures into negative numbers for each of the employee outcomes! The contrast with worker influence is perhaps a fairer comparison. *Management*-Perceived Worker Influence accounts for only 6% to 16% of the variance in the employee outcomes. The figures are comparable for *Employee*-Perceived Worker Influence aggregated to the company level of analysis. By any standard, then, our results are highly significant—statistically, conceptually, and, we believe, practically.

Conclusion: What the Results Mean

At the outset of this chapter, we reiterated several hypotheses that all seemed very plausbible. Yet only some were supported by the data. Here, we return to our results to discuss why the pattern of results emerged as it did.

Company Contribution to the ESOP

Our strongest, most certain, and most surprising results are for the Size of the Company Contribution to the ESOP. The larger the company's contribution to its ESOP, the more satisfied employees are—with the ESOP, with their work, and with the company in general. The strong effects of ESOP Contribution are not explained by any other ESOP or company characteristics. Nor is Contribution significantly related to any measure of management style or worker participation. Finally, Contribution is a "clean" and objective variable.

The direction of causality is clear; employee attitudes could not possibly influence the size of the company's ESOP Contribution.

For all these reasons, the Contribution results are strong and certain. But surprising? Why are they surprising? The Contribution results seem obvious enough to us now, but when we began our research, no researcher had so much as suggested that the financial or monetary aspects of the employee ownership plan might be important for employee attitudes. All of the research and theory emphasized worker control and worker involvement. These were supposed to be the primary characteristics and benefits of employee ownership.

Our Contribution results counter this emphasis. The results strongly support what we call an "extrinsic gratification" model of the effects of ESOP employee ownership. Employees who receive large financial benefits from their employer apparently respond to their employer with enthusiasm, commitment, and longevity. In short, employees appreciate their high compensation and the company that provides it.

One of the more interesting manifestations of this is that the larger the Company Contribution to an ownership plan, the less likely an employee is to want to leave, even though his or her ESOP nest egg, available only on departure, may be very large. Some employers fear that this nest egg could encourage turnover, but the data suggest the opposite: employees do not want to give up a good thing.

Taking this line of reasoning to its logical extreme, one might conclude that a company need only provide its employees with a lucrative benefit plan in order to insure a high level of morale. While this is surely an overstatement, the state of the economy in the last several years may make employees particularly responsive to a relatively large deferred benefit. Still, it seems likely that the Company Contribution to the ESOP assumes a larger symbolic value beyond simple monetary value in the eyes of employees. At the most basic level, a large ESOP contribution makes good the company's employee ownership rhetoric. What good is an employee ownership plan if, at the very least, it is not lucrative? A large ESOP Contribution introduces an element of hope and excitement into what otherwise might appear to employees to be a dull, uninspiring plan: "If the company continues at this rate," an employee may suddenly realize,

"I could earn a lot of money this way!" At a more abstract, subconscious level, employees may view the Company Contribution to the ESOP as an indication that management values and appreciates them —enough to literally share the wealth of the company with them.

Given the Contribution data, it is tempting to argue that employees in ESOP companies must actually show higher morale and satisfaction than employees in non-ESOP companies. That is, we found that the more ownership employees get, the happier they are. So wouldn't employees who get some ownership be happier than those with none? Unfortunately, the study results cannot prove this. It's possible that poorly designed ESOPs cause employee resentment and dissatisfaction, while well designed, financially rewarding ESOPs cause increased satisfaction and loyalty.

In any case, the Contribution results counter the prevailing popular emphasis on worker participation and quality of working life factors as _the_ central determinants of employee satisfaction and commitment. Our results suggest that there's more to work enjoyment than just _intrinsic_ satisfaction. _Extrinsic_ satisfaction—the prospect of earning a significant amount of money—adds appreciably to overall work satisfaction. Thus, we think our results paint a very balanced picture: employee owners respond positively to both the financial benefits of their work (Contribution) and to its intrinsic rewards (Employee Ownership Philosophy, Worker Influence).

Employee Ownership Philosophy
Employee Ownership Philosphy, a measure of management's philosophical commitment to employee ownership, is also consistently significantly related to the employee outcomes. Philosophy is positively related to ESOP Satisfaction, Organizational Commitment, and Job Satisfaction, and negatively related to Turnover Intention.

As Employee Ownership Philosophy is a fairly subjective and ambiguous measure (at least compared to Contribution), we need to define our terms carefully. Just what does Employee Ownership Philosophy mean? Looking back to chapter 4, we see that the management official who is high in Employee Ownership Philosophy says that employee ownership is a "a central part" of his/her company's "management philosophy" and that employee ownership plays "a major role" in the company's "corporate culture and identity." Further, the high-scoring management official thinks that the company's employee ownership plan is more than just "a tax-saving or financing mechanism." Employee Ownership Philosophy is just that—a philosophy, a belief, an attitude.

Why does Employee Ownership Philosophy have such a big effect on employee satisfaction? How does a managerial attitude reap these effects? It's hard to tell, but our guess is that management's attitudes about employee ownership shape their behaviors towards employees. Management's commitment (or lack thereof) to employee ownership may be translated into action in a thousand ways. Does the company provide employees with stock voting rights? Does it give employees information about the financial performance of the company? Does it offer employees significant opportunities for participation and influence in company decisions? Does it go to great lengths to make sure employees understand and think about the ESOP?

The positive association of Employee Ownership Philosophy and the employee outcomes suggest that employees do respond favorably to the intrinsic rewards of their work. They respond favorably to being treated like owners—with respect, trust, and consideration. The results for Employee Ownership Philosophy vindicate popular and academic press attention to quality of working life, worker participation, and corporate culture.

Still, we hasten to add that our results for Employee Ownership Philosophy are less certain than those for ESOP Contribution. The measure of Employee Ownership Philosophy is subjective, and open to social desirability effects (managers wanting to look good by saying the right things). The correlations between Employee Ownership Philosophy and the various measures of worker influence and participation are somewhat inconsistent and confusing. The direction of causality between Philosophy and employee attitudes is not obvious; management may be supportive of employee ownership ideals because their employees show high morale and commitment to the company. And finally, our interpretations of the Employee Ownership Philosophy results are necessarily more speculative than are our interpretations of the Contribution results.

It makes sense to us that both money and participation (in the broadest sense of the term) influence employee attitudes. Our results suggest this. They don't prove it.

ESOP Communications

ESOP Communications, a measure of the number of ways in which the company educates employees about the ESOP, is significantly positively related to employees' satisfaction with stock ownership and significantly negatively related to employees' turnover intentions. Our interpretation of this finding is straightforward: the more employees understand and think about the ESOP (as a result of management's communications efforts), the more enthusiastic employees will be about the ESOP, and about staying with the company.

ESOPs are complicated, technical plans; employees may be suspicious or disinterested in the ESOP. ESOP benefits to employees are long-term and distant; employees may be apathetic or resentful. When management counters these employee sentiments with easily understandable information about the ESOP, employees respond well. In addition, an effective, active ESOP communications package seems to be part and parcel of the best companies' management practices. Companies that have an extensive ESOP communications program also tend to give employees more financial information about the company, and tend to be more participative than companies with less comprehensive communications programs.

And what of the other ESOP characteristics? Why don't they matter? We look at them now.

Percent of Company Stock Owned by the ESOP

The percent of company owned by the ESOP is not significantly related to any of the employee outcomes. This result contradicts previous research and theory, but it is more understandable when we realize that Percent has no bearing on either the financial or the intrinsic rewards of employee ownership. Percent is not significantly related to Contribution or to Stock Value. Nor is Percent significantly related to Voting Rights or to any of our measures or worker influence. Given these results, Percent would only make a difference in employee attitudes if employees somehow found it more satisfying to own 80% of company stock than 30% of company stock, even though owning a larger percentage of stock didn't give them any additional benefits from employee ownership.

The Reason the Company Established Its ESOP

The Reason the Company Established its ESOP is not significantly related to the employee outcomes; employees do not respond significantly differently to ESOPs established for different reasons. Like Percent, the reason the plan was established seems to have no bearing on the extrinsic and intrinsic rewards of employee ownership to employees. Reason is not significantly related to Contribution, Stock Value, Employee Ownership Philosophy, or Worker Influence. In other words, companies that set up their ESOPs for different reasons do *not* differ in the size of their contributions to their ESOPs, in their worker participation policies, or in the other measures.

Two additional factors may also help to explain the nonsignificance of the results for ESOP Reason. First, the Reason for ESOP Establishment is an ambiguous and troublesome variable. We counted seven reasons for ESOP adoption, but we did so rather arbitrarily. Perhaps we should have lumped together companies that set up ESOPs as employee benefit plans with those that set up ESOPs as employee incentives. Perhaps we should have lumped together companies that used an ESOP to buy out the private founder with those that used an ESOP to purchase the company during a corporate divestiture. Perhaps we should have simply distinguished ESOP Reason into two categories: Financial and Tax Savings vs. Other. The possibilities are endless, but the criteria for judging between these possible schemas are not at all clear. Thus, we may have chosen the "wrong" categorization of ESOP Reasons, though we have no conceptual argument to support that hypothesis.

A second additional explanation for the insignificance of the Reason results is statistical. We used analysis of variance to calculate the statistical significance of the Reason results. However, the larger the relative proportion of categories to sample size (for example, seven ESOP reasons for 37 companies) and the smaller the sample size, the more difficult it is to obtain statistical significance. Perhaps a larger sample size would have yielded significant results for ESOP Reason.

Voting Rights
ESOP Voting Rights is not significantly related to any of the employee outcomes. Employees in companies that do offer employees full ESOP Voting Rights are not more satisfied than employees in companies that deny employees full ESOP Voting Rights. Again, this result contradicts previous employee ownership theory. Two factors—one substantive, one statistical—explain the Voting Rights results.

First, ESOP Voting Rights are almost always quite minimal. Few issues come to vote. Further, non-managerial employees must know that the impact of any one individual's vote is insignificant, and employees rarely vote their stock as a block. Seven of the 13 companies in our sample that do offer full ESOP voting rights are publicly held (and hence required to provide full voting rights to employees). Employee owners in these companies often comprise a small minority—the average percent of ESOP employee ownership in the publicly held companies in our sample is 14.37%—so that the employee vote is unlikely to wield much influence. Finally, though Voting Rights is significantly related to Management-Perceived Worker Influence, it is not significantly related to Employee-Perceived Worker Influence. In sum, the value of ESOP Voting Rights is, in most cases, likely to be small and symbolic, and therefore insufficient to significantly influence employee attitudes.

Second, statistical factors again make it difficult to obtain a significant result. Voting Rights is a dichotomous variable, but only 13 companies passed through full Voting Rights. A larger sample size might show significant results.

Stock Value
Change in the Value of Company Stock is insignificantly related to the employee outcomes. Given the Contribution results, the Stock Value results are somewhat surprising. Change in the Value of Company Stock also influences the financial rewards of ESOP employee ownership. Shouldn't employees be more satisfied to own stock in a company whose stock is quickly rising?

Our only explanation for the Stock Value results is that, compared to the Size of the Company Contribution to the ESOP, Stock Value normally has a relatively small influence on the financial rewards that employees receive. For example, if an employee receives an ESOP contribution of 2% of salary each year, his or her ESOP account will still be quite small after five years unless the company shows phenomenal growth in stock value. If an employee receives a contribution of 10% of salary each year, his or her ESOP account will be relatively large after five years unless stock values decline sharply. Moreover, in our sample, only five out of 33 companies showed a decline in stock values in the two years preceding our employee survey, a factor that limited the variance in our measure. Finally, we should note that the Stock Value results are in the predicted direction; they are just not very large.

Worker Influence

Worker Influence is the last of our main independent variables. Worker Influence (both Mangement-Perceived and Employee-Perceived) is significantly positively related to the employee outcomes; the more influence employees have in company decision-making, the more satisfied they are.

Our results suggest that worker participation does not necessarily have to be formalized. Our measure of formal decision-making groups is not significantly related to employee attitudes. Further, we found that few of our study companies had formal programs to involve employees in company decision-making, though many were strongly committed to worker participation through everyday, informal mechanisms. This was especially the case for the smaller firms. In the next chapter, we discuss the methods for, and results of, involving employees in workplace decisions.

Practical Implications

You are a company president and you've heard about Employee Stock Ownership Plans. You've done a fair amount of research and you understand the technical details of setting up a plan. Now it's time to make your decision. Should you put in an ESOP?

We certainly can't make the decision for you, but we can offer you some practical suggestions. Do you want your ESOP to act as an incentive and reward for your employees? Is employee satisfaction an important consideration?

If so, put in an ESOP only if:

1. You are willing to make significant financial contributions to the plan. We can't specify an exact dollar amount, but we recommend giving annual ESOP contributions of at least 5%, and preferably 10%, of the covered employee payroll.
2. You are strongly committed to the idea of employee ownership. You should be ready to treat employees like owners, to bring them—formally or informally—into company decision-making.
3. You are ready to develop an active ESOP communications program involving, for example, newsletters and regular meetings for employee shareholders.

These three considerations, above all others, are most important. How you structure your ESOP—voting rights, vesting schedule, percent of company stock owned by the ESOP—is of secondary importance *if your plan offers a significant financial benefit to employee participants and if you feel—and demonstrate—your philosophical commitment to employee ownership.* An ESOP is never magic. It will not miraculously transform a sluggish company or a disgruntled workforce. But our research suggests that, *under the right circumstances*, an ESOP can have strong positive effects or employees' work satisfaction, their commitment to the company, and their plans to stay with the company.

Appendix 6A
Employee Survey Scale Items

General ESOP Satisfaction

Because of employee ownership, my work is more satisfying.

I really don't care about the employee ownership plan in this company. (Reverse)

I'm proud to own stock in this company.

Employee ownership at this company makes my day-to-day work more enjoyable.

Owning stock in this company makes me want to stay with this company longer than I would if I did not own stock.

It is very important to me that this company has an employee stock owner-ship plan.

Owning stock in this company makes me more interested in the company's financial success.

Employee ownership at this company gives me a greater share in company profits.

Organizational Commitment

I am willing to put in a great deal of effort beyond that normally ex-pected in order to help this organization be successful.

I find that my values and the organization's are very similar.

I really care about the fate of this organization.

I talk up this organization to my friends as a great organization to work for.

This organization really inspires the very best in me in the way of job performance.

I am proud to tell others that I am part of this organization.

I am extremely glad that I chose this organization to work for over the others I was considering at the time I joined.

I would accept almost any type of job assignment in order to keep working for this company.

For me, this is the best of all possible organizations for which to work.

Job Satisfaction

All in all, I am satisfied with my job.

In general, I don't like my job. (Reversed)

In general, I like working here.

Turnover Intention

How likely is it that you will actively look for a new job in the next year?

I often think about quitting.

I will probably look for a new job in the next year.

Employee-Perceived Worker Influence

How much say or influence do *non-managerial* workers in your company *actually* have over the following areas:

1. Social events
2. Working conditions
3. The way workers perform their own jobs
4. Pay and other compensation
5. Hiring, firing, and other personnel decisions
6. Selection of supervisors and management
7. Company policy (investment in new equipment, planning for the company future)

Desired Worker Influence

How much say or influence *do you think* that *non-managerial* workers in your company *should* have over the following areas?

1. Social events
2. Working conditions
3. The way workers perform their own jobs
4. Pay and other compensation
5. Hiring, firing, and other personnel decisions
6. Selection of supervisors and management
7. Company policy (e.g., investment in new equipment, planning for the company future)

7
Lessons from Employee Ownership Success Stories
Creating the Idea of Ownership

In the last chapter, we presented a quantitative analysis of what makes employee ownership work. In this chapter, we present intuitive and qualitative profiles of the highest-scoring companies and what they do to spread the idea and practice of ownership among their employees. We want to flesh out these bare statistical bones with a more intuitive and qualitative report on what our best companies do to spread the idea and practice of ownership among their employees.

We cannot stress enough, however, that our key finding is very simple and straightforward: employees will act more like owners if they see more stock in their accounts each year. Nothing matters more than how much stock employees get each year. This finding does not make for very interesting or subtle stories about how clever, dedicated managers created a brilliantly effective ownership program, or how determined employees bargained to create a truly innovative labor-management partnership. Its simplicity must not be deceiving, however. Unless employees get substantial amounts of stock ownership, it is unlikely (if not impossible) that they will really think of themselves as owners. No matter what else a company might do, it seems, ownership, per se, matters.

Nonetheless, for the most successful employee ownership companies, providing substantial annual contributions is usually only the foundation, basic as it might be, for ongoing efforts to create among the employees the idea that they really are not just workers, but owners. These companies do this in a variety of ways—participation programs, frequent communications, small group meetings, abolition of special perquisites for managers, informal contacts between managers and employee-owners, symbolic things such as calling everyone an "associate," developing a statement of principles, and other such efforts. What strikes us about what these companies do, however, is that it is not so much the specific structures of their programs that matter so much as the sincerity and vigor of the efforts behind them. These companies really believe in the idea of ownership, and it is this belief that seems to be communicated to workers. Company management constantly seeks to reinforce this concept, and the reinforcement seems to count more than the quality of any individual program. Doing something, even if the desired success is not always achieved, is seen as better than doing nothing. These companies are always trying to improve, to reinvent their corporate cultures to make them fit their employee ownership character.

This is bad news and good news. It is bad news because it means you cannot simply set up some kind of formulaic approach to ownership and reap the benefits. On the other hand, it is good news because it means that many companies that really want to accomplish something with employee ownership can do so if they try enough. Each company needs to determine what is appropriate for its own circumstances, often through a process of trial and error. It is something like training for a marathon. The concept is simple—get up and run a long way every day—but the execution takes a lot of commitment and effort. While there are useful guidelines to make the training more efficient, there are no magical formulas that can make it easy. Making an employee ownership plan work is also simple in conception, but requires a lot of effort and commitment to make people think and act as owners.

The companies included here are those whose employees scored the highest on our measures of commitment to the employee ownership program. They are not presented in any particular order, for we do not want to suggest that the company that scored the highest is necessarily more successful than the one that scored the next highest, and so on. Our measures are not fine enough for that. As a group, however, these companies are clearly more successful than the other companies in the study. While the last chapter identified the factors that are generally identified with making employee ownership work, this one will allow us to look more specifically at individual programs in individual companies. Because each of these companies is responding to its own unique circumstances, however, the cases presented in this chapter are not meant as models for others to copy so much as examples that we hope will inspire people to do what these companies have done—figure out what will work for them. The success these companies have had should, we think, convince a lot of people that the effort is well worthwhile.

Chickens and Eggs:
Does Financial Success Make Employee Ownership Work or Does Employee Ownership Create Financial Success?

All of these success stories are financially successful as well, whereas the companies that scored the lowest on measures of employee attitudes were all in financial difficulty. Does this mean a company must be financially successful for employee ownership to work? Or does it mean that when employee ownership works, companies are more financially successful? Unfortuantely, we cannot say for sure, but we suspect that the answer may be "both."

Our judgement is that, at a minimum, more financially successful firms are in a better position to do the things that make employee ownership work. They can make substantial annual contributions, spend resources on things that make work more enjoyable, experiment with employee involvement programs, and so on. On the other hand, troubled firms may not be able to afford many of these things, and may be cutting payrolls at the same time. That suggests that troubled firms cannot expect much from employee ownership unless they turn around quickly. Other companies, however, will find that financial success is no guarantor of employee ownership success. They have to build on that economic foundation to do the kinds of things the companies described here do. In the language of logicians, being financially secure is a necessary, but not sufficient, condition for making employee ownership work. This kind of relationship does not show up very well in correlational analyses, and thus we found no significant relationship between financial performance and employee ownership success. What that means is that we cannot say that the more successful you are, the more employees will like being owners. What does seem true is that if the company is in financial difficulty, employee stock ownership will not make a difference.

Seven Case Studies

American Recreation Centers

People often think of employee ownership as something meant to save gritty industrial plants—steel mills for instance—or, at the other extreme, as a means to hire and keep people in glamorous high-tech companies. In fact, most employee ownership companies are much more prosaic. They do things such as make picture frames, print magazines, or, as at American Recreation Centers, operate bowling centers.

After all, a business like bowling-center management, with widely dispersed facilities and a need to create a pleasant atmosphere for customers, can use dedicated, responsible employees as much or more than a steel mill or a software company. American Recreation Centers, founded in 1961 and located in Sacramento, California, is a firm that has taken this to heart, and with considerable financial success. Their total sales have increased about $1 million every year from 1979–1984, the years for which data are available. They have also increased their profits by about $800,000 in this period. And the company has made a substantial contribution of stock to the ESOP trust every year since its inception in 1974, making it one of the earliest ESOPs. The plan held 25% of the company stock at the end of 1983.

ARC also provides for early entry into the plan and has an accelerated vesting schedule. Employees may begin participating after 500 hours of employment (this brings in part-time employees) whereas the common practice is after 1,000 hours. The workers are 100% vested after six years, compared to ten years in most ESOPs. The company treats the employee shareholders exactly like all other shareholders. This includes distribution of quarterly and annual reports. Most important, the annual proxy solicitation is given to every eligible employee shareholder, thus providing the opportunity to share in the election of the Board of Directors and other activities that require a shareholder vote. ARC also pays dividends on the stock. Robert Feuchter, company president, feels that these factors contribute to the employees' satisfaction with the company and with their jobs.

Feuchter reports that the company is dedicated to the idea of employee ownership, and makes it a central part of the company culture. He said, "I'm a great believer in people owning stock in the companies they work for. I used to work for (another company), and it was clear that you were a hired hand. I always wanted to own something." He believes that this attitude has contributed to an improvement in a number of factors including productivity and profitability, employee attitudes about management, and cooperation among the employees themselves. He also thinks that employee ownership has made employees more interested in the company's financial success and more satisfied with their jobs.

ARC also makes a major effort to educate the employees about the plan and to keep reinforcing the idea of ownership. The company:

1. discusses employee ownership in orientation for new employees;
2. describes the employee ownership plan in an employee handbook;
3. regularly mentions employee ownership in the company newsletter;
4. describes employee ownership in a slide show for employees;
5. holds small group meetings about employee ownership;
6. hangs posters around the company; and
7. has informal conversations with employees about the employee ownership plan.

None of these things is unusual or difficult and most companies do two or three of them. Doing them all, and doing them repeatedly, is not so common.

In addition, American Recreation has a committee to address and maintain good employee-management relations. Representatives from all sectors and levels of the company participate in this activity from the non-supervisory personnel to the CEO. This is no easy task in such a large company, about 800 employees, which serves a wide area. But ARC's management thinks it is worth the time and effort.

Half the managers at ARC are women, which is "unlike most of the industry," but ARC made a conscious decision to achieve this. "There's an incredible amount of talent on the female side of the ledger," reports Mr. Feuchter. This decision to provide opportunities to participate in a professional job and in stock ownership to a group which has historically been without either of those may account for the slightly higher job satisfaction scores among women. In addition, workers in a high turnover industry, like this one, are usually not included in this kind of plan. ARC makes it easy. The employees apparently perceive this and appreciate it. They return this appreciation to their company, providing benefits to everyone. "Strike."

Fastener Industries
Industrial weld fasteners are nuts and bolts with small "projections" on them that allow the fasteners to be welded onto pieces of equipment too thin to be threaded themselves. They are on the insides of file cabinets, computers, sinks, and all sorts of other things. The first thing you notice when you walk into the Berea, Ohio fastener factory, the leading industrial weld fastener manufacturer in the nation, is the insistent banging of machines hammering and cutting pieces of rolled steel into thousands of nuts and bolts, often at the rate of 200–400 per minute.

The second thing you notice is that all the machines are painted different colors. Some time ago, during a slack period, the plant manager told the employees they could repaint the machines in their section in colors of their choice, a small thing, but indicative of how things work at this company whose 115 employees own 100% of the stock.

The ESOP was established in 1980 to buy the shares of the family that had owned the company for decades. After the last family member to run the business decided to retire, an ESOP seemed like a logical alternative. The company had always been very employee oriented, and had operated a generous profit-sharing program. With the consent of the participants, that plan was converted to the

ESOP. Its assets, along with a bank loan, were used to buy out the owners. Rich Biernacki, company treasurer at the time of the conversion, became president. In this model ESOP, Biernacki has been a model president.

The ownership culture is a prevailing force in this company. First of all, the plan itself is considerably more liberal than most. All of the stock was transferred to the ESOP at the outset, making the company 100% employee owned immediately; employees are eligible to participate in the plan after one month of service, are immediately vested, and have full voting rights on the stock. The company also provides financial consultation to employees about the best ways the stock or cash payout can be handled upon receipt by the departing employee.

Some of the unusual features at Fastener seem only natural to Biernacki and the employees. As mentioned, all eligible employees have immediate full voting rights, though only limited voting is required by law in a privately held company. "If you don't vote it, you don't really own it," Rich Biernacki told us. The employees take their voting rights seriously. Fifteen employees were nominated and ran for the board in the first election, although the employees chose four company managers for five of the seats. Biernacki sees no problem in being responsible to his workers. "If I can't convince them I'm right, then maybe I'm not," he told us.

Most companies have gradual vesting schedules to encourage workers to stay with the company. However, again Biernacki voices a strong view here, "I think one of the worst things that can happen is to have an employee who really doesn't want to work for the company but stays around to become vested."

Another unusual feature is that the largest shareholder holds less than 4% of the stock. Since stock allocation is based on compensation, it is clear that the salary ratio is quite low.

The working conditions could hardly be better. First of all, there is a 35-hour work week in the production department rather than the industry norm of 40 hours, and all employees are on salary. The workers are given quarterly financial reports, and they read them, according to Biernacki. "You can tell by the kinds of questions they ask at the annual meeting," he says. Bonuses based on profits are paid at the end of the year. 1983's bonus was three-fourths of a month's salary.

Fastener has made substantial contributions to the ESOP employee accounts, contributing the maximum of 25% the first three years and 15% in 1983.

Fastener was always profitable and was able to break even during the early 1980s at a time when closings in the industry were common. As is company policy, no one was laid off during this period, even though that meant reducing profits. The workers are paid a wage higher than the industry average. Biernacki seemed genuinely perplexed when asked about the pay differences between blue-collar workers and others, saying, "Those groups aren't even separated in my mind."[1]

Rich Biernacki meets monthly with the supervisors. These supervisors then meet with the shopfloor workers. The main purpose of these meetings is to keep everyone informed of mangement decisions. However, workers immediately involved in the decision are consulted beforehand. For example, if new machinery is to be purchased the workers actually using it will be consulted. Management's attitude is reflected in Biernacki's summation:

> I think it works both ways. He owns the place and expects to be involved, and you [the manager] respect that he owns the place, and you want him involved in it. You know he knows best; he can save you a lot of problems.[2]

Biernacki tells a story of a worker's watching a machine leave the plant one day. "Are we selling that or giving it away?" he asked. "Selling it," he was told. "O.K.," said the worker, "I just wanted to make sure we were getting something for *our* machine."

The president also meets every six months with a group of about 12 workers until the whole work force is included. Any relevant topic can be discussed. These small group meetings provide an opportunity for every employee to be heard, and for Mr. Biernacki to find out firsthand what is on the workers' minds. Unknown to Mr. Biernacki before he did it, this process is labeled "deep sensing" in mangerial theory. He just thought it was a sensible thing to do.

"Employee ownership is so important that our company would set up a plan even if there were no tax benefits," was the response given by Rich Biernacki when asked to describe the view about employee ownership at Fastener Industries. This is communicated and undoubtedly felt by all workers there. Turnover is virtually nonexistent (about 2–3% per year). In fact, as at a number of other successful companies, workers tell their relatives and friends about openings, making the company something of a large extended family. Like the bowling alleys of American Recreation Centers, the "nuts and bolts" of Fastener Industry are not the stuff of glamor and excitement. From what employees at Fastener told us, however, their company does a lot more right than make a good weld fastener. The example it has created for other companies to emulate seems pretty exciting to us.

Riverside Construction Company

Riverside Construction Company is something of an anomaly among this group of companies. Their scores on General ESOP Attitude, Job Satisfaction, and Organizational Commitment were among the very highest of all the companies studied yet the company demonstrated few of the characteristics common to what we are terming "successes" based on scores.

Riverside's contribution to the ESOP is healthy but not outstanding (10% of salary each year in 1982 and 1983); there is no formal worker participation in decision-making; financial information is not given to the employees; there are no voting rights attached to the stock; vesting does not begin for three years; stock is not distributed until retirement. When asked, Gordon Lounsbury, secretary-treasurer, said "Making employees owners makes sense, but we would not have done it if there were no tax or other financial benefits."

There is little discrepancy between degree of actual influence and desired influence by the workers in company decision-making at Riverside. According to the employee responses on the surveys, they don't have much, and they don't want much.

So what is the explanation for these exceptionally high ownership, commitment, and job satisfaction scores? We don't know. Though the company's financial performance is strong, this is not sufficient to explain the top or near-top scores on the aforementioned measures.

There are, however, a few things which stand out about Riverside. It is in an industry where there is much short-term employment, and there are considerable layoffs depending on the season and the workload. This kind of work environment would not seem to readily lend itself to worker ownership. Consequently, workers in this type of industry may have less of an opportunity to participate in an employee ownership company than those in some other industries. But Riverside does have a plan, and a successful one. It overcomes the problems of having people coming on and going off the payroll by requiring that workers work for the company for 1,000 hours to qualify to participate in the ESOP (a typical plan feature), but allowing them to stay in the plan if they work as little as 50 hours in any year (compared to 500 in most plans). To keep "floaters" out of the ESOP, vesting does not start for three years.

A second notable characteristic about Riverside in relation to worker ownership is that 85% of the workforce is unionized, and they participate in the plan. Union members are precluded from participating in a number of unionized ESOP companies. In some cases, this is because the company's management wants to limit the ESOP to non-union employees; in some, it is because contributions to other benefit plans for union members are high enough so that the company is not able to take a tax deduction for further benefits such as ESOPs. In still other cases, the union has asked not to be included in the plan. In any event, the union does have the right to bargain over inclusion in the ESOP. While Riverside is not unique in including union members in the plan, it is an important feature of their ownership program. Mr. Lounsbury told us "All our field employees are union. If we didn't recognize the union members, all we would be recognizing are the clerical, administrative, and management employees. We didn't think that was fair. We like to feel that it's all one unit."

The attitude of company management that "it's all one unit" suggests a company committed to the notion of a more cooperative workplace, one in which employee ownership is used as more than just a financial benefit for some workers. Indeed, even though there are no efforts or plans to have any kind of formal participation or communication programs, there is an informal network which appears to link the owner and management with all the workers and the workers with each other. The company president spends about 50% of his time in the field. He knows everyone on a personal basis. "If they're working nearby, employees will come over here to talk at the end of their shifts," Mr. Lounsbury told us.

Even though our research was as comprehensive and rigorous as possible, cases such as Riverside demonstrate that there are still a lot of idiosyncratic factors involved in making employee ownership effective. There will always be companies that do not conform to the norms that our statistical analyses describe, whose success stems more from something within the character of the company that is, apparently, hard to measure or even describe in some systematic way.

Hyatt Clark Industries

In these successful companies, employee ownership often seems to create an atmosphere of cooperation and good feeling between labor and management. In many of these firms, this environment predated the ESOP, and the ESOP simply reinforced it; in others, efforts to create this environment and set up an employee ownership plan came at the same time. But what would happen in a company in which labor-management relations had traditionally been hostile? Could employee ownership overcome a tradition of highly charged adversarial relations, one in which union leaders had built their reputation on an ability to stand up to management?

This issue has been put to the test at Hyatt Clark Industries, a New Jersey manufacturer of roller bearings for motor vehicles, primarily rear-wheel-drive autos. With 87.5% of its workforce organized by United Autoworkers Union Local 736, Hyatt had a reputation for some of the most contentious labor relations in the industry. In fact, that reputation was one factor in the 1980 decision by General Motors, Hyatt's former owner, to sell the plant.[3] GM's public reason was because the plant was too expensive. The bearings manufactured at the plant were becoming obsolete and the parts still needed could be gotten cheaper elsewhere. Labor could also be bought cheaper overseas.[4] When no buyer could be found, GM announced in March 1981 that it planned to close the plant. That announcement set off a shock wave through the community. James May, a union member, and now president of UAW Local 736 at Hyatt, read in *The New York Times* about a buyout by the workers of a plant in Ohio in a similar situation. He and his partner, shop chairman James Zarello, amidst skepticism and downright ridicule and antagonism from some, pursued the idea. Their first effort to raise money for a feasibility study by having each union member put up $35 failed by a narrow vote. A second effort, this one asking for a voluntary $100 contribution, gained the active support of local management, and succeeded. $100,000 was raised.[5]

The study indicated that with a 25% cut in pay and benefits the plan had a chance to succeed. After some thought, the union accepted this on the condition that stock allocations be made on an equal basis. Some haggling occurred, but management acquiesced. Financing was arranged, in part because General Motors agreed to purchase Hyatt's products for at least three years.[7]

The union received three seats on the board of directors in the deal.[8] However, voting rights to elect board members or on any other corporate business will pass through to the workers only after the $53 million purchase debt is retired in 1991.[9]

From the outset, Hyatt was thus a different kind of employee ownership company. The workers had actually made an investment in the company by accepting lower compensation. This created an expectation of ownership rights not necessarily present in other employee ownership companies. Also, this buyout has received more media hype to date than any other, further contributing to the implanting of the ownership idea in the minds of the workers who made concessions. Since the employees had long been suspicious of management anyway, many would see the ESOP as a chance to "really run the company."[10]

In October 1983, two years after the buyout, the company had made a remarkable turnaround from the downhill slide in the years just prior to the buyout. Employment increased from 800 to 1,200, and profits graced the bottom line again. Productivity rose an astounding 90%, largely due to changes in the way work was organized. A series of worker involvement programs was set up, the new president, Howard Kurt, began meetings with employees, and many status perquisites were abolished.[11] Our data indicate that the workers did feel like owners, with greater commitment to the organization, more motivation at work, and less desire to leave.

If a culture of ownership is present anywhere it should be present at Hyatt Clark Industries. After all, the employees do own 100% of the company stock, stock they in effect purchased through compensation concessions. This is unlike the usual arrangement of management installing an ownership plan as a "free" employee benefit.

The plan itself is a liberal one with only 60 days of employment required for participation and with allocation based on months of service rather than the more common method based on salary. The union was adamant on these points.

In addition to providing board seats to three union representatives, other efforts are made to keep workers informed and to have them participate in decision-making at least at the job level. Financial information is provided to the workers, and problem-solving groups called Employee Action Teams (EATs) have been established. Due to fluctuations in the internal labor force, these teams have not really been thoroughly tested. Semi-annual productivity bonus plans have been established along with profit-sharing.

Although all of these things suggest a company moving in the right direction on employee ownership, the old strains between labor and management are far from gone. They surfaced most bitterly in 1984 over the profit-sharing plan. That year, the company showed a $2.2 million profit entitling the workers to $600,000 in bonuses. However, a $14 million capital expenditure had also been authorized by the board. Something had to give; the money could not stretch far enough to cover both. The board, with dissenting votes from the two union leaders and their appointee, decided to postpone the bonuses. Productivity fell sharply. The shop chair said, "You can't expect workers to say 'I must continue to cooperate even though I'm exploited just so the company can do well.' That's just not human nature." Workers, in effect, declared a slowdown until the compensation issue could be resolved.[12]

General Motors, in the meantime, was deciding whether to renew its purchase agreement, an agreement without which Hyatt could not operate. The profit-sharing dispute had now lingered over into the new round of contract talks. Management wanted to keep wages down in order to invest more; workers said they needed some of the profits now, and argued that management was overcompensated anyway. GM said it would not renew its contract unless the dispute was resolved, and with this pressure, the two sides agreed to a wage increase of $.50 per hour. Management also agreed to a proposal to share more power with employees in areas of corporate decision-making.[13]

While this dispute has been the most serious, there have been others. The adversarial style of labor-management relations the company had for so long has clearly not been eliminated by employee ownership. If our survey had been taken at a time when the disagreements were most serious, we suspect the scores would have been much lower. On the other hand, the company has made considerable progress. It is far more productive than it ever was under GM, even with the periodic slowdowns. It has made money and created 700 new jobs. New decision-making structures have been put in place, sometimes only after hard bargaining, that have the potential to create a better environment for everyone.

Worker ownership cannot eliminate a poor market, the situation primarily responsible for General Motor's divestiture decision and the continuing bane of Hyatt's. Nor can the term worker ownership, with no substance, produce ownership feeling. Our finding in this particular case suggests that Hyatt's workers must have a say in mangement, must feel that their compensation is fair, and must believe that they have quality jobs in order to act like owners. They are working on it.

The Lowe's Companies

Upon retirement from the Lowe's Companies in 1975, Carl Valentine was presented with a check in the amount of $660,000.[14] No one was more pleased than Robert Strickland, Lowe's chairman, and no one was more surprised than the recipient himself.

The Lowe's Companies, a chain of retail and wholesale home center stores covering 19 states, is the largest company included in our high scorers, with more than 7,000 employees and 235 stores.[15] It reached $1 billion in sales in 1982. In the last two decades, Lowe's grew from six hardware stores to be the largest operation of its kind in the United States.

Bob Strickland thinks that it is no accident that this phenomenal growth began about the same time as the first sharing of ownership with the workers through a profit-sharing plan:

> How do I know it works? How do I know that Lowe's growth wasn't influenced more by geography, or the business we're in, or management skill, etc.? In the late 50s and early 60s, there were at least five companies like ours in the sunbelt—one in Virginia, one in South Carolina, one in Florida, and two in North Carolina. Same geography, same business, different management, of course,

but not bad management. Three of the companies didn't make it on their own and sold out. The fourth company is about one fourth our size, and they have just adopted an employee stock ownership plan. Survival of the motivated, and the productive.

In addition to Charles Valentine's success story, Lowe's has created millionaires out of 50 other employee owners.[16] Almost makes you want to put in your employment application today, doesn't it? But there is more to the story. Lowe's employee owners don't just sit around and wait to collect their money. In the words of the TV commercial, "they earn it."

In 1983 Lowe's was cited as being able to "publish a textbook on productivity"[17]—productivity brought about through motivation. This was motivation connected not only to the work itself but to keeping the ownership plan going. A couple of grave threats to the plan occurred during those decades of intensive growth. Fortunately, management was as motivated to keep employee ownership as Lowe's employee owners have been to keep Lowe's profitable.

The first threat to the plan came in 1960, three years after the establishment of the profit-sharing plan, which was later converted to an Employee Stock Ownership Plan. In 1960, Carl Buchan, who became the primary Lowe's stockholder after he bought out the other original family owners, died. "I desire to build this business into the largest and most successful in the world, owned and controlled by those who did it," was his legacy to the employees. With that as their beacon, the managers arranged for the profit-sharing trust to buy Buchan's shares with a loan obtained by the company. The workers obtained about 48% of the stock in this way.

In the 1970s Lowe's ownership plan was nearly a casualty of the company's success. The drastic increase in the stock value created an incentive for employees to leave the company, taking with them millions of dollars in profit-sharing benefits. At the same time, the law governing profit-sharing plans required that, in order to be "prudent," Lowe's diversify the plan's holdings out of Lowe's stock into other assets. In order to accomplish this, Lowe's sold 400,000 shares from the profit-sharing trust. These two factors depleted the trust to about 17% of the outstanding shares. There were also now more employees to share less stock, further reducing share value.

This reduction in employee ownership was demoralizing to the workers. However, the management again rallied to the support of the concept. After taking a careful look at the relatively new legislation encouraging worker ownership much more directly and soundly than ever before, they decided an ESOP would be a much better new vehicle for worker ownership at Lowe's. In 1978 the profit-sharing plan was frozen, and the ESOP was established. This new plan alleviated the problem of diversification to demonstrate fiduciary responsibility.

With this transaction, all participants in the profit-sharing plan were immediately vested. They were offered the accrued value of their profit-sharing accounts in cash or stock (the cash or stock would stay in the frozen profit-sharing plan). The employees overwhelmingly chose the stock. Management felt that this was "a real testimonial to their desire for Lowe's stock, and to the decision to switch to the ESOP." Why does management want to keep employee ownership around? They responded that they would set up a plan even if there were no tax benefits. In fact, Lowe's does have and had prior to the ESOP, a Stock Purchase Plan which provided no tax benefits to the company. Management reported to us that employee stock ownership had a positive effect on 11 of the 13 factors about which we asked:

1. productivity,
2. profitability,
3. employee attitude about the job,
4. employee attitude towards management,
5. employee interest in company progress,
6. cooperation among employees,
7. employee suggestions,
8. communication between employees and management,
9. quality of work,
10. employee turnover, and
11. recruiting new employees.

Management reported there was no effect on

12. absenteeism, or
13. tardiness.

Mr. Strickland also said that employee ownership is central to the company philosophy, a philosophy that says that workers should have the right to benefit from the profits they help to create. Merely receiving payment in exchange for your labor is not enough, according to Lowe's.

Why do the workers want to keep employee ownership around? Reason number one, in keeping with our research findings, is that there is money to be made in owning Lowe's stock. Charles Valentine was not the only person to receive a six-figure check upon leaving Lowe's. Nor was Mr. Valentine a retiree in the common conception of the term. He had worked at Lowe's only 17 years and was a relatively young man when he departed. He used his money to go into business for himself and now owns and operates a dairy farm and two cattle ranches.

Spence Bumgarner was Lowe's first six-figure retiree. He worked at the Lowe's Companies for 13 years and retired with $150,000. He said he was "surprised to death. They worked this thing up several years ago, kept telling us what a good deal it was; I didn't think it'd amount to anything, but it sure did." With his money Mr. Bumgarner was helping his children and fixing up his home, which "he let run down for 40 years," Mrs. Bumgarner said. Lowe's was getting a lot of that money back, according to Mr. Bumgarner, since he was buying his materials there, naturally. "Tell all of them I think Lowe's is the greatest."[18]

In 1975, Ferrell Bryan left Lowe's after 20 years at the age of 47 with nearly $500,000. He took half in cash and half in stock. Six months later, his $250,000 in stock was worth $350,000. He said he "couldn't get used to the idea at all." He wasn't the only one who couldn't get used to the idea. His wife refused to quit her job until they actually had the money and it was safely in the bank.

The Bryans bought a small farm, and Mr. Bryan said, "Anything I need for the farm or the house I go into the store in town. I know I'm going to get my money's worth. They've got the best goods and services around."[19]

Harold Ferguson was talked into coming to work for Lowe's by a cousin. He didn't want to work at a hardware store. Less than 20 years later, at age 44, he left Lowe's with $1.5 million. That's right, $1.5 million.[20]

Well, you say, these stories are phenomenal, but that's not such a big deal for company executives. Charles Valentine was a warehouseman. Spence Bumgarner was a lumber grader. Ferrell Bryan was a truck driver. Harold Ferguson was a warehouse worker and later a store manager.

In addition to making many people rich, Lowe's works at making employee owners know that they are stock owners. One way the company does this is by having committees for maintaining good management-employee relations, budget and financial control, and development of new products and services. Non-supervisory as well as managerial personnel are involved with these committees. They talk up employee ownership by using posters, newsletters, and informal conversations. They have also put together a video about the company plan.

Compared to other companies we have studied, Lowe's non-managerial employees feel they have little input into company decision-making. Nevertheless, Lowe's has been a remarkable financial performer, growing in two decades to the largest home center chain in the United States today. Louis Kelso, credited with originating the ESOP idea, described Lowe's as "the most successful example of what employee ownership might achieve." There is reason for Lowe's worker owners to believe, along with many others, that Lowe's will continue to prove Mr. Kelso right.

Virginia Textiles
Of all the ways to become an employee ownership company, starting up is the hardest. Using employee ownership in a start-up doesn't provide a market for a retiring owner; it doesn't save a firm which would otherwise close; it isn't practical as a way to raise capital; it doesn't serve to make wage concessions more equitable. Most start-up companies plow their earnings back into the company, and so have no taxable income against which they can take the deductions ESOPs offer. What employee ownership does offer new companies is a way to involve all the workers in capital ownership, and, as a consequence, economic democracy. And this, in the minds of some people, is the primary reason for worker ownership. Jerry Gorde, a founder and the president of Virginia Textiles, is one of those people.

Virginia Textiles is an alternative company started by an anti-establishment person. In 1976, Gorde was living in Bar Harbor, Maine with Wendy Herron, now vice-president for retail sales at Virginia Textiles. He received a telephone call from his mother telling him that his cousin was selling her small T-shirt business in Richmond, Virginia. Maybe he would be interested in "getting a job." Since he and Wendy were planning to leave Bar Harbor soon anyway, he said he would take a look at it, which he did. Gorde had acquired some business experience working in his father's business, the Miami Fruit and Syrup Company, some years earlier, but Wendy was still reluctant to take the project on. It represented everything she hated—schlocky T-shirts and business in general. But after taking a look at the books, Jerry was able to convince her that the company could be their ticket to economic freedom. Besides, after being on the road for four years selling leather crafts or working as a fisherman wherever he could, Gorde was ready for a change.[21]

Gorde had originally hit the road after serving on the National Council of the Youth International Party, the "Yippies," in the early 1970s. This affiliation ended in the summer of 1972 during the time both major political parties were having their national conventions in Miami. Gorde was in Miami along with other Youth Party leaders, Abbie Hoffman and Jerry Rubin among them, to bring to the attention of the "other party's" leaders, and the world, their shortcomings in serving the needs of the people. Gorde was convinced by Miami undercover police to be out of Miami by the next day. Thus began his four-year trek up, down, and across the United States, which eventually led him, along with his companion, to Richmond.[22]

Though running a business was the antithesis of Gorde's self-image, he brought with him the same values which had drawn him to the anti-war movement. Having his employees own and have an equal vote in corporate decisions was, he felt, the "best way to satisfy individual economic necessities and preserve personal freedom while maximizing profits." With that as their bottom line, Gorde, Herron, and Robert Tarren, a friend from the Yippie days, began trying to "build their own system." That was in September 1977. Today, Virginia Textiles is a $12 million company with five divisions including retail sales, screen printing, advertising specialties, wholesale distribution, and computerized embroidery. How did they get from there to here?

After paying his cousin $3,000, Gorde and his two partners sat around in their 10′ × 20′ purchase, the Dirt Shirt, waiting for drop-ins to choose a T-shirt and have a picture or their names printed on it. But they didn't sit around for long. Gorde liked a challenge, and this was a challenge. The first order of business was how to get more business. Gorde offered a local radio station T-shirts with the station's name on them in exchange for advertising time. It worked. The T-shirts started bringing in enough money to restock the inventory and pay the bills, which included $50 a week each in salary.[23]

Gorde and Tarren hit the streets selling while Herron ran the store. They came up with ideas like "Had a piece lately?" emblazoned on a T-shirt for a local pizza parlor. Though the pizza parlor was skeptical at first, the promotion was successful and the pizza place is still a customer. An "I only sleep with the best" T-shirt marketed to and sold in the Richmond Hyatt Hotel was another best seller until corporate higher-ups called into question the meaning some might construe. Gorde's Yippie experience as a negotiator served him well. At the end of the year there was a small profit. 1978 heralded the addition of another division, doubled sales, tripled profits, and an increase in staff.[24]

Sales passed $1 million in 1981. By that time they had an additional 1,000 square feet of space, purchased more sophisticated equipment, and added an advertising specialties division to the custom screen printing and retail sales units. Gorde thought it time to strike for the biggest move yet, a $500,000 loan for expansion into larger quarters and more enterprises. He and his associates put together a good-looking business profile to present to lenders and got the money from the state's largest bank. That helped birth the wholesale distribution and embroidery sections. The wholesale division alone brought in $3 million in sales in fiscal 1983. Fiscal 1984 saw $12 million in sales. That is a 94% average growth rate every year for the five years from 1979 through 1984.[25]

For the last three years the company made the *Inc.* magazine list of the 500 fastest-growing privately held companies in the United States. One of our Union's most socially and politically conservative states, Virginia, and the capital of the Confederacy, Richmond, named Jerry Gorde, former Yippie and present unconventional businessman, Small Businessperson of the Year in 1983.

While all this was taking place around, and in part because of, Jerry Gorde, what was taking place inside Jerry Gorde? Were his values changing along with the business? It doesn't look that way.

At first, bonuses were paid to the workers to enable them to buy stock in the company. An outright gift of stock would have been taxed as personal income. However, the stock purchases were still made with after-tax dollars. Then Gorde heard about a federally legislated plan to encourage broadened ownership which provided for employees to receive company stock with no personal outlay of cash. He decided to investigate further.

One of the first things he did was to attend a conference about ESOPs in the spring of 1982. To his surprise and chagrin, he discovered that many of the companies in which these plans had been established considered their employees only as a liability involved in getting a tax deduction. Gorde thought this was a gross abuse of the concept and felt compelled to share that feeling with other attendees during a panel discussion. Fortunately, this experience did not deter him from using an ESOP as a means for sharing ownership. Since the ESOP is a flexible tool which can be democratically structured while facilitating stock distribution to all workers, it served the purpose well at Virginia Textiles.

The employees vote their stock and will be able to borrow against their equity as it builds. As of September 1983, 16% of the stock was owned by the employees through the ESOP. All workers get an extensive description of the plan, which is written so as to be easily understood. Gorde, like many of the leaders in these outstandingly successful companies, is totally committed to the rightness of this idea. Ownership can mean taking the lumps sometimes as well as getting the goodies, however. During the economic dip of the early 1980s, Gorde asked and the workers agreed to a pay reduction (which was returned to them in the next quarter). There were grumblings, but it was either that or layoffs during the slow period.[26]

All in all, the workers feel great about being able to participate in capitalism on their terms. Jerry Gorde, by employing worker ownership at Virginia Textiles, is helping to provide this opportunity. As he and others are discovering, there is more than one way to make a contribution.

Quad/Graphics

"Where in the world is Pewaukee?" It is the center of the United States if you look on the map printed by Quad/Graphics, a 2,000-employee company located in Pewaukee, Wisconsin.[27] Founded in 1971, Quad/Graphics is the brainchild of Harry V. Quadracci, who had the notion that "business is management and workers . . . joined together in a common bond of trust, working together to become something more than they ever hoped to be."[28] Quadracci implements this notion in a number of ways, one of which is an Employee Stock Ownership Plan established in 1974, the year legislation codified the concept.

The Spring Fling, now a 10-year tradition at Quad/Graphics, symbolizes Quadracci's idea of what a work environment should be. Every year all mangement personnel "retreat" by taking the day off to regroup, socially and professionally. Rather than close down for a day, the plant remains operational. Who is running the show? The other employee owners, that's who. What could go wrong? Everything, says Quadracci, from a misplaced ad to a miscalculated ink hue. Why is Quadracci willing to take this risk? Because he lives his beliefs that responsibility "should be assumed and shared. Our people shouldn't need me or anyone else to tell them what to do."[29]

That trust has not been misplaced. The workers act as though Quad's 17 presses worth more than $68 million belong to them, because they do. They act as though every shipment affects their livelihood, because it does. They act as though every order is their personal responsibility, because it is.

In 1970, Harry V. Quadracci walked away from the printing firm where he had served first as corporate counsel, then as vice-president and general manager of the Wisconsin division, to form his own printing company.[30] He has been "walking away" ever since. *Inc.* magazine's cover story of October 1983 about Harry Quadracci and Quad/Graphics was, in fact, called "Management by Walking Away." Mr. Quadracci has been called a natural manager. But he himself says that he reads just about everything on management theory that comes along and uses those parts which fit into his philosophy.[31]

Quadracci is a doer, not just a reader. One of the first things he did in 1972, Quad/Graphics' first operating year, was to install a full-color printing press. Though the conventional wisdom at the time was to remain flexible, Quadracci's intuition told him that magazine photo printing, like television, was heading toward color.[32] That hunch paid off. Quad/Graphics has maintained a compound sales growth rate of between 30–40% per year. The industry average is less than 10%.[33] From the 11 original founders, and a 20,000-square-foot plant housing one press, Quad/Graphics now boasts over 2,000 employees, 50 times the floor space of the original plant, two additional operations in Wisconsin, and one on the East Coast. From the now six divisions, magazines including *MS, U.S. News and World Report, Mother Jones, Harper's, Playboy,* and *Newsweek*[34] are printed with company-manufactured ink and hauled in company trucks to their destinations.[35] "You know what the purpose of the division is. Now you figure out how to make it work," was the guiding admonition Quadracci gave to the employees as each division was established.[36]

Another story reflecting Quadracci's style describes how he told the drivers in the trucking fleet that they were to be partners in a new division, DuPlainville Transport. Not only were they to haul the magazines out but were to be responsible for increasing the back-haul revenue to expand the fleet. When asked what they should transport back, Quadracci reportedly said, "How should I know? I don't know anything about driving an 18-wheeler," and walked away. There were some setbacks, but they got it rolling and made the operation lucrative enough to expand the fleet as planned. Mr. Quadracci did intervene, however, when he felt that the truckers were buying more trucks than their division profits could support.[37]

Although well-known outside the company, the community, and even the industry for its innovative practices, technologically and managerially, Quad/Graphics has another distinction. An employee stock ownership plan, which now holds approximately 37% of the company stock, is at the heart of the company philosophy and culture. A large part of the impetus behind the start-up of Quad/Graphics by Quadracci and his co-founders was the desire to diminish any class division among workers. Quadracci calls the workers "partners," a manifestation of this belief in the stock ownership concept.

In order to instill and reinforce the company ownership culture, all new hires have "mentors" for a year or even two. Performance takes precedence over seniority, new recruits are told. There is a two-month probation period during which the company and the new hires have a chance to get acquainted well enough for either to decide this is or is not for them. Employees are treated with respect, and they are expected to return respect to their work, their equipment, and their co-workers. Some things are not tolerated, among them missing work and sloth. This process of integrating the new workers into environment, though informal, is to be taken seriously. "Think Small," an employee-initiated-and-run job participation program, grew out of this procedure of absorption. In addition to these informal and formal ways of integrating the workers into the company, various training courses on all phases of the work itself are provided by other workers, including Mr. Quadracci. Employees are encouraged to further their formal education, and all managers are expected to and do have a working knowledge of contemporary management theory.

This "family" (the term used in an in-house publication) atmosphere is further reinforced through numerous other means. These include providing luxurious facilities and a company sports center, and offering on-site college courses. Company-sponsored sports activities make up a large part of the social life of the "family." "Think Small" dinners are hosted at the Quad lodge every year for all employees; twelve employees are invited at a time until the entire work force has participated.[38]

A recent addition to the list of ownership rewards is a company-owned 40-acre campground and recreational park complete with a lake, where the annual picnic will be held from now on, and where the Quad kids can attend camp. Lessons in word-processing and toad-catching are some of the camp's offerings. From the tranquil to the zippy, Quad also added sports car racing to its activities. The Quadmobile and team were cheered on at parades and other events as well as at the track.[39]

All of these activities and the success they connote have not been lost on the business world. A vice-president at one of Quad's customers says that mentioning that "Harry is thinking about" something in the presence of other printers is a sure way of getting their attention. Awards for innovation have been won by some of the divisions.[40] *The 100 Best Companies to work for in America* cited Quad. Harry Quadracci was also named in 1984 one of the most memorable businessmen ever interviewed by *Inc.* magazine. He was also named the 1984 "Outstanding Wisconsin Businessman" by Heritage Wisconsin.

As these awards signify, Quad/Graphics got to be the printer of the most, over 90 weekly news magazines, by being the best. Our research indicates that the workers would agree. The word "best" came up again in a conversation between Mr. Quadracci and a friend who is also a competitor. The friend said, "Anybody who visits your plant knows that your employees intend to be the best printers around."[41] Our work indicates that Mr. Quadracci would disagree with that. He would say that they already *are* the best printers around. Why? Because they own the place.

Conclusion

Looking at the companies portrayed in this chapter, one cannot help noting how financially successful they have been. But one other thing, we think, should be equally striking. Each of these companies sees people as its most important resource. The employees are considered more of a family than just hired hands. In fact, in a few of these companies, that is almost literally true: many of the employees are related to one another, for relatives are quick to tell other relatives of job openings. Saying that "people are our most important resource," of course, is so common that it seems little more than a bland homily. Almost every corporate executive could be counted on to say something like that about company employees. What makes these companies different, we think, is that their management really believes and acts on it.

The companies in this chapter vary in their lines of business and reasons for establishing their plans. There are three manufacturers, two service organizations, and two sales companies. They range from a start-up to family transfers to a buyout. In a couple of the companies, the plans were established simply as employee benefits. In these firms, the present major stockholders are still active in the company and are not thinking about using the plan as a retirement vehicle just yet. The point is that no pattern of establishing plans in certain kinds of industries or for any one dominant purpose has evolved. So we cannot say that ESOPs work best in retail businesses as opposed to service organizations or to raise capital as opposed to providing a market for a private owner. We can say that they appear to work best when there is a commitment by management to the concept and that commitment is demonstrated and reinforced through various means.

One other thread we have noticed and commented on many times in the last several years is that there is often a strong, dynamic, charismatic leader who is making this egalitarian imprint on the company. One of our researchers reported that he felt as though he had been through a wind storm after an interview with one of these companies' CEOs. This kind of dynamism is the extreme, but is often present and is apparently inspiring. It inspires others to believe in and to try to make ownership work. There is, of course, an irony here, for it seems that in some cases one of the best ways to create a more equitable workplace is to find a strong leader. When the inertia and habit ingrained in people's more traditional expectations about how work should be organized are considered, however, the usefulness of having such a strong, change-oriented leader becomes more obvious.

When the elements present in these companies—a strong commitment to ownership, determined leadership, and innovative ways of involving employees in the company—are combined with large contributions to employee ownership plans, employees emerge with a direct and vital interest in their company's welfare. That is a powerful combination. It provides the basis for making employee ownership not only a just, but also very sensible, way to run a business.[42]

8
Cooperatives and Other Plans

This chapter describes the cooperatives and companies with plans other than Employee Stock Ownership Plans (ESOPs) that we studied in the course of this project. The results presented in the preceding chapters were based only on our ESOP companies.

Cooperatives and companies with other kinds of employee ownership plans were not included in the data analyses of the ESOP companies because we could not make valid comparisons between ESOP companies and non-ESOP companies. There are several reasons for this. First, people who choose to work in a cooperative are often making that choice because they want to work in an employee owned and controlled company, even if they have to make some financial sacrifice to do so. In an ESOP firm, many employees would have come to work for the firm before the ESOP was introduced; even among those who came later, we suspect, the presence of a plan would typically be only one among many considerations in choosing a workplace, and perhaps not the most important. This self-selection makes it inappropriate to compare the employees of a cooperative with the employees of an ESOP.

A second consideration is that almost all the companies included here require at least some employee financial commitment in order to become an owner or cooperative member. Most ESOPs, by contrast, simply contribute ownership shares to employees. In some cooperatives, buying stock is a condition of employment; in others, it is voluntary. Either way, people in these companies are making a choice to be owners, either by making voluntary purchases or by choosing to work for the firm. Again, this presents a problem of self-selection that makes the attitudes and behaviors of employees in these companies not directly comparable to those in ESOP firms.

This is unfortunate, for it would have been interesting to see if the form of ownership makes a difference in employee attitudes and behaviors. Does being required to put up some of your own money make you a more committed owner? Does working in a company where decisions must be made democratically make ownership more meaningful? People have certainly argued that this is the case, but any results we might find here in answer to these questions would be clouded by the doubt that the poeple who work for these firms, or choose to be owners within them, already had more positive, or at least different, attitudes towards employee ownership before they went to work for their company.

It is also unfortunate because we were not able to study enough of these other forms of ownership to allow us to do the kind of statistical analysis that we performed earlier. We cannot say with any confidence that coops, for instance, work better if they follow certain sorts of guidelines and policies than others. Nonetheless, the experiences of these companies do shed light on how employee ownership works. In this chapter, therefore, we will present several case studies of the more interesting cooperatives and other non-ESOP companies we studied.

Several things strike us about these firms. First, in the cooperatives, a great deal of energy is devoted to developing systems of corporate governance. In almost every case, the cooperatives started out with the intention of making almost every decision by consensus among all members. As the coops grew, however, and as more and more time was spent discussing how to run the company, and less and less time was spent running it, the coops developed systems in which decision-making was delegated to individuals or committees. The membership retained ultimate control, but was less involved in every decision.

Second, although almost all of the firms described here are very democratically structured, this has not, contrary to conventional wisdom, prevented at least some of them from being very financially successful. Philips Paper, a company in which employees buy stock directly and have a considerable say in company affairs is one of the most profitable firms in its industry. The Solar Center, which is a cooperative with an ESOP, has been one of the few solar firms to stay profitable in an increasingly difficult environment for solar energy. Denver Yellow Cab, with 1,000 employees, the largest worker cooperative in the United States, is also one of the more successful taxicab companies. While we can hardly generalize to say that a democratic structure has caused the success of these firms (although they might argue it has), we can certainly say that their success indicates that worker involvement at all decision-making levels is not incompatible with making a lot of money.

Finally, the patterns that we saw emerging in the ESOP companies seem to hold here as well, although we cannot confirm this statistically. The companies that scored especially high on our employee survey among the non-ESOP firms also seem to be firms that make substantial annual contributions (or allow employees to buy large amounts of stock at a discount), that have a real commitment to ownership, and that, obviously among these firms, are very participative.

Worker Cooperatives: Blending Ideology and Business

ESOPs were essentially unknown until Congress provided them with specific statutory existence in 1974. Cooperatives, on the other hand, have been around at least since the 1840s, when the "Rochdale Pioneers" in England created the first model laws for both worker and consumer cooperatives. Consumer cooperatives grew quickly after that, and are a substantial part of the economy in a number of European countries. Producer and marketing cooperatives, such as Sunkist and Land o' Lakes, dominate many agricultural sectors in this country. Credit unions, another form of cooperative, play a major role in banking. Worker cooperatives, however, have been much harder to establish, especially in the United States. In non-worker cooperatives, member fees are typically very low, and the fact that everyone has one vote to govern the coop is often mere formality. In fact, these frequently very large organizations are run little differently than any other corporation. In a worker cooperative, membership fees are often larger, as they form part of the company's capitalization. Requiring that everyone have an equal say becomes more difficult as well because the smaller size of worker cooperatives means that members may really make an effort to run the company. In a marketing coop with thousands of widely spread members, for instance, this is not likely to happen. Finding management people, investors, and other key business players willing to accept this condition is a serious problem for worker coops. In addition, cooperative laws typically operate at the state level, and are more appropriate for agricultural coops than worker coops. Only seven states, Massachusetts, New York, Connecticut, Vermont, New Hampshire, Oregon, and Maine, have separate incorporation laws for worker cooperatives. Most cooperatives are set up according to the state corporate laws. Still, there are hundreds of worker cooperatives in the United States, and the very fact that they do express the purest combination of worker ownership and control makes them worth studying. Can businesses operated this way make it in the business world?

The second chapter provided details on how cooperatives are defined and organized. The basic point to remember, however, is that cooperatives are primarily defined by their internal governance: only workers can be members, only members can vote, and all members receive one and only one vote. In addition, some share of net earnings is returned to members annually.

All of the cooperatives of which we are aware follow a similar pattern. They are established by a group of like-minded people who wish to work in a democratic organization. People with this, rather than money, as a primary motivating factor gravitate to cooperatives. There is usually a standard entry fee paid by beginning workers who wish to be cooperative members. The fees range from a nominal $5 to several thousand dollars and are set by the present coop members. Most coops also try to manage all company affairs on a cooperative basis, often consensually. Especially in seasonal businesses, labor is hired in the form of support workers who are paid a wage but do not share in the profits or membership.

Common Ground
Common Ground Restaurant, which is located in Brattleboro, Vermont, was founded in 1971 and was converted to a cooperative in 1977. The original founders wanted to sell and found a buyer in the workers. Common Ground follows the cooperative pattern in their

structure and operating procedures. Worker-members are admitted through a two-thirds majority vote of the present members. They must demonstrate their potential as coop members through their work and discussions with members. The membership fee is $5. In addition each new member must purchase a share of stock for $200. Non-member support workers are also hired for a wage as needed.

Common Ground has 15 worker-owners who make decisions consensually through a committee. All members can serve on the committee on a rotating basis. Before the committee was established the cooperative was in existence for about four years, with decisions being made consensually, lackadaisically, or if there was no disagreement, by default. For example, if someone had an idea, s/he talked about it to the other workers, maybe getting suggestions. If the others did not disagree, or did not disagree strongly, and the idea originator had the ambition to go forward, the idea became a policy. That, for instance, was how Common Ground's catering service got started. Workers knew each other pretty well, making it easier to make consensual decisions.

After about four years in business it started looking as if the business might not survive, so the workers decided to take things more in hand, and established the governing committee. The company became more financially stable, a feat the workers attribute to the more formal decision-making mechanism, which also provided for task accountability. Before the committee, things often seemed to fall through the cracks because nobody assumed the responsibility for doing them or everyone assumed that someone else was doing them. Another advantage provided by the committee was that the worker-owners found that they provided sounding boards for each other for ideas, gripes, and merely communing. The committee continues to be the only governing body. There is no board of directors and no levels of reporting. Decisions relating to the jobs themselves are made at the job level. Jobs are rotated on an informal basis by agreements made between individual workers.

We've been told the service is slow at Common Ground, but the food is good and the atmosphere pleasant. Brattleboro, Vermont, by all accounts, is conducive to relaxation. Given the goals of the members, this all fits quite well. The members can set and abide by their own rules, something more dear to them than status, external recognition, or money. For people who are very motivated, but not by the usual economic goals, finding a niche like Common Ground is what success means.

Denver Yellow Cab

Taxicab companies are especially well suited for worker cooperatives. Cab drivers often own or lease their cabs, making them more like individual entrepreneurs than employees. They need common services, however, such as insurance, maintenance, and dispatching. By forming a cooperative, they can provide themselves with these services at reasonable cost. Taxicab cooperatives can now be found in several major cities, including Salt Lake, Los Angeles, Sacramento, and San Francisco.

Denver Yellow Cab is the largest taxicab coop, and the largest worker coop. With over 1,000 employees and 80% of Denver's cab business, it is also the largest 100% employee-owned business in the Mountain States region.

The company had been in business for decades before becoming a cooperative. In the 1970s, however, it was bought and sold by a series of owners. The drivers (who are 90% of the employees) had long wanted to buy the company. Moreover, they had a $200,000 strike fund their local union had accumulated, money that could be used as a downpayment on the $2,000,000 they needed to buy the company. In 1980, they made an offer which the owner accepted and became the new owners.

All the drivers must join the coop by paying $1.50 per shift worked. Other employees can join as well, on the same terms, but are not required to do so (most now have). The company owns 300 of its 400 cabs, with 100 being owned individually by drivers. All the members pay fees to the coop for services provided—insurance, fuel, dispatching, and so on. They also pay to lease their cabs, unless they own them. They receive no salary, so their earnings depend entirely on what they can make on the street.

All the coop members have an equal vote for the board of directors, which has hired a professional management team. At the time of our study, all the board members were drivers. In the first years of operation, the board intervened regularly in management decisions, resulting in financial decisions that were often confused and ill-advised. At the time of our study, for instance, the company could not provide us any information about their financial status because they were not sure what it was. The board subsequently decided that it would set up a four-person executive team and give that team much more room to maneuver. That has now been replaced by a more conventional management structure. Apparently, this approach has succeeded, as the company has become quite profitable.

This is not to say it is now like a conventional company. That is hardly the case. The board still clearly governs the company, and the workers still are very interested in company affairs. In fact, Denver Yellow Cab was distinctive among the companies we studied in that the employees were more concerned with the participation benefits of ownership than the financial ones (partly because the coop will return relatively little money to the members, most of whose income comes from driving). At the time of our study (early 1983) there was a lot of ferment in the company, with many workers dissatisfied with how things were being run. Worker job satisfaction scores were towards the low end of the scale relative to other companies surveyed. Scores on how much influence the workers thought they had in the company were lower than in most firms where employees have no role in decision-making. By contrast, they scored very high on the measure of how much influence they would like to have in the company, one of the larger discrepancies we found. In other words, workers were very interested in making the company democratic, but thought it had not yet reached that point, despite its cooperative structure.

After we did our survey, things at Denver Yellow Cab did seem to settle into a more stable pattern, and it might well be that if we came back, we would find better results. Even at the time of our survey, the company had already cut turnover from 200% (average in a cab company including the old Denver Yellow Cab) to about 25%. Moreover, the employee owners had compiled the best safety record of any cab company in the country. Despite the recession at the time, and the internal management problems, the company was already profitable.

Although Denver Yellow Cab is larger than the other coops, it too has gone through a similar pattern of starting with a very open, almost chaotic system of governance to one that is more structured. They have not given up on democracy; they have worked to create a system in which it can mesh with the company's financial needs.

The Solar Center

In 1977, Peter Barnes, West Coast editor of *The New Republic* at the time, and five of his friends decided it was time to do something about their feelings about the way the economic system was working. They thought that workers should own and control the company for which they worked and that companies should produce more socially useful products. Rather than just talk or write about it, they formed their own worker cooperative, The Solar Center.[1]

The structure is similar to other cooperatives. New members have to make a cash commitment to the company. Workers make decisions on a one-person, one-vote basis; in practice, all decisions are made by consensus.

For about three years, the founders led the nearly idyllic existence they had envisioned, selling almost anything related to solar energy from do-it-yourself kits to expertise.[2] In order to remain competitive they finally settled on designing, selling, and installing solar water-heating systems for commercial buildings. Later, they moved into cogeneration.

As a conventional cooperative, the Solar Center not only succeeded, but flourished. Sales are now between $1.5 and $2 million, and there are 23 employees. They are a long way from the original notion of needing only to borrow Peter's pick-up truck from time to time and using a friend's garage for storage if necessary, or from being able to make every decision informally.[3]

By 1980, the Solar Center had grown in size and sales to the point where its informal structure was becoming more of an obstacle than a pleasure. While the members' fundamental principles remained the same, there were now more employees and more diverse viewpoints and more complex financial considerations with which to deal. The haphazard method of bringing in and buying out owners, for instance, was a chore.

A more structured decision-making process was needed as well. The informal, consensual style that had worked before was just too cumbersome now. It was apparent that to survive the Solar Center had to accept the organization it had become. The organization demanded it, and the marketplace demanded it. Should the members face it, or should they throw up their collective hands? They faced it.

Enter the Constitution, which was to establish:

> a permanent process for admitting new owners and buying out old ones; to delegate authority to people who were elected by and accountable to the employee-owners; to distinguish between policy decisions, which would be made by the elected representatives or by all the owners, and administrative decisions, which would be made by managers; to prevent 'tyranny of a minority,' while assuring that consensus on major policy decisions would be sought before voting would occur; and to equalize voting power, regardless of how much stock people owned.[4]

An ESOP was set up to meet the first of these goals, that of transferring ownership from the company and departing employees to new employees. Having workers contribute their after-tax earnings to buy stock seemed irrational, when an ESOP would allow them to buy it with pre-tax dollars without impinging on the cooperative governance system. An ESOP would also allow the company to take tax deductions for the stock it contributed to the workers. Under this arrangement new hires are still required to make a cash investment of $3,000 to purchase stock. In addition to the purchased shares, stock is distributed to each individual employee account each year of employment, based on months of service.

On the governance question, committees were established so that all employees were not required to be involved in every decision. Overall authority, however, still rested with the entire membership.

Peter Barnes offers five lessons he "learned by experience" for others interested in starting a worker owned and operated business.[5] They are:

1. *Growth is inevitable, so accept it, plan for it, and enjoy it.* Remaining small is a romantic notion which does have advantages. Growth also has advantages—excitement is generated, more areas of responsibility are provided, and a livable income is generated.
2. *Democratic organizations need leaders, and leaders need to be supported and rewarded.* Entrepreneurs, among other things,

envision and create new possibilities, bring together diverse
resources, and inspire others. These individuals should be encouraged primarily by intrinsic rewards—the thrill of creating
something out of nothing, recognition, and the satisfaction of
helping others learn and grow—and secondarily by monetary
rewards.

3. *Authority must be matched to responsibility.* In order to get
things done this concept must be practiced at the individual
level. In a democratic structure managers are worker-owners
who are ultimately accountable to their peers for carrying out
the policies set by all worker-owners.

4. *Get sophisticated, not cynical.* Hold onto your basic values.
But also approach situations with a mind to taking the best
and leaving the rest. This can be an exciting challenge to your
creativity and even your success.

5. *Never forget to make the organization, and its values, self-
renewing.* There are three parts to this. First, if power and
responsibility are to be shared, risks must also continuously
be shared. Requiring new owners to make an investment
comparable to the previous owners' is probably the best way
to do this. Second, new owners must be welcomed and integrated into positions of responsibility. Third, education is
essential. Most individuals have little or no experience in or
even knowledge of a worker-owned and operated business.
Instruct them about democratic practices and more especially
about your/their company and its history.

Our employee survey results indicate that the employees are
very enthusiastic about the company and the opportunities it offers.
This enthusiasm seems well-placed. The Solar Center didn't just
happen. It was and continues to be worked at by those enthusiastic
worker-owners.

Freewheel Bicycle
Running a coop means opening yourself up to the possibility of a
great deal more dissension than would be the case in more traditional workplaces. Although many workers might disagree with
company policies, there are not too many other companies where

they can act so fully on their complaints. How a coop handles this greater potential for internal dissension can determine how it will meet its goals. Freewheel Bicycle is a good case in point.

Freewheel Bicycle started out in 1974 with eight workers and, like the majority of cooperatives, no formal management structure. They operated this way for about seven years, at first working when they wanted to work and paying themselves barely livable wages. They sold bicycles and accessories and made repairs. In 1979, they started carrying cross-country skis; in 1980, camping equipment; and in 1981, exercise equipment. Sales have steadily increased from $46,000 in 1975 to $870,000 in 1984. There are now 13 worker-members with seasonal support workers of about the same number.

As many coops report, decision-making by all member-workers ultimately became too cumbersome and took away from actual work time. Consequently business suffered. So a more formal management structure was devised and put in place. Since 1981, there have been three reporting levels: employees to supervisors to board of directors.

The six-member board is elected by all the coop's members. Qualifications for serving on the board are that the person must be a manager, have retail sales experience, and possess the expertise needed on the board at the time. The board meetings are open to all members, who can make suggestions. There are two worker participation groups at Freewheel along the natural division of sales and repairs. Decisions about how to handle the work itself are made in these groups. Any issue which cannot be resolved at this level is referred to the board. Worker-owners are also consulted about the selection of managers and long-term company policy issues.

All this has not meant that Freewheel has been without vigorous controversy, including picketing by former members. But disagreement is not necessarily unhealthy. How that disagreement is handled tells the tale. As has been indicated in other cases reported in this book, the perception of doing well or not doing well depends on who is doing the perceiving.

Freewheel is, one, still in business; two, it has increased its sales every year; three, it has systematically added to its product line over its relatively short existence; four, it has generated jobs. This is all being done in a democratic workplace while providing a product and service in line with the values of the members. Freewheel has, apparently, handled its own disagreements well.

Starflower

Eugene, Oregon and Brattleboro, Vermont (home to Common Ground Restaurant, the first company profiled in this chapter) are almost mirror images. Both are in the upper corners of the country. Both are set in luscious green hills populated by tall pines. Both became an oasis for 1960s counterculture business establishments. Both contain vestiges of this move to live alternatively. Starflower, a natural foods producer and distributor located in Eugene, Oregon is one of these.

Starflower was started by a husband and wife in 1972 as a feminist coop. It had most of the attendant characteristics; it was set up with social goals in mind, one person/one vote, initial consensual decision-making, and a working probation period for entrants. It did not, however, require an entry fee.

Starflower followed the cooperative pattern of having to adapt to a more structured operating procedure to survive. While it is true for any organization, conventional or alternative, that only the dynamic ones are able to compete, it is fair to say that Starflower was more than dynamic—it was, at the time of our study, in turmoil. A number of stabilizing changes have been made since our last contact with them in the spring of 1983, two years ago.

Their hiring policy of giving priority to those most likely to be shunned by conventional businesses—gays, single mothers, and minorities—has been terminated. It did not provide the kind of skills needed, as they finally admitted. Even insuring that women be provided access to jobs traditionally and sometimes more easily done by men (heavy lifting, for example) is no longer favored. Salaries are now more competitive so the benefit of taking food is no longer given.

Starflower started out with no hierarchy and rotated workers in jobs. It was the first natural foods distributor in the geographic area. However, competitors started cropping up in 1978. By 1980 they were in a financial crunch and a decision had to be made. They could continue with a totally participatory management or create more of a division of responsibilities. With some outside support, Starflower decided to go with management changes.

A worker-elected five-member board of directors with staggered terms of one to three years is now in place. At first only worker-owners were eligible. To fill a void in expertise, outside board members now serve. They have also established working teams for bookkeeping, sales, warehouse, trucking, and purchasing. These teams have four to six members who meet regularly.

Three managerial positions were created in 1978 to facilitate a move into larger quarters. These positions were made permanent since it was apparent that things worked better with them. The managerial positions were rotated and people were asked to stay in them at least two years. But according to member Jan Tobin, they "wore people out, because here you were, directed to run the company . . . but you weren't allowed to make any decisions. Your hands were tied." Consequently, Starflower stopped rotating the members in those jobs and started hiring managers from the outside in the early 1980s. "Management definitely runs the company now. Cooperative ownership doesn't necessarily mean cooperative management," Sandy Zimmerman, sales and marketing manager, told us recently.

There is also a council with a representative from each team, one board member, and one manager. The council hears grievances and is in the process of writing a company "bill of rights." Another 1980s addition has been an alienation committee, which serves to counsel members.

Starflower is following the rules proposed by Peter Barnes, even though they may not have ever seen them. After some years of trial and error, they have created a structure that has succeeded in adapting their internal structure to their unique set of goals. They provide wholesome products. They provide a versatile, dignified, and safe workplace. They provide money to social and political causes. And their 30 worker-owners reap $34 million in sales.

Jan Tobin sums it up, "People want Starflower to be here . . . sometimes we wonder if we want to be here. And yet I love it. . . . We do business in a different way, we really do."

Other Plans

Bureau of National Affairs
Coops are not the only way of making people owners. Some businesses have simply decided they wanted to share ownership and have

come up with their own unique way of doing it. One of the most notable examples of this is the Bureau of National Affairs (BNA).

Where would Washington, D.C. be without the Bureau of National Affairs? The same place as Pewaukee, Wisconsin before Quad/ Graphics put it on the map. One or more of BNA's 50 publications can be found on the shelves of nearly every government office, law firm, trade association, and public interest group in Washington. These publications report on almost everything which is recordable, including taxes, patents, energy, labor, environment, and safety.

David Lawrence, BNA's founder, first tried this idea in a newspaper format in 1929. Advertisements, the mainstay of newspapers, could not support the cost. So he went to publishing the facts, cut and dried. It turned out facts were what people wanted. BNA is 55 years old, and for two-thirds of that lifetime it has been employee owned. When Mr. Lawrence decided to sell in 1946, he wanted the workers to have the company. A stock purchase plan was set up. Lawrence had another business he sold to the employees—*U.S. News and World Report.* Those employees recently sold out, making themselves quite rich in the process.

BNA has done quite well itself. It has established several service subsidiaries, such as a tax branch and a seminar program, in response to the seemingly endless desire for information about what Washington is up to. Its 1982 sales volume was $92 million, and the company is valued at $88 million. It has approximately 1,300 employees. Offers of up to two and one-half times the appraised value of its stock have been made to the worker-owners, but they don't want to sell.

Stock purchase through payroll deductions is available to full-time employees after one year and to part-time employees after five years. Two-thirds of the eligible employees participate in owning 100% of the stock. Dividends are paid and the employees can vote their stock. In addition to being able to own stock, BNA has a profit-sharing plan, which covers all employees, and a pension plan.

BNA's president, William Beltz, reports that the company is totally committed to employee ownership and tries to communicate this to the employees. He thinks that Mr. Lawrence was right to think the employees deserved the company, and could be expected to treat it right. The views of Mr. Beltz and Mr. Lawrence seem to be justified by the company's performance.

Financial information is routinely provided to employees. In fact, unlike most privately held companies, BNA is quite candid about its business affairs. Weekly meetings are held in each operating department for all workers in that department. They are generally a forum for information exchange primarily relating to tasks. There is little employee input into decision-making at BNA. But compared to other companies studied, BNA employees, on the whole, do not desire a lot of influence in this area. The communication efforts Mr. Beltz mentioned must have an impact. The employees did indicate that they enjoy their work more because they own stock. They are quite aware of the financial benefits of owning stock and are quite positive and enthusiastic about the provision.

The next time you look at a BNA report, remember it was probably composed by employee owners who are providing you with the most comprehensive information available, so that you will keep filling those shelves, and their company will keep growing.

Phillips Paper
One of the more common figures in employee ownership is the benevolent entrepreneur, the sympathetic business owner whose genuine affection for his or her employees translates into a desire to see them eventually own the company. To some people, this kind of behavior seems little more than a kind of benighted indulgence destined to prove that, in the hard world of the market, nice guys finish last.

No one would dispute that notion more vigorously than Gil Phillips, the principal owner of Phillips Paper Company in San Antonio. It would be tough to argue with him. Phillips is making his employees owners (they will eventually own all the stock), provides a profit-sharing plan, pension plan, personal and car loan plan, and tuition reimbursement plan, and, on top of it all, pays more than competitive salaries. He also has set up a variety of committees that allow employees to make many of the company's decisions. Despite this—Gil Phillips would say because of this—Phillips Paper is five times as profitable as it was when all these programs were started in 1973, when Phillips bought the company from his uncles. Its sales per employee are substantially higher than its competitors', and retained earnings have increased from .5% to 2.3% of sales.

Gil Phillips had been a "populist idealist" since his youth. Later, when he read about worker-managed enterprises in Yugoslavia, he decided that at least certain features of that system should be transported here. After he bought Phillips Paper, he went about putting these principles into action.

Phillips Paper employs 42 people distributing paper to fast-food chains and other outlets. When San Antonians munch fried chicken at Church's, they are eating off plates distributed by employee owners and decision-makers. Under the Phillips plan, employees receive bonus shares after their fifth, tenth, fifteenth, and twentieth year of service. In addition, they are encouraged to purchase stock out of their profit-sharing benefits. The nine-person board includes six non-managerial employees elected by the shareholders. A stock ownership plan committee governs the plan, and three of its five members are elected by the employees. Day-to-day operations are governed by four employee committees. There is one committee for sales, one for warehouse and local delivery, one for office staff issues, and one for state-wide delivery. Committees meet as needed. They elect a representative to an operations committee, which also has two company officers. This committee can act on anything recommended by the job committees, and its decisions are final unless overruled by the board. That, however, has never happened. Phillips does not join the job committees unless invited. Finally, a management committee of five non-mangement employees meets regularly to decide on issues such as sick leave, special events, and vacations.

The committee system injects considerable democracy into the company, but it does so in a very clearly structured way, with well-defined responsibilities. Because the system works so well, Phillips is freed to work on the things he thinks he does best, mainly sales.

Phillips designed the stock ownership system himself. Now that he is thinking of moving on to something else, however, he has found the new provisions of the tax law for ESOPs especially attractive and plans to set up an ESOP to buy out his stock. The ESOP will replace the existing plan. Not surprisingly, his hope is to use the money to invest in new employee-owned enterprises.

Gil Phillips is, by anyone's definition, a "nice guy." His employees told us their friends could not believe that there were jobs as good as those they had, a reaction their high scores on our survey confirmed. But Phillips is also a very good businessman who believes that when employees are treated as owners, and given ownership responsibility, they will be much better employees. The success he has had in creating a business that is at once very profitable and very rewarding for those who work there suggests he, and not the hard-nosed "realists" of the business world, is right.

Conclusion

There is no question that as long as ESOPs have the tax advantages they have, most employee ownership companies will use ESOPs. Cooperatives and other forms of employee ownership are not going to fade away, however. Some companies are too small to make the legal costs of ESOPs worth the tax advantages they provide; other companies, for idiosyncratic reasons, will find the ESOP structure does not suit their needs. While some worker cooperatives will, as the Solar Center did, incorporate an ESOP into their cooperative structure, most will find ESOPs too expensive or legally cumbersome to be useful. Still others will not have enough taxable income to make an ESOP worthwhile, will not understand ESOPs, or will simply not like them.

While it seems unlikely that cooperatives and other forms of ownership will ever make a significant penetration into the marketplace, they have an importance beyond their mere numbers. Perhaps most notably, they are a continuing demonstration that companies can create employee ownership arrangements that are not dependent for their success on the blessings of the federal tax code. While coops do have some tax benefits, these are rarely of more than minor importance to the operation of these firms, and very few companies are set up as coops out of a desire to capture these benefits. This is even more true of such hybrid arrangements as those we found at Phillips and BNA. While many of these non-ESOP companies do not succeed, many do, and that is a continuing demonstration that employee ownership can, entirely on its own merits, be a profitable way to run a business. This may take on special significance if the tax breaks for ESOPs are ever withdrawn.

Cooperatives and some of the hybrid forms are also important because they take employee ownership to its logical limits—employees actually owning and controlling their companies on an equal basis. Cooperative supporters are properly fond of likening this notion to the democratic system. After all, when our founding fathers suggested a governance system based on equal participation of all citizens (or at least all white, male citizens), that was considered a pretty radical and impractical idea too. If employee ownership can work in these companies to achieve the goals of their members, then a very important principle will be established, one that can have considerable significance for other employee ownership efforts. Although these other efforts might not go so far as the cooperatives, being able to point to the success of the latter will make more modestly democratic structures seem more acceptable.

The companies reviewed here suggest that cooperatives can, in fact, succeed, both in conventional terms and in the terms of their members. This is not to say that most cooperatives do succeed. We simply do not have adequate evidence from this or other studies to address that question. It *is* to say that democratic ownership and business success are not, by definition, incompatible.

Finally, these companies suggest that the basic findings discussed in the chapters on ESOPs are relevant here as well. Most of these companies did quite well on our survey. Most of the employees in these companies are also receiving a significant portion of their total compensation in ownership, just as was the case in the ESOP firms. At the same time, each of these companies is obviously strongly committed to the idea of ownership, and provides employees with significant participation opportunities. While we cannot make the same kind of conclusive statements about the relationship of these factors here as we could for the ESOP firms, it does appear that these non-ESOP firms support our general findings.[6]

9
Work, Ownership, and the New Economy

When the agricultural economy gave way to the industrial, the country needed a new structure to accommodate the changed mode of production. In agriculture, the basic units of production, the farms, could be economically owned by individual families. The new factories and companies, however, often became too large to be owned by single families. Investors were needed to provide the capital to build the plants, buy the machines, and make the products. But these investors would be very different kinds of owners than the farmer with a piece of land. Unlike the farmers, the investors could not be expected to put their personal assets at risk to back their investment in the firm. After all, they might own only a small piece of the company. If it failed, their personal liability could far exceed their investment. Moreover, unlike the farmer, these investors could, at best, only expect partial control over the company's operations. In fact, most did not want to exercise that control—they wanted to hire managers to do it for them. So the limited liability corporation was invented. It would be owned by those who could afford it, not by those who, as on the farm, worked it; if it failed, only its own assets were at risk, not all the assets of its owners. It could be managed by professionals and staffed by workers.

This system of employees and owners worked fairly well for a long time. Immigrants from other lands joined emigrants from the countryside to supply the labor for the new productive order. Unions were created to give the employees a measure of control over their economic lives. An adversarial model of labor-management relations was developed to determine how to divide the wealth. Wages rose, and the U.S. working class became, on the whole, fairly prosperous, at least compared to workers elsewhere. Our own internal market was so vast that it could absorb almost anything we produced. Our own businesses worried little about the need to compete abroad; foreign competitors found our market too distant or too tough to crack. For the U.S. worker, a good job meant a secure, well-paying one, one that could provide the resources for a good life, and an even better life for one's children. America's entrepreneurship, productive capability, and skilled workforce were a powerful combination.

But times have changed. The world is catching up, or racing ahead in some cases, and competition is tougher. Our distance from other markets has shrunk as transportation has become more efficient and as a growing number of products are made less from the resources of the earth and more from the resources of the mind. A more educated workforce is looking for more from work; a more worried management is looking for more from workers. Our post-depression vision of a government that could manage the economy to sustain economic prosperity while increasing social equity has given way to a debate about what the government should stop doing first. We seem now to be forced to choose between policies that stimulate growth, but sacrifice equity, and policies that make society more equitable, but at the cost of jobs and economic competitiveness.

Serious as these problems are, we are not among the doomsayers who would suggest that we are about to become another fallen kingdom. We do argue, however, that we very much need a "social invention"[1] that can move us away from a system appropriate to the industrial revolution towards one more appropriate to the emerging postindustrial economy of the late twentieth century. We need a system that encourages growth while fostering equity, not one that insists that one side's gain is the other's loss. We need a system that provides a workable structure for labor-management cooperation, one that provides incentives for employees to assume more responsibility and initiative. If new industrial technologies eventually reduce the amount of labor needed in society (much as the industrial revolution did), we will also need a system in which people can earn from owning, not just working. Otherwise, we will end up with an economy made up of a small number of very wealthy owners, a larger number of highly paid workers, and a much larger group of poorly paid service workers, the underemployed, and the unemployed. Indeed, we are already moving in that direction, with the acceptable "natural" rate of unemployment much higher than a decade ago, with fewer and fewer highly paid working-class jobs, and with a widening inequality of wealth.[2]

Not surprisingly, we believe that employee ownership can be that social invention. It can be to the postindustrial world what corporate ownership was to the industrial—the structure that accommodated a transition to a new economy. Used well, we believe it can spur economic growth while spreading economic justice. It can provide the motivation and rewards to create a more productive, cooperative economy. Ultimately, it could even provide a source of significant ownership income for millions of people, making the transition to an economy in which less work is needed much easier to accomplish.

What is so appealing about employee ownership is that, much like corporate ownership before it, it seems so logically and intuitively right to so many people—people of all political and economic persuasions. Its main enemy is inertia. Moreover, our study indicates that implementing an effective employee ownership program does not require any magic formula, any special set of economic circumstances, or any long-worked-for mastery of arcane management techniques. The message from successful employee ownership companies is really very simple: contribute significant amounts of stock to each employee on a regular basis and treat your work associates more like partners than hired hands. How you do this, in fact, may matter less than the sincerity with which you try it.

The New Capitalists

We have made some strong claims for employee ownership in this chapter and this book. We believe the evidence supports these claims. First, we have contended that employee ownership is a more equitable way to organize work. Equity is an important value rooted in the history of the United States. Our rhetoric, if not always our practice, proclaims that equal efforts deserve equal rewards. Whether through civil rights legislation, universal public education, the progressive tax system, or any number of other policies, we have affirmed our belief in the rightness of equity. We have looked at the matter more practically as well, holding the notion that if more people believe society will treat them equitably, more people will be willing to make the kind of efforts that keep society productive.

We have affirmed our belief in equity in its other meaning as well—ownership. Homesteading, reclamation, mortgage interest deduction, FHA and VA loans, small business loans, and other policies were all meant to encourage the broad ownership of wealth. A nation of owners, we believed, would be a nation of more responsible citizens.

At least at work, however, fewer and fewer of us are owners, and while income distribution has improved somewhat, most kinds of wealth are owned by relatively few people. We have simply failed to do much about the inequity of ownership, an inequity that was part of why people came here in the first place. Equally important, we have created a system in which if people work harder or better than they are paid to work (which, after all, is what helps give companies a competitive edge), the surplus they create is captured by someone else.

By making employees owners, therefore, we can create a better equation between performance and reward, an equation that can be very motivating. This, of course, is a second major argument for employee ownership. A non-owning employee simply has much less incentive to avoid waste, suggest new ideas, work harder, or work efficiently. This can be especially important in the growing number of companies that seek or need to involve employees more in decision-making. When employees are given more responsibility, they need more incentive to assume it. This increased motivation can be an important supplemental, if not determining, factor in keeping companies competitive. Employee owners should also be more likely to stay with their companies, something of particular concern to high-tech firms. At the same time, it can be very important where jobs are being "de-skilled"—that is, where people are doing less sophisticated work than they are capable of doing. Ownership can help maintain at least some level of employee commitment.

A third potential virtue of employee ownership is that it creates a better identity of interests between society's economic needs and shareholders' wants. Currently, most publicly held stock is controlled by large institutions or wealthy investors. Their interests are maximized individually if the companies they own maximize short-run profits. That way, they can move their investments around from one company to another. Companies more interested in the longer term may lose these investors. Long-term strategies may impose investment costs that decrease a company's short-term worth. Since there is no way to predict in advance how successful these strategies will be, investors will often only see the short-term decline in earnings these costs impose. Their reaction is, in many cases, to sell and invest in something with greater short-term potential. Yet this pressure for short-term rewards is not in society's best interest, for only a long-term strategy can keep us competitive. Employee shareholders, by contrast to outsiders, are better served by this long-term approach. Keeping a job is more important to them than maximizing short-run returns on their stock.

Fourth, employee ownership can encourage a transition to an economy in which less labor is needed. Our current system makes that transition difficult. Elaborate approaches are often taken to limit job loss when new technologies are introduced: approaches that will make some companies think twice about the costs of introducing innovations. Even if these approaches succeed within a company, however, they may do nothing to limit job loss in society. A plan that calls for reductions through attrition, for instance, still means fewer jobs in that firm.

Of course, economists argue about whether these new technologies really cost jobs or actually create more new ones. While we have seen an increase in what economists consider the "natural" rate of unemployment from about 4% in the 1960s to 6% or even 7% in the 1980s, it is too early to know for sure what technology will ultimately do to the amount of work needed.

What we can say, however, is that there is at least a good chance that the historic trend of reducing the number of hours people need to work to produce progressively higher standards of living will continue, and perhaps even accelerate. With broad employee ownership, there would be every reason to encourage this trend, not brake it. As owners, employees could look forward to a time when they need to work even less to earn as much, for a growing part of their income would be from ownership. That would help keep us competitive, while giving more people more time and money to pursue other things of interest—family, hobbies, culture, education, entrepreneurship.

Finally, and most controversially, employee ownership can help democratize society. Political and social democracy are obviously important values in this country. All our public and most of our private organizations are supposed to work that way. We have not, however, extended that notion to the economic sphere, as some of the founding fathers thought we should.[3] As corporations become larger and larger, it seems that the incongruity of the non-democratic corporation becomes more troublesome. Business is making more and more decisions that affect the public and public policy— decisions to relocate, to close, to follow one investment policy or another, to adhere to or violate certain health or environmental standards, to support civic activities, and so on. In the "free market" system of economic models, no firm would be large enough for its decisions to have such important public impacts. In the real world, this is obviously not the case.

At the same time, work has become the primary community for many people, replacing the neighborhood, town, or extended family. If people are to live democratically, it could be argued, these primary communities need to be democratic as well.[4]

For both these reasons, creating a more democratic society may require creating more democratic corporations. Employee ownership has been the best way to accomplish this. No other approach has succeeded in democratizing the firm so well. Employee owners have a more direct and legitimate stake in corporate policy than any other group except, perhaps, shareholders. They are probably the only group, in fact, with enough of a stake to make participation in corporate governance worthwhile. Perhaps most importantly, there is no reason to believe that the more democratically organized employee-owned companies are at any competitive disadvantage, and some reason to believe they actually may perform better than their more traditional counterparts.

If employee ownership accomplishes any of these objectives, it should be considered a success. But has it demonstrated that it can? Or does? On some points, we think the answer is self-evident. There are, for instance, virtually no U.S. firms that allow any significant employee input into corporate policy other than those with employee ownership plans. Similarly, employee ownership appears to be making the ownership of wealth more equitable. There is no evidence, and we have no reason to believe, that most employee ownership firms' compensation packages are much different than those of comparable conventional companies—except that on top of everything else, employees get stock. If this is true, then employee ownership must be contributing to a broader distribution of the ownership of wealth. The hundreds of employees at Lowes' Companies who have left with six-figure amounts or more, for instance, would certainly agree with this. For many of these people, their only other chance at such wealth would probably be a lottery.

Employee motivation and the resulting changes in corporate performance are more difficult issues. There is some evidence that employee ownership firms perform better, but it is not conclusive. Our research suggests that ownership can improve motivation and job satisfaction if handled well, but we cannot yet prove that most employee owners are more motivated than most non-owners. It does seem logical that employee ownership firms will pursue longer-term strategies, but it could also be argued that workers will instead press for short-run wage increases at the cost of reinvestment. This is an issue that needs much more research.

There is, in other words, still much to be learned about just how employee ownership performs. Because the widespread use of the concept is relatively recent, it will be some time before we can make a complete assessment. Nonetheless, even at this early point, there is persuasive evidence that employee ownership is achieving at least some of its major goals, and may be fulfilling others as well. It is not a bad beginning.

Making Employee Ownership Work Better

Working or not, employee ownership is clearly growing, and growing very quickly. The burden of our study has been to learn what can make that growth most productive. In the process, we have learned a great deal about employee ownership and about work in general.

We find what we have learned very encouraging. Making employee ownership succeed is not that complicated. You don't have to be big or small; you don't have to be capital intensive or labor intensive; your line of business isn't very important; the presence or absence of unions is not a critical factor. A poorly educated workforce makes communicating the employee ownership plan harder, but not impossible; otherwise, workforce characteristics do not seem crucial. A company that consistently loses money, or has very flat earnings, will have a tougher time, but frankly, these companies are not going to stay around for long anyway.

What does matter is pretty straightforward:

1. Make regular, substantial contributions to the ownership plan. We cannot stress this enough: spreading wealth is the key to making employee ownership work. Most of the companies that scored the highest on our surveys contributed an amount equal to 10–25% of pay every year to their ownership plan. Employees see ownership primarily in financial terms, so the more they get, the better. Nothing will matter as much as this, though other things are important too.

2. Seek to involve employees in decision-making. Even though most employees are primarily interested in the financial side of employee ownership, most will also feel more like owners if they have some say at work. Moreover, some employees will respond more strongly to non-financial factors. Providing these participation opportunities is easiest and most important at the job level. After all, employees know a lot about their jobs, so why not give them more responsibility for them? Involving employees at higher levels can help too, though. Employees are usually very conservative shareholders, and normally do not want to participate in management decisions, so management's fears here are largely unwarranted. Employee input at these levels may provide both helpful new ideas and information, as well as an important symbol of ownership.

3. Treat people like owners, not employees. Participation programs help here, but more can be done. Employee owners are partners in the business. They are more likely to act that way if they are treated that way. Day-to-day interactions with and between employees matter. Symbolic things, such as calling all employees "associates" or "managers" or eliminating

status perquisites for top employees can, if done sincerely, make a big difference.

4. Make repeated and careful efforts to make sure employees know what their ownership plan means.

The first and most important of these criteria—lots of stock—is simple to do, although gathering the will to do it is understandably not so easy. The other elements need more work, time, and experimentation, but mostly they need effort. Most of the most successful companies we studied have designed their employee owner relations efforts themselves, using common-sense notions and their own instincts. What distinguishes their efforts is that there is, in the words of the authors of *In Search of Excellence,* a "bias for action."[5] These companies kept trying things until something worked, and they did a lot of different things to keep reinforcing the notion of ownership.

If a company does all these things, success is still not certain. Not much in business is. Any reasonably healthy company that follows this course, however, is at least very likely to see results.

Our research has also taught us something about work. When we started this project we, like other researchers, expected that "intrinsic work motivation" or some such abstract notion, would be very important in determining how employee ownership works. High levels of employee input and even control, we thought, would be very important factors. We also expected that the whole set of factors that would contribute to the success of employee ownership would be complex, consisting of several things that might vary from company to company. We did find that participation matters, and other parts of our research, not elaborated here, confirmed the notion that challenging, interesting work makes for more satisfied, motivated workers. What really opened our eyes, however, was the preeminence of financial concerns. Our data suggest the simple conclusion, often glossed over in the literature, that most people work first to make money, not to seek personal fulfillment. If the workers we studied could buy more control or more interesting, participative work, we suspect they would not pay a great deal for these things.

To some advocates of employee ownership, these findings will be disappointing. We don't think they should be. Many jobs will never be as fulfilling as researchers might like. Moreover, responding to financial incentives is not an ignoble motive. After all, ownership has always been an important American value, for it provides people with the means to make a better, more secure life for themselves, one in which they and their families can have more options.

This is not to say that our study shows such programs as job enrichment, employee involvement, and workplace democracy are unimportant, for they clearly can make a difference. What it does say is that those who are concerned about making jobs better must remember that to the people they are trying to help, "better" means, above all, "more money." We would argue that the wealth distribution features of employee ownership make it a very effective means of making work better.

The Future of Employee Ownership

When the National Center for Employee Ownership was started in 1981, one of us made a call to someone who turned out to be away. The person answering the phone for him took a message, and when told the name of the organization, replied in all sincerity, "I didn't know people could still own employees." The concept of employee ownership has come a long way since then. While not yet exactly a household word, it has gained considerable currency and legitimacy in business, union, and political circles.

On the other hand, employee ownership has a very long way to go before it begins to achieve the kind of economic transformation of which we have suggested it is capable. Whether it will ever approach that end depends on several factors. Certainly, the most important of these is the retention of at least some significant tax incentives. Sweeping tax reform, worsening budget deficits, or any number of other factors each could lead to cutbacks or eliminations of important incentives. At the same time, employee ownership must continue to prove itself in the marketplace. If it doesn't, the tax incentives will surely fade away. Even while the tax breaks are available, many companies will not set up plans because they will not see the tax incentives as, in themselves, enough of a reason to proceed—they will want evidence that corporate performance will be enhanced as well. The role of unions could be critical as well, especially if they decide, as a few have, to take an aggressive role in promoting the idea. Our best guess is that employee ownership will continue to grow, that there will be a fairly rapid learning curve as more companies learn to use it well, and that the kinds of economic challenges that we have discussed earlier will continue to make employee ownership appealing. With such a short history, though, our prognostications are little more than ways to pass the time.

A more useful way to pass the time is to initiate a debate about what the future of employee ownership should be, and how that future can best be encouraged. There are at least four schools of thought.

One school might be called the "purist" approach. In this view, the key task is to create a few very good models of employee ownership, models that can demonstrate how well the concept can work. The best existing model is the Mondragon Cooperative system of Spain, where 18,000 workers in over 80 worker cooperatives have established a very successful and democratic system with little assistance from the government. The argument is that employee ownership can and should simultaneously achieve economic growth, social equity, and workplace democracy. Unless it achieves these multiple objectives, the purists fear, it may soon be seen as little more than a passing financial or organizational gambit, one usually established by management for its own self-interest. Ownership without control, for instance, is seen as the corporate equivalent of taxation without representation; participation or even control without ownership is seen as potentially manipulative or cooptive.

These concerns are not just moral, however. They are practical as well. If too many people feel they are cheated by employee ownership, it can never achieve a firm footing in society. A better approach, say the purists, is to create effective models which, by their very success, can encourage others to follow the same path.[6]

This approach has a strong ideological appeal to many people, but the process it proposes is a slow one at best. Its emphasis on fully realized democratic companies turns away many businesspeople who might be willing to share ownership, but not yet control. Still, in the last decade, some very encouraging progress has been made to establish these kinds of models. The efforts of the Industrial Cooperative Association (ICA) in Somerville, Massachusetts, the Center for Community Self-Help (CCSH) in Durham, North Carolina, and the Philadelphia Association for Cooperative Enterprise (PACE) have been largely responsible for this success. CCSH, for instance, has established a network of worker cooperatives in North Carolina, ICA has helped fashion a city strategy for worker ownership in Burlington, Vermont, and PACE has worked with a local union to start a group of union-initiated worker-owned firms in Philadelphia. Each group has also succeeded in starting a loan fund for worker cooperatives.

These efforts can create working models of what can be achieved, models that can be extremely important in providing evidence and guidance for other employee ownership programs. In time, they may also succeed in creating practical alternative economies in a number of local areas. They are not intended, however, to bring employee ownership, in some form, to thousands of companies.

While this approach relies mostly on private efforts, another approach calls for more direct government action. Advocates of this view contend that business will never voluntarily give up "real" ownership or power to workers, and that government must intervene.[7] Mandatory pre-notification of plant closings, state or federal financial assistance for buyouts, an industrial policy that would have some worker ownership component, and similar policies usually form the core of this strategy.

While the government obviously is involved in promoting employee ownership, much of this approach seems impractical to us. While several states do support employee buyouts, the considerable efforts to pass plant closing legislation have made little headway, even in more favorable political times. Broader industrial policy with an emphasis on employee ownership also seems unlikely. A modest industrial policy in Rhode Island (one without any employee ownership provisions) was defeated by a 4–1 margin in a recent referendum, despite wide support from political leaders.

But even if we could have the government mandate employee ownership, would we want it to? We think not. As our study indicates, employee ownership works best when people—mangement and labor—work at it. If employee ownership is imposed from above, it will at the least be resented by the very mangement people whose support is required for it to work well. Without this support, there would be more and more examples of employee ownership not accomplishing much. Either supporters of the idea would then lose interest, or the political climate would change, and the requirements for employee ownership would be replaced by some new nostrum.

Both the purist and governmental models basically come at the idea of employee ownership from the view of labor. On the other side, there are many who promote it from the viewpoint of management. Management, they argue, sets up these plans, so it is management that must be persuaded to do so. Most of that persuasion will need to be financial, primarily in the form of tax breaks. The greater the incentives, the more plans there will be; the more plans there are, the more workers will be owners. Large plans are better than small ones, but almost any plan is better than none at all, especially since the more companies that establish plans, the broader the constituency will be for the tax breaks.

This is a somewhat exaggerated description of this view but, to varying degrees, it characterizes the approach of many of the professional consultants in this field. While these people differ in their views on what role employees should play in a company, and in the emphasis they place on employee motivation in "selling" employee ownership, they would all agree that the key thing is to get stock in the hands of employees. That is an emphasis our research indicates is justified. To reach this goal, it is important to avoid loading onto employee ownership too many requirements, such as mandatory voting rights, that might prevent people from setting up plans.

This approach has helped spread the idea of employee ownership very quickly. But there is a danger here too, if this approach is followed in its undiluted form. If a company sees employee ownership primarily or even exclusively as a clever financial gimmick with lots of tax breaks, and nothing more, it is unlikely to do the kinds of things that make sure employee ownership reaches its potential. Just as with the second approach described earlier, political supporters of employee ownership may become disillusioned with its performance, and the tax incentives may vanish. At least some companies will use the tax breaks to set up plans that are not in the best interests of workers, but that support management's self-interest (such as terminating a well-funded pension plan for a higher-risk ESOP to help fund a takeover defense in an economically shaky company). That kind of use will be well-publicized, causing further deterioration of public support. Unions may also become skeptical if they see employee ownership being used primarily for narrow management interests. The press, which has been essential to the spread of employee ownership, may start writing more critical stories about the idea. Employee ownership would not be the first idea overhyped by its promoters as a great savior only to end up as little more than an item in some future trivia game.

Our research and experience suggests to us that all of these approaches have some merit, but none can stand on its own. Ultimately, we believe, employee ownership must be able to demonstrate its worth in the market. Heavy as the burden may be, it must show management and the public that it can add to the bottom line, and it must show employees and their representatives that it can make work more rewarding, financially and otherwise. Other social inventions—corporate ownership, the family farm, pension plans, employee involvement programs—similarly had to meet market tests of their worth in order to survive.

We believe the same argument applies to employee participation and control in employee ownership firms—they need to prove themselves in the market if they are ever to be broadly supported. Since the step from ownership to ownership *and* control *and* participation is shorter than the step from neither to both, we think that mandating such a policy would be counterproductive. Moreover, even if companies only share ownership, if they share enough of it, this can, in itself, satisfy the most basic goal of both employees and the employee ownership concept.

In order for employee ownership to establish itself in the market, we believe several things are necessary:

1. *Laws that stimulate people to try employee ownership in a variety of corporate settings.* Tax laws are the most obvious, but aid to employee buyouts can help in selected cases as well. These laws, of course, already exist, but unless they are kept on the books for a substantial time, too few companies will overcome their inertia and skepticism and give employee ownership a real trial. Care must be taken, however, not to make these laws so attractive (or mandatory) that they are used too often in the damaging ways suggested above.

2. *An active public awareness campaign.* State and local governments can and are helping here, and could do more. Con-

sultants are also beginning to organize seminars and other public relations efforts. This is an area that needs constant attention, however.

3. *Good stories.* Employee ownership very much needs its heroes: the Lowe's Companies warehouse workers leaving with hundreds of thousands of dollars in stock; the W.L. Gore Associates, People Expresses, and Science Applications posting remarkable growth rates; the Allied Plywoods and Fastener Industries prospering through common-sense, employee-oriented management; the Workers Owned Sewing Companies and Women's Community Bakeries providing work and control for people who would otherwise find them hard to get; the Weirton Steels and Hyatt Clarks saving jobs and communities. These companies form a kind of employee ownership folklore, one that can be handed down to reporters, other companies, employees, and the public.

4. *Broad dissemination of good information about what makes employee ownership work.* This, of course, is why we wrote this book. We need more research, more debate, and more experimentation, though, if we really are to accomplish this objective. That means that for those who want to become involved in employee ownership, there are many roles to play—employee, consultant, promoter, researcher, reporter, entrepreneur, union leader, public official. Ultimately, it means creating a diverse infrastructure of people and organizations who know what employee ownership is and can be.

Even if all of this happens, employee ownership will still face obstacles. Inertia is surely the greatest, but outright opposition will emerge as well from those who feel their interests are threatened. We cannot predict how serious these problems will be, but we do believe that if we can do the realistic things outlined above, employee ownership will, in the next generation, be a common and permanent feature of the economy.

Conclusion

When European immigrants first came to this country, many came looking for a chance to own their own capital. We built an extraordinarily successful political and economic system on that foundation.

But this foundation has been steadily deteriorating as work and ownership are connected for a decreasing proportion of our population. Fortunately, in the last decade, we have seen a revival of the ownership idea. There are not many ideas that create social justice, promote economic growth, and appeal to most everyone politically, but employee ownership does. We are not naive about the obstacles employee ownership faces, but its progress so far has surpassed the most optimistic projections of a few years ago. We believe it provides a solution to a variety of our social and economic problems, a solution we cannot afford to ignore.

Appendices

Appendix I
Employee Ownership Cases

The cases that follow were developed in late 1984 to provide a brief overview of how some of the more interesting employee ownership companies operate. Any information about such things as sales, percent of the company owned, and number of employees is obviously subject to change.

These companies were not selected as representative of employee ownership. Rather, they were selected to provide readers with examples of some of the more creative and important uses of the idea. Only some of the companies were included in our research sample.

CASES INCLUDED

Alaska Commercial Company
Allied Plywood Corporation
American Recreation Centers, Inc.
Antioch Publishing Company
Atlas Chain Company
Brooks Camera Company
Bureau of National Affairs, Inc.
Chrysler Corporation
The Common Ground
ComSonics, Inc.
Denver Yellow Cab Cooperative
Eastern Airlines
Fastener Industries, Inc.
W.L. Gore and Associates
Hunter Associates Lab
Hyatt Clark Industries, Inc.
The Journal Company
Leslie Paper Company

The Lowe's Companies
North American Tool and Die
The North Face, Inc.
O&O Supermarkets
Parsons Company
People Express
Phillips Paper Corp.
Publix Supermarkets
Quad/Graphics
The Record Factory
Riverside Construction
Rural/Metro, Inc.
Science Applications International Inc.
The Solar Center
Transcon, Inc.
Up-Right, Inc.
Weirton Steel Company
Western Airlines
Workers Owned Sewing Company

ALASKA COMMERCIAL COMPANY

Product/Industry	Retail sales (general stores). SIC: 5399
Plan	ESOP (1984); plan owns 33%.
Coverage	All employees after one year with 1,000 hours service.
Background	Alaska Commercial is the oldest retail company in the state, founded in the 1800s as the Russian American Company. It very successfully operates general stores in 23 communities throughout Alaska. In 1977, the company was acquired by the non-profit Cooperative Community Enterprise Development Corporation (CCEDC). CCEDC sought to use the stores as a means of providing local employment and services to communities that often lack institutions to provide them. The stores function as meeting places in villages, and return part of their profits to the various village corporations in the form of bonus rents. Since ACC was acquired by CEDC, its sales have increased from $9 million to $52 million, a compound rate of 26% per year. It now employs 380 people. As part of its development strategy, the company has set up a leveraged ESOP to purchase 33% of the stock.
Plan Structure	Allocation is made by salary; vesting is at 20% per year until completed; distribution is at a break in service. Employees vote their stock on a one-person, one-vote basis.
Participation Features	Employees elect one-third of the board and a variety of other programs are being set up at the store level for employee input.
Company Performance	The ESOP is just getting underway, so its impact on company performance cannot be gauged.
Contact	Sam Salkin
Alaska Commercial Company
1011 E. Tudor Rd., Ste. 120
Anchorage, AK   99503

ALLIED PLYWOOD CORPORATION

Product/Industry	Wholesale of plywood and other building materials. SIC: 5211, 2435, 2436
Plan	Profit-Sharing Plan (1951)
Employee Stock Ownership Plan (1976)

Coverage	All 25 full time employees participate; ESOP owns 85% employees own 15% directly.
Background	Company founders began profit-sharing plan to encourage employees to identify their own fortunes with those of the company and to reward them for company profitability.
	Founders used the ESOP to buy their shares when they retired. This arrangement was appealing to them because it had certain tax advantages and would keep the company independent. Owners felt an obligation to employees not to sell to a conglomerate.
Plan Structure	Allied distributes monthly cash bonuses based on profits. These bonuses are equal for all employees. Individuals also receive an annual cash bonus which depends upon their seniority, job class, days worked that year, and performance.
	All employees participate in the ESOP after one year. Complete vesting takes ten years, with 30% after three years and 10% each year thereafter. The ESOP repurchases shares of retiring employees at book value. Even though Allied is now 100% employee owned, the company will continue to contribute new shares to the ESOP so that new employees also become owners.
Participation Features	The company holds monthly meetings of all employees to discuss ideas and complaints. Workers elect three employees to the seven-member board of directors, one from the office and two from the warehouse. Election is by one person/one vote. Employees vote their shares on major issues. For instance, they recently voted to purchase a new computer system. The board is considering passing through all voting rights.
Company Performance	In 1982 the ESOP leveraged the purchase of the last 40% of Allied from its former owners. The company successfully paid off the loan by 1984 and was considering passing through dividends on the stock. Allied expected sales to grow 20% in 1984 to $12 million.
More Information	"The Allied Plywood ESOP." ESOP Association of America.
	"Case Study: Allied Plywood Corporation." *Employee Ownership*. June 1982. National Center for Employee Ownership.
Contact	Robert Shaw, President Allied Plywood Corporation 4740 Eisenhower Drive Alexandria, VA 22304 (703) 751–5800

AMERICAN RECREATION CENTERS, INC.

Product/Industry	Bowling Centers and Real Estate Management. SIC: 7933, 6522
Plan	Employee Stock Ownership Plan (1974)
Coverage	Majority of 850 employees covered; 25% owned.
Background	ARC is publicly traded company that operates 23 bowling centers and develops and manages commercial real estate. It employs 800 people (450 full-time). The company was founded in 1961. The company's philosophy is that base pay should be minimal, but incentive pay substantial. Thus, there are a number of bonus, commission, and profit-sharing plans. Half of its managers are women, which is unusual for the industry.
	The ESOP replaced a profit-sharing plan because the company wanted employees more involved with their work, and because they could contribute more to the ESOP than to the profit-sharing plan (since they could contribute company shares instead of cash if they wanted).
Plan Structure	Employees become eligible to participate in the plan after they have worked 500 hours in one year and have attained age 18 or higher. The 500-hour rule allows part-time employees to participate (in most companies, 1,000 hours are needed). Vesting is on a six-year schedule, starting at 20% after two years. Employees have full voting rights and are paid a dividend on their shares.
Participation Features	Employees vote their shares on all issues. There are also monthly meetings at each bowling center to discuss any issues that employees or managers might bring up. The interest in these meetings varies greatly, depending in part on how the managers handle them.
Company Performance	ARC has been a very profitable firm, with average net operating margins of 20% and return to equity of 18.6%. The firm's public shareholders have benefitted as well, with an average stock increase of 31% per year since the ESOP was started—6 to 10 points per year better than competitors.
More Information	Ira Wagner. "Report to the New York Stock Exchange on the Performance of Publicly Held Companies with Employee Ownership Plans." NCEO: 1984. $12.50.

Contact Robert Feuchter, President
American Recreation Centers
P.O. Box 60729
Sacramento, CA 95860
(916) 488–8206

ANTIOCH PUBLISHING COMPANY

Product/Industry	Manufacturer and distributor of bookstore products. SIC: 2731
Plan	ESOP (1979); plan owns 34%.
Coverage	All full-time employees with one year or more of service.
Background	Antioch was founded in 1926 by Ernest Morgan, a socialist-activist printer. Control was passed to Lee Morgan in 1971, who expanded the company's line from bookplates to a variety of bookstore sideline items. The company now has 30% of this market. Sales have doubled every three years since then. The company currently employs 120 employees.
Plan Structure	Antioch's ESOP now owns 34% of the company, and Morgan hopes it will own at least 50% within the next ten years. Vesting begins at 40% after four years and reaches 100% after ten. Employees must have reached the age of 50 and have left the company before they receive their stock. Allocation is according to salary.
Participation Features	Employees vote their stock on issues which require more than a majority vote. Non-management employees elect two of the nine board members. Employees receive financial reports and board minutes and participate on safety committees.
Company Performance	Since the ESOP was established in 1979, sales have grown 150%. Morgan says that the ESOP has made it much easier to attract and retain good employees and has made employees much more interested in the company.
More Information	"Antioch Publishing Company." *Employee Ownership.* March 1984.
Contact	Lee Morgan, President Antioch Publishing Company 888 Dayton Street Yellow Springs, OH 45387

ATLAS CHAIN COMPANY

Product/Industry	Manufacturer of precision roller chain for agricultural and construction equipment and other industrial uses. SIC: 3531, 3523.
Plan	Employee Stock Ownership Plan (1983)
Coverage	All 85 employees participate; 100% owned.
Background	After several consecutive years of losses Renold PLC, a British-based conglomerate, decided to divest its Atlas Chain Company subsidiary. Renold could find no buyers and ceased to manufacture roller chain at the plant in March 1983. The UAW formed a "Save Our Jobs Committee." The committee collected $200 from each employee to help finance a feasibility study. Later, the committee invited management and other non-union employees to join them in their effort. By October 1983 employees agreed to wage cuts and rule changes and raised $7 million in financing to buy the company's assets.
Plan Structure	The Atlas Chain ESOP allocates stock annually according to each employee's months of service that year. Employees become fully vested in their accounts over 5 years if they are 55 years or older or over 10 years if they are less than 55. Years of service with Renold count toward vesting. Atlas distributes stock to employee accounts as it pays off its loan.
	After the old plant closed, the pension plan was terminated and the participants were fully vested. Atlas Chain now has a contractual provision to review every six months the feasibility of opening negotiations for a new pension plan, but the employes have chosen, for the time being, to rehire laid-off employees rather than fund the retirement plan.
Participation Features	Employees elect five of seven members of the board of directors. In August, 1986 Atlas will pass through full voting rights on all ESOP shares. Until then, unallocated shares will be voted by the Board.
Company Performance	After three quarters of operation as an employee-owned firm, Atlas's attorney reported that the company was doing much better than anyone had anticipated.
Contact	Don Hayes, President Atlas Chain Company Fourth and Pacific Streets West Pittston, PA 18643 (717) 655–1401

Bill Scott, President
UAW Local 271
Atlas Chain Company

BROOKS CAMERA COMPANY

Product/Industry	Franchise of Retail Camera Stores. SIC: 5946, 5733
Plan	Employee Stock Ownership (1971); 100% owned.
Coverage	200 employees participate; approximately 250 employees total.
Background	Rather than sell his shares to an outside buyer, which might have jeopardized the company's future, the retiring owner was convinced by one of the employees to establish an ESOP. The deal involved converting a profit-sharing plan into an ESOP and borrowing to purchase the rest.
Plan Structure	To try to reduce the relatively high turnover rate that is common in the retail camera trade, the Brooks Cameras ESOP has a vesting schedule under which a person who leaves before completing three years of service forfeits the stock allocated to their account.
Participation Features	Brooks holds periodic meetings with small groups of employees to discuss the company's progress and whatever is on people's minds. Brooks management believes that the key to motivating employees to begin thinking and acting like owners is to pass through dividends immediately to the owners.
Company Performance	Brooks has grown to be the dominant photo retailer in the San Francisco area with 18 different locations including its own photo-finishing plant and distribution center.
More Information	ESOP Association Profiles: "The American Dream: A Double Whammy" by Karen Young for the National Center for Employee Ownership. Unpublished.
Contact	Joseph Dee, President Brooks Cameras 239 Utah Avenue South San Francisco, CA 94080

BUREAU OF NATIONAL AFFAIRS, INC.

Product/Industry	Newsletter publishing, printing, data processing, and other services. SIC: 2731, 8111

Plan	Direct purchase through special trust; plan owns 100%. Also has PAYSOP and 401(k) plan.
Coverage	70% of employees own stock (excluding PAYSOP); no employee owns more than 5%.
Background	BNA was founded by David Lawrence in 1929, and sold by him to its employees in 1947. Lawrence also owned the U.S. News and World Report Company, which he also sold to the employees. BNA currently has over 1800 employees. It has been a frequent target of takeover inquiries, as it has been a profitable company. Although one serious suitor offered considerably more than the then current market price of the shares, BNA has resisted, wishing to remain employee owned.
Plan Structure	An option to buy stock is granted to all full-time employees after one year and part-time employees after five. More than two-thirds of the employees buy stock (91% of management; 60% of non-management). Management owns 64% of the stock; non-management employees own 36%. The company also has a pension plan, profit-sharing plan, 401(k) plan, and a PAYSOP. On retirement, employees may exchange their voting stock for non-voting stock.
Participation Features	Employees have full voting rights on their stock.
Company Performance	BNA has been a very profitable company for several years, with steady growth. Since it has been employee owned for so long, it is difficult to evaluate what the impact of employee ownership has been on company performance. Employees seem relatively satisfied with the plan.
Contact	William Beltz, President BNA 1231 25th Street Washington, DC 20037 Washington-Baltimore Newspaper Guild 1511 K Street NW, Suite 926 Washington, DC 20005

CHRYSLER CORPORATION

Product/Industry	Automobile manufacturer. SIC: 3711, 2295, 2899, 3399, 3519, 3714
Plan	ESOP (1980); plan owns 12%.
Coverage	All employees employed between 1980 and 1984.

Background	When Chrysler neared bankruptcy in 1979, it asked the government for a $1.5 billion loan guarantee. As a condition of that guarantee, the company was required to contribute $162.5 million worth of its stock to an ESOP in four equal installments. The plan was established in 1980 and terminated in 1984 when the company and the union agreed not to continue it. Because of the increase in company stock prices, the stock ended up being worth approximately three times the $162.5 million. The importance of the Chrysler ESOP extended beyond what it provided to the employees, however, because it was the first instance of trading stock for wage concessions (as also required by the law), a pattern that has become very common since then.
Plan Structure	The shares were allocated equally to all employees, who will receive them when they leave the company.
Participation Features	The stock, by law, carried full voting rights. The company has established a number of job-level employee involvement teams, although these teams were not related to the ESOP.
Company Performance	The company's recovery is legendary, but it would be impossible to judge what, if any, contribution the ESOP made to this recovery. At the end of 1984, the union and the company decided that other benefit plans would be more important.
More Information	"Chrysler's Fate May Hinge on Employee Stock Ownership Plan." *Barron's*. Dec. 17, 1979. pp. 4–7.
Contact	Mark Hardesty, Assistant Director of Research United Autoworkers Union 8000 E. Jefferson Detroit, MI 48214 Chrysler Corporation P.O. Box 1919 Detroit, MI 48231

THE COMMON GROUND

Product/Industry	Restaurant. SIC: 2099
Plan	Worker Cooperative (1977)
Coverage	13 of 23 employees participate; 100% owned.
Background	The Common Ground was originally an investor-owned corporation. Area residents bought shares in 1971 to establish a

natural foods restaurant appealing to their "political and philosophical tastebuds." In 1977 the shareholders sold to the employees.

Plan Structure | The cooperative employs both members and non-members. Potential members must demonstrate, through discussion and work, that they are committed to the values of the cooperative. Then the membership votes on admission, with a two-thirds majority needed for acceptance. New members must pay a $5 membership fee plus purchase a $200 share of stock. All workers share profits and tips equally and the ratio of highest to lowest paid is 1.3 to 1.

Participation Features | The Common Ground has no board of directors and no hierarchical management structure. A policy committee settles disputes and sets financial and long-term policy. Members may choose to sit on the policy committee. All employees may participate in other committees including hiring and grievance, menu, pricing, scheduling, and maintenance.

Workers have job autonomy and may take responsibility for new areas. For example, several workers produced a cookbook and another managed the expansion of a catering service.

Company Performance | The Common Ground has lasted longer than many alternative foods restaurants and is now in its seventh year of employee ownership. The members' scores (1984) on measures of job satisfaction, organizational commitment, work motivation, and job effort are among the highest NCEO has recorded.

More Information | "A Co-op Restaurant: All From Scratch." *The New York Times.* December 7, 1983.

Employee Ownership. National Center for Employee Ownership. June 1984.

Contact | The Common Ground
25 Elliot Street
Brattleboro, VT   05301

COMSONICS, INC.

Product/Industry | Manufacturer of accessories for cable television and communications. SIC: 3662, 4899

Plan | Employee Stock Ownership Plan (1974).

Coverage | 61% of 116 employees participate; 48% owned (7/31/84).

Background	The company's founder and owner believed that "the idea of participatory ownership and management is something that would work." Putting his ideas into practice, he created a very participatory management system and established an ESOP that will own 100% of the company by 1986.
Plan Structure	All 21-year-old full-time employees participate in the ESOP after one year of work. Allocation is by salary and vesting begins at 30% after five years, increasing at 7% per year until 100% at the 15th year.
	ComSonics also has a profit-sharing plan which distributes 50% of profits over an employee-set target.

Participation Features	An employee committee advises employees of all issues before the ESOP trust and collects votes of the following basis:
	   Minor Issues—vested shares held by the trust
	   Major Issues—all shares, vested or not.
	"Major" and "minor" are as defined by state law. All non-vested shares are voted by the Board on minor issues.

	Workers are encouraged to request meetings on any issue and they form committees which, depending on the issue, have either volunteer members or all workers of a particular job class. Such committees discuss and decide on production, hours, budgets, and corporate objectives. One committee recently decided whether to have two or three shifts and set the shift pay differentials.
Company Performance	In 1982 *Inc.* magazine listed ComSonics as one of the nation's 500 fastest growing small companies.
More Information	"ComSonics, Inc." ESOP Association of America.
Contact	Warren Braun, President ComSonics, Inc. P.O. Box 1106 Harrisonburg, VA 22801

DENVER YELLOW CAB COOPERATIVE

Product/Industry	Taxicab company. SIC: 4121
Plan	Cooperative (1979); plan owns 100%.
Coverage	All drivers; 60% of non-driver employees.
Background	During the 1970s, Denver Yellow Cab experienced a series of strikes over the union's status at the company. In 1978, its

owners sold it to Metropolitan Transportation Company, which quickly decided to resell it. The union had been interested in the possibility of a worker buyout for some time, and had accumulated a $100,000 strike fund. In 1979 negotiations were completed.

Denver Yellow Cab was and is the largest cab company in Denver, and also operates several smaller transit services. It employs over 1,000 drivers, most of whom lease their cabs from the company. Another 100 employees work in dispatching, service, and other non-driving jobs. The drivers make their income from fares and tips; the cooperative makes most of its income from the provision of services to drivers, including leasing them the cabs, insurance, dispatching, and mechanical servicing.

Plan Structure

All employees are eligible to participate in the coop by contributing $1.50 per shift over five years. The total amount of this payment is held in a non-interest-bearing account and returned to the member at departure from the company. All drivers and most of the "inside" workers must participate, but participation for workers in two of the smaller bargaining units is voluntary. When the company's loans are repaid, some form of profit-sharing may be instituted.

Participation Features

Each member has one vote in coop affairs. The board of directors is made up entirely of employees elected by the members. In addition, several other committees have been established to handle negotiations, grievances, and other company policy matters. Members of these committees are elected or appointed according to a random process. Almost all management people were former drivers.

Company Performance

Since the coop was formed, many of the drivers have faced difficult times due to the recession, which reduced the number of people using taxis. The coop, which makes its money from leasing and other fees, however, has made a profit, and the recovery is now helping the drivers. Since the formation of the coop, turnover has dropped from 200–300% to about 20%. The company has also established the best safety record in the industry.

More Information

Chris Gunn. *Workers Self-Management in the United States.* Ithaca, NY: Cornell University Press, 1984. pp. 157 ff.

"Denver Yellow Cab." *Employee Ownership.* December 1983.

Contact	Alan Cowley, Chairman of the Board
	Denver Yellow Cab Cooperative Association
	3455 Ringsby Court
	Denver, CO 80216
	(303) 292–6464

EASTERN AIRLINES

Product/Industry	Airline. SIC: 4511
Plan	Stock held in four special trusts for all employees except pilots; stock is owned directly by employees through these trusts (pilots are negotiating over their trust); employees own 25%.
Coverage	All employees except newly hired flight attendants subject to a new wage scale.
Background	In the early 1980s, Eastern's economic fortunes deteriorated. In 1983, its president, Frank Borman, told the company's 37,000 employees that unless they took wage cuts, the company would be forced to file for reorganization under chapter 11 of the bankruptcy laws. The employees had made concessions before, however, and were concerned that concessions be used effectively. They argued, therefore, that if they were to make concessions, they would have to receive stock in the company and influence in its management decisions in return. Labor relations at the company had deteriorated during the preceding years, and neither side trusted the other. The problem was finally resolved after the unions brought in their own specialists to evaluate the company's books and concluded that some actions were needed. A mediator was then brought in to help find a resolution. Part of that resolution turned out to be a substantial ownership plan and what is probably the largest role for employees in any non-majority employee-owned company.
Plan Structure	Eastern's plan is unique. It provides workers with 25% of the voting shares and $260 million in preferred stock in return for $292 million in wage concessions. The stock is allocated on the basis of how much of a cut each employee took. The employees also agreed to a 5% productivity increase, which will work out to a $75 million savings. The stock will be distributed to employees in the next few years.
Participation Features	The Transit Workers Union (TWU) and the International Association of Machinists (IAM) each nominate a member of

the Board, while the pilots and non-union employees, subject to an earlier agreement, recommend two members, neither of whom can be associated with Eastern or its unions. The board has 19 members. A joint union-management committee has been established to review Eastern's business plans, and employee involvement teams are being set up at the job level.

Company
Performance

Labor relations have improved significantly, but the productivity gains will not exceed the 5% specified in the contract. On-time departures and arrivals have increased 20%. The company has now returned to profitability. Nonetheless, it asked for additional concessions in 1984.

More Information

"Air Workers Give and Get Concessions." *In These Times.* December 21–January 10, 1984.

Contact

Jack W. Johnson, Sr. Vice-President
Eastern Airlines
Miami International Airport
Miami, FL   33148
(305) 873–2211

Charles Bryan
International Association of Machinists
4349 NW 36th Street
Miami, FL   33142

Robert V. Callahan, President
Local Lodge 553
Transport Workers Union
7370 NW 36th Street, Suite 412
Miami, FL   33166

Larry D. Schulte, Master Chairman
EAL–MEC
Air Line Pilots Association
201 Madeira Avenue
Coral Gables, FL   33134

FASTENER INDUSTRIES, INC.

Product/Industry

Manufacturer of nuts, bolts, and fasteners for automobiles and appliances. SIC: 5013

Plan

Employee Stock Ownership Plan (1980).

Coverage

All 125 employees participate; 100% owned.

Background	Fastener had been family owned since 1905 until the last family member decided to retire in 1979. Employees voted to convert a profit-sharing plan to an ESOP to buy part of the company. The company itself borrowed money to buy the remaining shares from the family. As the company repaid the loan it contributed shares to the ESOP.
Plan Structure	New employees participate in the ESOP after one month of work and are immediately 100% vested in their accounts. The ESOP allocates stock according to pay, but salaries are so close that no one employee owns more than 4% of the company. Fastener employees work seven hours per day and earn wages higher than the industry norm.
	Employees may sell their stock back to the ESOP up to 15 months after leaving Fastener. After that the ESOP is no longer required to repurchase stock, although it maintains the right of first refusal. The company gives retiring employees four hours of free consultation with company lawyers or CPAs to determine the best strategies for investing retirement benefits.
Participation Features	Employees have full voting rights on their shares. The company president believes, "If you don't vote the stock, you don't own it." Employees elect the board of directors.
	Each worker meets the company president once every three months with 10 other randomly selected employees. Plant managers meet with employees monthly. Employees consult with managers about machinery purchases and other decisions.
Company Performance	During the recent recession Fastener built up inventory rather than lay people off. Even so the company broke even while other firms in their field took losses. It is now making very good profits.
More Information	"A Democratic ESOP—The Experience of Fastener Industries." *Employee Ownership*. June 1981. National Center for Employee Ownership.
	"Fastener Industries—A Model ESOP." *Employee Ownership*. December 1983. National Center for Employee Ownership.
Contact	R.G. Biernacki, President Fastener Industries, Inc. One Berea Common, Suite 206 Berea, OH 44017 (216) 243–0200

W.L. GORE & ASSOCIATES

Product/Industry	Manufacturer of high tolerance wires and synthetic fibers, most notably "Gore-tex." SIC: 3357, 2295, 2621, 2891, 3679, 3842
Plan	Direct Purchase Plan (1959) Associate Stock Ownership Plan (1973)
Coverage	All 3,000 associates participate; ESOP owns 10%, associates own an additional 85% directly.
Background	Bill Gore enjoyed working as a research team member at Du-Pont before starting his own company in 1958. He believed an entire company, not just the research scientists, could operate as a team. Gore says the objective of the company is "to make money and to have fun doing it." Gore insists on making it clear that the company has no "employees," only associates.
Plan Structure	Gore does not disclose plan information.
Participation Features	Associate ownership fits well with Gore & Associates' unusual management structure. Associates receive stock through the ESOP and have full voting rights. They elect a nine-member board of directors.
	W.L. Gore has no pyramid management structure. Every one is an associate and according to Gore "all of us are non-managers." The company describes its management as a lattice structure where every associate has direct access to every other associate.
	New associates have sponsors until they have settled into a job they like at the company. Each Gore plant has less than 200 employees in order to maintain a friendly atmosphere.
Company Performance	From 1977 through 1982 Gore's earnings grew at an incredible compound annual rate of nearly 40% per year. Sales in 1983 were over $250 million.
More Information	"The Un-Manager." *Inc.* August 1982.
Contact	W.L. Gore Gore & Associates 555 Paper Mill Road Newark, DE 19711 (302) 738–4880

HUNTER ASSOCIATES LAB, INC.

Product/Industry	Technical instruments manufacturer. SIC: 3811
Plan	ESOP (1977); plan owns around 30%.
Coverage	All employees 21 or over with 1,000 hours of service.
Background	Hunter Associates Laboratory set up its ESOP out of a belief that as true associates, employees should have a share of corporate growth, and that as owners, associates would be more concerned and productive. The company currently employs about 135 people. Hunter Lab is the only company in the world exclusively devoted to the measurement of product appearance. It develops its products from the R&D stage to marketing.
Plan Structure	ESOP stock is distributed according to salary and vests at 40% after four years, increasing 10% per year to 100% after ten. Stock is distributed at a break in service. The company operates a profit-based pension plan and a 401(k) savings plan. Employees do not vote their shares.
Participation Features	Hunter managers believe the ESOP is a vehicle for increasing awareness, pride, and a real sense of worker participation. Thus, they think it is very important to be able to pass dividends through to employees, as will be encouraged by the new tax law.
Company Performance	Hunter had been growing steadily. Open lines of communication and knowledge of the operation of the ESOP directly affected the ability of Hunter Lab to work its way through the 1982 recession and to grow more rapidly in the years since.
Contact	Phil Hunter Hunter Associates Laboratory 11495 Sunset Hills Rd. Reston, VA 22290

HYATT CLARK INDUSTRIES, INC.

Product/Industry	Manufacturer of tapered roller bearings (automotive). SIC: 3562
Plan	Employee Stock Ownership Plan (1981)
Coverage	All 1500 employees participate; 100% owned.

Background

In August 1980 General Motors announced plans to close its unprofitable Hyatt roller-bearing plant. Local UAW union leaders, joined later by plant managers, began an effort to buy the plant in order to save jobs. In exchange for ownership, workers accepted a 25% pay cut, new work rules, and a 50% reduction in benefits. Also, Hyatt put together a financial package including $33 million in loans to leverage the buyout, a $10-million non-voting stock sale to General Motors, and a three-year purchase agreement with GM. In 1981 the new firm, Hyatt Clark Industries, was underway.

Plan Structure

The ESOP trust holds 100% of the common stock. In 1991, when Hyatt's loans are repaid, shares will become fully vested and workers will receive voting rights. Shares are allocated equally to all employees.

In addition to the ESOP, Hyatt has established a productivity bonus plan and a semi-annual profit-sharing plan.

Participation Features

Hyatt has had difficulty in the transition from a traditional management and labor-relations style to a more democratic and participatory system. Nevertheless, employee ownership has introduced employee involvement in decision-making. The union has three of ten seats on the board of directors: two union officers and one designated outsider.

Workers meet regularly in productivity teams, similar to quality-of-work-life teams, and discuss day-to-day problems, propose solutions, and post them in common areas. Also, four times a week, ten self-selected hourly workers meet with the president in round-table discussions open to any subject.

Company Performance

Since the changes in work rules and the adoption of many employee suggestions, productivity at Hyatt is up by 80%. With the revival of the national economy, especially the increase in automobile sales, the company made a profit in 1983. Employment at Hyatt returned to its pre-recession level of 1500 workers in 1983, almost double the 800 workers when the ESOP was established.

More Information

"Hyatt-Clark Industries, Inc. Buyout." Harvard Business School Cases: 9–383–122 and 0–484–042.

Contacts

Howard E. Kurt, President
Hyatt Clark Industries, Inc.
1300 Raritan Road
Clark, NJ 07066
(201) 499–6500

Jim May, President
UAW Local 736
80 Central Ave.
Clark, NJ   07066
(201) 381–2459

THE JOURNAL COMPANY

Product/Industry	Newspapers, Broadcasting and Printing. SIC: 4832, 2711
Plan	Employee Stock Trust Agreement (1937)
Coverage	About 2,000 employees own 90% of the company.
Background	In accordance with the will of the deceased majority shareholder, who hoped to have ownership and control of the Journal remain local, the Journal trust was started. Employee ownership grew from 25% to 90%.
Plan Structure	The stock is sold to employees with three years of service using a complicated formula which spreads ownership among all employees based on salary and seniority. The Stock Trust Agreement prevents the ownership of stock from passing into the hands of individuals who do not have direct involvement in the Journal. Retirees must sell one-tenth of their holding within a year of retiring and a like amount each year until all stock is returned to the trust fund. In event of death all shares must be sold to the trust fund.
Participation Features	In 1943, a plan for a unitholders (stockholders) council of 24 members to represent employee owners' interests was proposed and accepted. No major executives are eligible for election to the body, which serves as an advisory body to management. Each of seven major areas of the business elects members to the Council to serve for two years. In addition, each area elects one unitholder to serve on the company Board of Directors.
Company Performance	The Milwaukee Journal, a five-time Pulitzer-Prize-winning newspaper, began diversifying in the 1960s. The Journal Company now owns one additional newspaper, three weekly newspapers, printing companies, two commercial television stations, radio stations, a microwave common carrier, an audio-visual company, and "shoppers" (advertising papers).
More Information	"Employee Ownership." December 1981
	Werner Severin. "The Milwaukee Journal: Employee Owned Prizewinner." *Journalism Quarterly.* Winter 1979.

Contact   Thomas McCollon, President
                        The Journal Company
                        Box 661
                        Milwaukee, Wisconsin 53201
                        (414) 224–2000

LESLIE PAPER COMPANY

Product/Industry	Wholesale paper distributor. SIC: 5110, 5111, 5086, 5112, 5113
Plan	ESOP (1975); plan owns around 75%.
Coverage	All full-time non-union employees with one year of service.
Background	James Leslie's grandfather founded Leslie Paper in 1894. In the late 1960s, Leslie decided that the paternalistic structure of the company had created "dependency and cynicism among employees" and that innovation had become very difficult. The company's performance was deteriorating. Leslie thus told his father that either he would purchase the company or leave. His father agreed to the sale in 1969, and soon thereafter Leslie set up an employee ownership program, later to become an ESOP. The firm now employs 200 people.
Plan Structure	Details on plan structure were not available. The teamster employees, a minority of the workers, do not participate in the ESOP as they have their own benefit plans, and the ESOP contributions would put their total benefits over legal maximums.
Participation Features	The company has now become very open and participative. Employees are encouraged to suggest ideas and act on them. Drivers, for instance, suggested that the computerized route structures were inefficient and devised a more efficient system of their own. Employees conducted their own warehouse safety inspection, and came up with changes that lowered insurance costs.
Company Performance	The company has performed extremely well since setting up the ESOP, growing at a compound rate of 20%, despite no increase in employment, a record that indicates a considerable increase in productivity.
Contact	James Leslie
Leslie Paper Products
P.O. Box 1351

Shelard Tower
Minneapolis, MN   55440
(612) 540–0700

Miscellaneous Drivers and Helpers Union
Local #638
3001 University Avenue
Minneapolis, MN 55414

THE LOWE'S COMPANIES

Product/Industry	Wholesale/retail building materials. SIC: 5411
Plan	Profit-Sharing Plan (1957, effective 6/1/56) Employee Stock Ownership Plan (1978)
Coverage	All full-time employees participate; 30% owned.
Background	The founder began a profit-sharing plan in 1957 and planned to sell blocks of his stock to the plan periodically during his lifetime. He died unexpectedly in 1960. The profit-sharing plan took out a loan to buy the company from his estate, then made a public offering of shares to pay for the loan. The profit-sharing plan retained 48% interest.
	During the 1970s many employees retired with huge profit-sharing accounts: $400,000 to $3.5 million. Also, the profit-sharing plan began diversifying investments in accordance with "prudent man's rule." As a result, the percentage owned by employees fell to 17% by 1977. Management introduced an ESOP in 1978 in order to rebuild employee ownership of the company.
Plan Structure	All employees participate after January 1 or July 1 after completing 500 hours. Vesting begins at 10% after the second year, builds at 5% per year until it reaches 50% after the tenth year, and continues at 10% per year until it reaches 100% after 15 years. Allocation is according to salary.
	Lowe's generally contributes between 12% and 15% of payroll annually.
Participation Features	Lowe's employees vote allocated shares; a board-selected ESOP committee votes unallocated shares. Board members are selected by shareholders. Each of Lowe's 250 stores elects a representative to an ESOP Advisory Committee which hears

management reports and makes recommendations. Employees receive information on company finances and long-range plans. Stores hold employee meetings at least once a month.

Company Performance

Lowe's has experienced phenomenal growth under employee ownership. The company had 6 stores in 1957; today Lowe's is the largest building supplies retailer in the United States. Sales reached $1.4 billion in 1982.

More Information

"The Lowe's Companies ESOP." ESOP Association of America.

"ESOPs of the Home Improvement Industry." *Building Supply News.* August 1982.

The 100 Best Companies in America to Work For. Robert Levering, Milton Moskowitz, and Michael Katz. Reading, MA: Addison-Wesley Publishing Company, 1984.

Contact

Edgar M. Spears
Director, Personnel Operations
Lowe's Companies, Inc.
P.O. Box 1111
North Wilkesboro, NC   28656
(919) 667–3111

NORTH AMERICAN TOOL AND DIE, INC.

Product/Industry

Computer components contract manufacturer. SIC: 3544

Plan

Employee Stock Ownership Plan (1978)

Coverage

Full-time employees participate; percent owned not available.

Background

Hundreds of the parts produced at North American Tool And Die have a tolerance of ± 0.001 of an inch (1/4 thickness of human hair). Therefore, the success of the company depends entirely on employees caring a great deal about the quality of their performance. Sharing ownership through the ESOP was seen as one tool to insure high employee motivation.

Plan Structure

Employees must be at least 24 years old, work a minimum of 1,000 hours per year, and be on the payroll at the end of the year in order to be eligible to participate.

Participation Features

Monthly meetings are held to recognize the "Super Person of the Month" and to provide information on the performance of the company and its plans for the future. Compensation reviews are held twice a year to present the opportunity to employees for a one-on-one performance review with their bosses.

Company
Performance

In the six years since the inception of the plan the company's sales have tripled, profits have increased by six times, and turnover has dropped sharply. The customer rejection rate has dropped from 6% to 0.2%.

More Information

"How To Build Employee Trust And Productivity." Harvard Business Review. January–February 1983. Vol. 61 no. 1.

Contact

Thomas Melohn, President
North American Tool And Die
999 Beecher Street
San Leandro, CA   94577
(415) 632–9263

THE NORTH FACE

Product/Industry

Manufacturer, wholesaler, and retailer of outdoor equipment and apparel. SIC: 2389

Plan

ESOP (1975); plan owns around 14%.

Coverage

Full-time employees with over 1,000 hours of service.

Background

The North Face is a 525-employee company established in 1967. It makes high-quality outdoor products and has 50% of the tent and backpack market and 20% of the apparel market. It operates 17 retail stores in five states, as well as manufacturing its own product. Half of its employees are immigrants from 30 different countries.

The company's ESOP was set up both to provide liquidity for its shareholders and to motivate employees.

Plan Structure

Stock is allocated according to salary and vests at 20% after the end of the second year and 10% per year thereafter. Employees do not vote their stock and receive it at a break in service. Up to 25% of the vested portion of an account can be withdrawn in emergency cases.

Participation
Features

The company has a long tradition of allowing employees to have meetings about any subject they want. Employees have the right to petition management about issues they think need resolution. The company also makes an extraordinary effort to communicate with employees about the ESOP and the company, an effort required by the fact employees speak 11 different languages. Translators are present at the meetings.

Company
Performance

The company has grown quickly since setting up its ESOP, but management believes employees are still not sufficiently aware of how the ESOP works and that the plan has not yet had a strong impact on company performance.

More Information

"The North Face." *Employee Ownership.* Sept., 1983, Arlington, VA: Nat'l Center for Employee Ownership.

Contact

Kevin Smith, Personnel Manager
The North Face
999 Harrison St.
Berkeley, CA   94710

O&O SUPERMARKETS

Product/Industry

Retail grocery. SIC: 5411

Plan

Worker Cooperative (1982)

Coverage

Store 1: 66% of 38 workers participate; 100% owned.
Store 2: 61% of 33 workers participate; 100% owned.
(note: percentages are changing, generally upward)

Background

In 1982 A&P announced that it was laying off 2,000 workers by closing most of its stores in Greater Philadelphia. In crisis negotiations the union got A&P to agree to reopen more than 50 of the stores through a subsidiary, Superfresh. Superfresh offered employees a profit-sharing plan in exchange for wage concessions.

The union deal with A&P also included a right of first refusal option for employees to buy any stores which Superfresh might decide to close in the future. Employees in two stores decided not to join Superfresh but to buy their stores from A&P and set up the first two Owned and Operated (O&O) Supermarkets. The two O&O markets have similar structures but are separate corporations.

Plan Structure

Worker-members buy into the cooperative by purchasing one $5,000 share through payroll deductions. This membership fee is the base of members' individual internal capital accounts. The cooperative periodically adds profits to or deducts losses from these accounts.

In each profitable accounting period the market allocates 30% of its after-tax income to a collective account. Then, the cooperative pays interest (not to exceed 12%) on that portion of the members' capital accounts representing the $5,000 membership share. Finally, the market allocates any remaining profits to individuals' accounts in proportion to hours worked that period. The cooperative defines hours worked as both paid hours and volunteer committee hours.

If losses occur the coop deducts 30% of the loss from the collective account, pays no interest on member shares, and deducts the remaining 70% of losses from individual accounts. Capital account deductions are also according to hours worked, perhaps creating a perverse incentive for workers to volunteer less when the business is in financial difficulty.

Participation
Features

In each O&O workers participate on standing and ad hoc committees and attend employee meetings. Members elect the board of directors in both stores on a one member/one vote basis. Ten members and two outsiders serve on the board which hires a non-member manager.

The O&O cooperatives have defined the authority of the manager, the board, and the general membership along three dimensions: time, money, and number of members affected. Decisions on matters of less than one year, less than $3,000, or affecting less than seven members, are the manager's domain. The board decides matters between one to three year's duration, $3,000 to $10,000, or affecting seven to 50% of the members. All other decisions are reserved for the general membership.

In 1982 all full-time employees purchased shares and became worker-members. Since then, the two stores have hired a number of part-time and some full-time non-members. In 1984 a committee of workers began looking for a way to include non-members in participation, profit-sharing, and ownership.

Company
Performance

Since becoming worker owned the O&O's have outsold the A&P markets they replaced. Roslyn, the first store, has increased sales by 40%, and Parkwood Manor, the second store, by 20%. The Parkwood O&O has even opened a second market.

More Information

Dennis Clark and Merry Guben. *Future Bread*. The O&O Investment Fund. Philadelphia, PA 19106.

"Workers Take Over the Store." *The New York Times Magazine*. September 11, 1983.

Contact

Martin Gusoff, President
O&O Supermarket
925 Easton Street

Roslyn, PA   19001
(215) 572–6876

Joe Offner, President
O&O Supermarket
12311 Academy Rd.
Philadelphia, PA   19154
(215) 824–3131

Wendell Young, President
UFCW Local 1357
210 East Courtland Street
Philadelphia, PA   19120
(215) 457–5200

PARSONS COMPANY

Product/Industry	Construction and Engineering. SIC: 8911
Plan	ESOP; plan owns 100%.
Coverage	All full-time employees after one year of service.
Background	The Parsons Company is one of the largest construction and engineering firms in the country. It was publicly owned through 1984, although its ESOP owned 26% of the voting stock. With the passage of the Deficit Reduction Act of 1984, it saw an opportunity to become 100% employee owned. The new law allowed banks to deduct 50% of the interest income they received from a loan to an ESOP, thus reducing the interest rates the company needed to pay (since the bank would pass through some of the benefit). Parsons' management felt it no longer needed the reporting burden of being publicly held, since it was generating enough of a surplus each year to finance its own growth. Moreover, it felt employees would be more supportive of long-term investment policies than outside shareholders. Management also had long believed that employees should be more like partners than employees.
Plan Structure	Details on the plan structure are not yet available, but the plan will most likely follow conventional ESOP design. The employees will have full voting rights on their allocated shares.
Participation Features	Information on participation programs was not available at press time.

Company Performance	The company had a 19% increase in earnings in 1983 over 1982, despite the depression in its industry. It has been a consistently profitable firm.
More Information	"The Tax Magic That's Making Employee Stock Plans." *Business Week.* October 15, 1984. pp. 158–159.
Contact	William Leonhard, President Parsons Company 100 W. Walnut St. Pasadena, CA 91124 (213) 440–2000

PEOPLE EXPRESS

Product/Industry	Airline. SIC: 4511
Plan	Stock Purchase (1981); employees own around 33%.
Coverage	All full-time employees.
Background	People Express has been the fastest-growing airline in history. Established after airline deregulation, the company has an unusual and highly publicized philosophy based on employee participation and responsibility. It now employs 4,000 people and continues to grow. Its market strategy is to offer the lowest fares in any market, and to make a profit by keeping its own costs down and its seat occupancy rate high.
Plan Structure	All full-time employees are required to purchase stock in the company. Each employee must buy a specified minimum number of shares at a sharp discount, and can buy additional shares at lower discounts. Stock can be purchased outright or over a period of years through payroll deductions. Employees cannot sell the stock for a period of years, but the company is considering plans that would require employees not to sell their stock while still employed. Base pay is much lower than that of the pre-deregulation airlines (but similar to the post-deregulation carriers), but is augmented by two profit-sharing plans which contribute about 15% of pay.
Participation Features	The company calls all its employees "managers" and organizes them into teams for each area of operation (flight, customer service, etc.). These small teams handle their responsibility without supervision. Customer service managers, for instance, handle check-in, in-flight services, ticketing (done on board), and so on. Teams decide how to organize this work

and can rotate jobs. Employees are also cross-utilized, expected to do work in different areas of the company periodically. The stock is voting stock, and shareholder meetings are held quarterly to discuss company affairs. There is very little staff management, and what management there is is promoted from within.

Company Performance

The company's success is already legendary. Many employees have already accumulated $100,000 to $200,000 worth of stock, and the average ownership per employee is close to $40,000 (1984). There are more than 100 applicants per job.

More Information

"People Express," in Robert Levering, Milton Moskowitz, and Michael Katz, *The 100 Best Companies in America to Work For."* Reading, MA: Addison-Wesley, 1984.

Contact

Donald Burr
People Express Airlines
Newark International Airport
Newark, NJ   07114

PHILLIPS PAPER CORPORATION

Product/Industry

Distribution of food-packaging products. SIC: 5113

Plan

Employee Stock Purchase/Bonus Plan (1973)
Profit Sharing Plan (1973) (1983)

Coverage

74% of 42 employees participate; 18% owned.

Background

Current president Gil Phillips bought the company from the original partners in 1973. Phillips introduced the plan in order to provide an incentive to workers and to promote the point of view that workers also ought to be owners.

Plan Structure

After two years of service employees may purchase stock from Phillips at 85% of book value. Purchases can be through payroll deductions. Employees also receive bonuses after 5, 10, 15, and 20 years.

The profit-sharing plan allocates 7.5% of the previous year's profits to employees according to seniority. In January 1983 the plan began awarding an additional 5% of profits, provided the company retains a cash surplus. This 5% is distributed equally among employees. If employees purchase ten or more shares within two weeks of the profit distribution they receive a bonus of ten shares.

Employee owners are immediately vested, but must hold bonus shares for two years. In addition, they may sell shares only back to the company or to other employees.

Phillips Paper also offers workers a pension plan, a personal loan plan, a car purchase plan, and tuition for work-related education.

Participation Features	The board of directors consists of the president, two other officers, and six non-managerial employees elected by the workers. Also, all workers belong to one of four job committees. Job committees are similar to quality circles and cover several functional areas including sales, office, warehouse and local delivery, and statewide delivery. Employees also have a majority of seats on an operations committee and a management committee. The board can veto committee decisions, but has never done so.
Company Performance	Profits as a percent of pre-tax sales rose 538% in the three years after the plan started, compared to the three years before. Sales per employee are higher than in any of the publicly traded companies in the industry. Employees responding to the NCEO survey showed an unusually high degree of job satisfaction, significantly higher than most other companies sampled.
More Information	*Employee Ownership.* June 1983. National Center for Employee Ownership.
Contact	Gil Phillips, President Phillips Paper Corporation P.O. Box 20067 3000 East Houston Street San Antonio, TX 78219 (512) 227–2397

PUBLIX SUPERMARKETS

Product/Industry	Supermarkets. SIC: 5411
Plan	Direct purchase plan (from outset); profit sharing; ESOP (1975); direct purchase plan owns 84%; profit sharing 10%; ESOP 6%.
Coverage	All full-time employees for ESOP; all employees are eligible to buy stock.
Background	Publix, with 15,000 full-time and 15,000 part-time employees in 262 stores, is Florida's largest supermarket chain, and

one of the industry's most successful firms. Its founder believed that employees should be owners and set up a plan under which employees could buy shares. It later set up a profit-sharing plan and then an ESOP as a mechanism for broadening ownership.

Plan Structure

84% of the stock is owned by 6,500 employees. There are limits on how much each employee can buy, so that stock can be dispersed. Another 10% is owned by a profit-sharing plan and 6% by an ESOP, both of which are organized along the usual lines. The individually held stock carries full voting rights, and the company will buy it back when employees leave. There is also a bonus plan equal to two weeks' pay and a profit-sharing plan at each store which allocates 20% of profits to employees.

Participation
Features

The company does not have formal participation programs, but does provide detailed financial information to its employees. Employees are also expected to participate in the promotion of the store, which many apparently do.

Company
Performance

Publix has been very successful. Its stock value increased from $10 in 1960 to $360 in 1983. Many employees have left with a half-million dollars in stock.

More Information

"Publix Supermarkets," in Robert Levering, Milton Moskowitz and Michael Katz, *The 100 Best Companies in America to Work For*. Reading, MA: Addison-Wesley, 1984.

Contact

Keith Billups, Vice-President
Publix Supermarkets
Box 407
Lakeland, FL   33802
(813) 688–1188

QUAD/GRAPHICS

Product/Industry

Printing. SIC: 2752

Plan

ESOP (1974); plan owns about 20%.

Coverage

All full-time employees after one year of service.

Background

Founded in 1971, Quad/Graphics has quickly become one of the major printers in the United States, printing *Playboy, U.S. News, Harpers,* and a variety of other major publications. It set up its ESOP both to purchase shares from the original owners and as part of its unique management philosophy, which stresses a high degree of employee involvement.

Plan Structure	Stock begins vesting at 40% after four years and vests at 10% per year thereafter; allocation is according to salary and stock is distributed at a break in service. Employees can take an early withdrawal for specified needs. Employees do not vote their shares. The company also offers a profit-sharing plan worth about 10–12% of salary.
Participation Features	The company is one of the most participative firms we have encountered. Employees work three-day, 12-hour weeks. One day a year, management leaves the plant altogether, leaving the running of the company to the employees. Employee groups are frequently asked to define their own areas of responsibility and create their own entrepreneurial centers. Departments set many of their own policies without interference from top management. Supervisors are kept to a minimum, and employees are expected to supervise themselves. The company also offers a variety of educational and other benefit packages as employee incentives.
Company Performance	The company has been a leading performer in its field, with growth rates of 30–40% per year, and profits to match. The company believes that employee ownership is an integral part of its overall philosophy, and that that philosophy is what makes it successful.
More Information	"Management by Walking Away." *Inc.* October 1983. pp. 68–76.
Contact	Harry Quadracci, President Quad/Graphics DuPlainville Road Pewaukee, WI 53072

THE RECORD FACTORY

Product/Industry	Retail trade. SIC: 5733, 5999
Plan	ESOP (1976); plan owns 96%.
Coverage	Employees with at least 83 hours of service in one year.
Background	Established in 1971, the Record Factory has now grown to 32 retail stores in Northern California. The previous owner decided to sell in 1976, and the store's managers proposed an ESOP to buy it. The owner loaned the ESOP the funds to buy the shares. The company now employs 350 people, most of whom are less than 40 years old, and many of whom are part-time.

Plan Structure	Vesting is at 40% after four years and increases gradually to 100% after ten; allocation is according to salary; stock is distributed at a break in service. Employees do not vote their shares.
Participation Features	The store's management calls its style "informally participative." Top management seeks the input of store managers, and the managers seek the input of the employees.
Company Performance	When the ESOP was established eight years ago, the company had 10 stores; it now has 32. Profits have shown similar growth. Management believes the ESOP reduces theft, a major problem in the industry, and makes it more likely that employees will stay with the company, despite the low pay that typifies retailers in this field.
More Information	"The Record Factory." *Employee Ownership.* March 1983.
Contact	Barbara Hardman, Vice-President The Record Factory 99 Park Lane Brisbane, CA 94005

RIVERSIDE CONSTRUCTION

Product/Industry	General engineering construction for streets and highways. SIC: 3241
Plan	ESOP (1981); plan owns about 25%.
Coverage	Full-time employees.
Background	Riverside was formed in 1967 as a partnership. It has grown considerably since then, and anticipates further growth with the new construction created by the gas tax. It now employs 75 people. The plan was set up as an employee incentive and a means to encourage workers to stay with the company. As is common in the construction industry, employment fluctuates depending on the contracts the company currently has.
Plan Structure	Allocation is according to salary, with vesting starting at 30% after three years and increasing 10% per year thereafter. Stock is distributed at retirement and employees do not vote their shares. Key employees have a bonus plan. There are separate pension plans for union and non-union employees. The company has contributed near the limit for annual ESOP contributions.

Participation Features	The company has no formal participation programs, but the president spends a great deal of time in the field talking with individual employees.
Company Performance	The company has grown from a very small firm to its current size in just ten years. Management believes it has always had a good rapport with employees, and that the ESOP adds to this. They also think it is helpful in retaining good people. The employees we surveyed were quite enthusiastic about the plan.
Contact	Gordon Lounsbury, Secretary-Treasurer Riverside Construction 111 Main Street Riverside, CA 92501 (415) 391-7540

RURAL/METRO, INC.

Product/Industry	Private emergency services. SIC: 8999
Plan	ESOP (1978); plan owns around 63%.
Coverage	All full-time and part-time employees with over 200 hours.
Background	Rural/Metro is the largest provider of private fire protection in the country, focusing primarily on Arizona. It also provides ambulance service, security services, and security product sales. It was established in 1948 and now employs over 1,300 people. Its ESOP was established as a mechanism to transfer ownership from the principal owner and as a means to provide employees, who have a great deal of responsibility and minimal direct supervision, with an incentive.
Plan Structure	Stock is allocated according to relative pay and is distributed at separation. The company does not pass through voting rights.
Participation Features	There are no formal participation programs, but employees are expected to assume considerable responsibility for their jobs, and employees have been very involved in product design and service innovations.
Company Performance	Since the ESOP was set up, company sales have more than tripled, and a loss situation was turned around to one of substantial profits. While the company does not credit all of this to the ESOP, it believes the ESOP has made a very important contribution.

Contact   Jim Bolin, Vice-President
                        Rural/Metro Corporation
                        P.O. Drawer F
                        Scottsdale, AZ   85252

SCIENCE APPLICATIONS INTERNATIONAL, INC.

Product/Industry   Diversified high-technology research, development, and
                        manufacturing. SIC: 7374

Plan   Direct Purchases and Bonuses (1969)
                        Profit-Sharing Retirement Plan (1973)
                        Stock Bonus Retirement Plan (1981)

Coverage   90% of 6,000 employees participate; 20% owned by retire-
                        ment plans, an additional 64% owned directly.

Background   Science Applications began in 1979 as an employee-owned
                        firm for philosophical reasons but also to provide an incen-
                        tive to employees. At first the company offered stock as a
                        bonus to key employees. Later, it offered stock to all em-
                        ployees through profit-sharing and wage deductions.

Plan Structure   The company contributes funds to the profit-sharing retire-
                        ment plan ($5.7 million in 1982). The profit-sharing plan
                        also accepts voluntary (after-tax) contributions from par-
                        ticipants. Employees choose from among a Fixed Income
                        Fund, a Diversified Fund, and a Company Stock Fund for in-
                        vestment of their profit-sharing accounts. The Profit-Sharing
                        Committee selects professional investment managers to
                        manage the Fixed Income Fund and Diversified Fund.

                        Stock Bonus Funds are invested in company stock. Retiring
                        employees may hold their shares, sell them back to the com-
                        pany at book value, or trade them in a limited market
                        through one broker-dealer.

Participation   Employees vote their shares and elect the board of directors.
Features   The board has 15 members, 8 of whom specifically represent
                        non-managerial employees.

Company   Equity per share grew from $.40 in 1973 to $4.20 by 1982.
Performance   Employment growth has also been phenomenal, from 300 to
                        3,600 employees during the same 9-year period. Company
                        executives "absolutely" attribute company performance to
                        employee ownership.

Contact	Stephen P. Meyer
	Corporate Vice-President and Treasurer
	Science Applications
	P.O. Box 2351
	La Jolla, CA 92037
	(714) 456–6040

THE SOLAR CENTER

Product/Industry	Marketing/installation of solar hot-water systems for apartment buildings. SIC: 1711, 1731, 1799
Plan	Worker Cooperative (1976)
	Profit Sharing Plan (1976)
	Employee Stock Ownership Plan (1978)
Coverage	All 25 employees participate; 100% owned.
Background	Five founders contributed $5,000 each to start up as a cooperative. They believed that a workplace "should blend democracy with efficiency." In 1978 the coop set up an ESOP to take advantage of tax breaks. The Solar Center is one of a few companies which blends cooperative and ESOP structures.
Plan Structure	There is a 12-month probationary period before new workers can become member-owners. Workers vote to accept new members. New members invest $3,000 in the Solar Center, which can be paid through payroll deductions. The ESOP allocates stock according to hours worked.
	Cash profit-sharing is based one-third on shares owned, one-third on months worked that year, and one-third on total months at Solar Center.
Participation Features	Workers vote one person/one vote. Workers elect an executive group which meets frequently to make decisions. The entire membership meets monthly and takes semi-annual retreats for long-term planning.
Company Performance	Despite changing government policy and energy needs the Solar Center's sales have grown steadily from $800,000 in 1978 to over $2 million in 1982. The number of member-owners has doubled to 25 since 1979.
More Information	*The Solar Center Employee Owner's Manual.* Available from the National Center for Employee Ownership. $8 members; $12 others.

"The Solar Center: A Case Study." *Employee Ownership.*
September 1984. National Center for Employee Ownership.

Contact   Janis Medina, President
                   The Solar Center
                   1115 Indiana Street
                   San Francisco, CA   94107

TRANSCON

Product/Industry	Trucking. SIC: 4213
Plan	ESOP (1983); around 49% owned.
Coverage	All employees taking concession in 1983.
Background	Deregulation in the trucking industry caused severe economic problems for many unionized firms, all of whom were now faced with new, non-union competition. Transcon is the nation's tenth largest carrier, and had a net loss in 1982 of $8.8 million. Transcon both needed to reduce costs and to raise new capital for better equipment. In 1983, therefore, it went to its unions and asked for a voluntary 12% pay cut over the next five years in return for 49% of the company and representation on the board of directors. The cuts were to be made outside the union contract; employees who chose not to make them would remain with the company but not receive the stock. Over 90% of Transcon's 3,670 employees agreed.
Plan Structure	Stock is allocated to all employees who agreed to the concessions on the basis of those concessions; distribution is made at termination; vesting is immediate. The company is retaining its pension plan. As a publicly held company, the employees are entitled to vote the shares allocated to them on all issues.
Participation Features	Employees elect three of the 13-person board, and can elect additional members as their voting share increases. Employee involvement teams will be set up at the job level, and the company is making a strenuous effort to communicate how ownership works to the employees.
Company Performance	Transcon president Joe Hall says flatly that the ESOP saved the company. The company has returned to profitability and has been able to embark on a major investment program. Productivity is also up.
More Information	"Another ESOP Fable." *California Business.* March 1984. pp. 55–60.

Contact | John Hollingsworth, Vice-President
Transcon Lines
P.O. Box 92220
Los Angeles, CA   90009

UP-RIGHT, INC.

Product/Industry | Manufacture and marketing of metal staging and mobile work platforms. SIC: 3441, 3446, 3494, 3523, 5074

Plan | Profit-Sharing Plan (1952)
Employee Stock Ownership Plan (1975)
Pension Guarantee Plan (1981)

Coverage | All U.S. employees participate; 40% owned.

Background | The company founder instituted a profit-sharing plan in 1952 to promote his philosophy that every worker should participate in ownership. The plan received one-half of profits above 5% of annual sales. The plan invested one-half of its assets in Up-Right stock. In 1975 the profit-sharing plan converted to an ESOP in order to distribute a larger share of profits to employees.

Plan Structure | The ESOP defines two contribution plans. The Stock Purchase Plan must contribute 8% of covered payroll each year. The Stock Bonus Plan may contribute an additional amount of equity depending upon company profitability. Contributions to the ESOP from either plan may be cash or stock.

ESOP shares are allocated according to salary and are vested at 6.66% per year, with full vesting in 15 years. Employees may partition to withdraw part of their equity for (1) downpayment on first home, (2) emergency medical expenses, (3) educational expenses, or (4) living expenses during layoff.

The Pension Guarantee Plan establishes a floor benefit value for retiring employees. The pension plan kicks in to make up the difference between the value of an employee's holdings and a defined minimum retirement benefit. Up-Right created the Pension Guarantee to protect employees from low stock prices during a period when its over-the-counter stock price was particularly volatile.

Up-Right also has a Productivity Bonus Plan for manufacturing employees.

Participation Features	Voting rights are passed through on all allocated shares as required by law in publicly traded firms, although voting was passed through even when Up-Right was closely held prior to 1980. The ESOP committee has always voted unallocated shares in the same proportion as allocated share votes. Employees receive a proxy solicitation for the annual stockholders' meeting.
	Up-Right schedules periodic employee meetings to discuss both the ESOP and general operations of the company. The ESOP committee publishes a special bulletin for employees and is very open about sharing corporate information.
Company Performance	Up-Right experienced its first loss in 1981 during the recent recession but has been recovering in 1982 and 1983 with modest profits. Dividends were paid (but not passed through) until 1983 and may resume in 1984 (with pass-through to employees). Bonuses had been paid nearly every quarter until 1983.
More Information	*Employee Ownership.* September 1983. National Center for Employee Ownership.
	"The Up-Right ESOP." ESOP Association of America.
Contact	Donald Reichert Vice-President, Administration Chairman, ESOP Committee Up-Right, Inc. 1013 Pardee Street Berkeley, CA 94710 (910) 366–7347

WEIRTON STEEL COMPANY

Product/Industry	Integrated steelmaker. SIC: 3312, 3479
Plan	ESOP (1984); plan owns 100%.
Coverage	All employees.
Background	Weirton Steel was a division of National Steel. In 1982, National announced that it would either reduce Weirton to a small finishing mill or sell it to the employees. The employees and Weirton's management formed a joint study committee to evaluate the possibility of a buyout. The company had been profitable most of its history, but had posted either unimpressive earnings or losses after 1974. The company is the

economic cornerstone of the Upper Ohio Valley, employing 7,000 people in a community of 26,000. An extraordinary effort was made by the employees and the community to save the company.

The feasibility study for the buyout indicated the company could be profitable if the employees took a 32% pay cut. Weirton employees, however, had been the best paid in the industry. Later, this figure was reduced to 20% because National agreed to assume certain pension and retiree health costs. National was willing to do this because they would be responsible for pension costs if Weirton were to close within five years (a legal and contractual requirement). These could amount to over $700 million, so National obviously wanted Weirton to succeed.

Weirton obtained most of the $386 million it needed to finance the buyout from private sources. It now must raise another $700 million to modernize the company. The buyout agreement was complicated, with the new company making an initial downpayment of $70 million, with further promissory notes due to National in 1993 and 1998.

Plan Structure

Stock is allocated according to salary, but employees will vote their shares on a one-person, one-vote basis, and vote them on all issues. Until stock is distributed in 1988, the stock will be voted by the trustee of the ESOP according to the direction of employees. Employees are eligible after working one hour in one year. The initial board has three union-picked representatives, with the remaining nine members chosen by the firm's financial advisors. Employees will be able to elect a majority of the board in five to seven years.

A profit-sharing plan will begin in the year following the year in which the company attains $100 million in net worth; if the company attains a net worth of $250 million, a second plan would begin with higher benefit levels. Both plans would provide substantial additional income.

Participation Features

Employee participation teams are being set up at all levels of the company on a gradual basis. The company has a strong commitment to participative management, and formal employee involvement programs, including training for participation, are being set up.

Company Performance

During its first three quarters as an ESOP company, Weirton increased employment from 7,000 to 8,000 and reported $48 million in profits, the highest profits per ton in the industry.

It also has added 200 new customers to its customer base. Employment has fluctuated somewhat with industry demand.

More Information   Jonathan Rowe. "Weirton Steel: Buying Out the Bosses." *Washington Monthly*. January 1984. pp. 34–38.

"Making Money—and History—At Weirton." *Business Week*. November 12, 1984. pp. 136–40.

Contact   Robert Loughead, President
Weirton Steel Company
Weirton, WV   26062

Walter Bish
Independent Steelworkers Union
Weirton Steel Company
Weirton, WV   26062

Charles Cronin
Manager, Corporate Public Relations
Weirton Steel Company
Weirton, WV   26062

WESTERN AIRLINES

Product/Industry	Commercial passenger airline. SIC: 4511
Plan	401(a) Employee Stock Plan (1983) Profit-Sharing Plan (1983)
Coverage	All 10,500 employees participate; 32% owned.
Background	With airline deregulation, Western faced new competition from low-cost carriers and the company suffered four straight years of losses totaling $200 million. In order to bring costs down the company and its unions negotiated the Western Partnership in 1983.
Plan Structure	Employees accepted wage cuts between 10% and 18% in exchange for 32% of the company's stock. A special trust, similar to an ESOP trust, holds the employees' stock. Because the plan is not technically an ESOP it cannot borrow money.

The profit-sharing plan will last at least until it distributes $2 million to employees. Employees will receive 15% of Western's first $25 million in pre-tax profits and 20% of pre-tax profits over $20 million. On a $30 million profit the average employee would receive $475.

Participation Features	Employees can vote their stock on major corporate issues such as mergers, tender offers, sale, or formation of a holding company. They also elect two members of the board of directors. A "Partnership Committee" with employee representatives monitors the plan. The company held employee meetings to describe the plan and employees may call a toll-free number for more information.
Company Performance	Western's plan is too new to evaluate other than to report that labor and management are committed to the effort and believe it is essential to the company's future. The concessions were originally for one year but have recently been extended and deepened.
More Information	"Western Fights Back." *Air Transport World.* April 1984.
Contact	John F. Thelen Director, Compensation and Benefits Western Airlines P.O. Box 92005 World Way Postal Center Los Angeles, CA 90009 (213) 646–2345

Union Representatives on Partnership Committee:

Susan Edwards
Association of Flight Attendants

James Shields
Air Transport Employees

Ken Green
Transport Workers Union

Joel Jensen
Air Line Pilots' Association

Ray Benning
International Brotherhood of Teamsters

WORKERS' OWNED SEWING COMPANY

Product/Industry	Garment sewing. SIC: 2342
Plan	Worker Cooperative (1979)
Coverage	All 60 full-time employees participate; 100% owned.
Background	In 1966 a group of 800 residents of rural Bertie County, North Carolina purchased shares to start Bertie Industries (BI),

a cut-and-sew factory which did subcontracting for garment manufacturers. As a mostly minority-owned business in one of the ten poorest counties in the country, BI received grants, loans, and management assistance from the Small Business Administration.

At its height, the company employed about 120 low-skilled workers. But the company was poorly managed, had very low productivity, and in 1976 the SBA withdrew its support. Two years later, BI went bankrupt.

Tim Bazemore, one of BI's founders, and a team of consultants from the Twin Streams Educational Center and the University of North Carolina decided to restart the business as a worker cooperative. The new business, the Workers' Owned Sewing Company, opened in 1979.

Plan Structure

At first Bazemore owned all of the shares in the coop. By 1981 he began selling $100 shares to employees through $2 to $5 per week payroll deductions. Each full-time employee must hold one and only one share which does not increase in value.

The company records any increases (or decreases) in equity in employees' individual internal capital accounts. Employees sell their $100 share and withdraw the value of their capital accounts when they leave Workers' Owned.

Workers' Owned members can earn productivity incentives to supplement their minimum-wage salaries. They may also borrow up to $150 interest-free from a company loan fund to meet their personal expenses.

Participation Features

All worker members vote to elect the seven-member board of directors which is composed exclusively of workers, makes major business decisions, and votes to hire or fire the plant manager. Employees also have bi-monthly lunch meetings and vote directly on many issues. For instance, in the summertime they voted to begin work at 5 AM in order to finish before the heat of mid-afternoon.

Company Performance

Workers' Owned made its first profits eight months after opening. In 1983 the cooperative started doing direct manufacturing for K–Mart and Sears instead of subcontracting for other manufacturers. Since then sales have increased dramatically to $600,000 in 1983 and almost $2 million in 1984.

Contact

Tim Bazemore, President
Workers' Owned Sewing Company
Windsor, NC
(919) 794–2708

Appendix II
Suggested Readings

LEGAL AND PRACTICAL GUIDES

Dennis Clark and Merry Guben. *Future Bread*. Philadelphia: O&O Investment Fund, 1983. $6.95.

   Describes how the "O&O" (owned and operated) worker-owned supermarkets were established in Philadelphia, and provides detailed, step-by-step guide on how to form a worker cooperative.

David Ellerman. "What is a Workers' Cooperative?" Industrial Cooperative Association, 249 Elm Street, Somerville, MA 02144.

   A good brief dicussion laying out the ICA's innovative cooperative structure model.

Robert Frisch. *ESOPs for the 80's*. Rockville Center, NY: Farnsworth Publishing Co., 1981. $25.

   A detailed look at ESOPs presented in layman's language.

Industrial Cooperative Association. *ICA Model By-Laws for Worker Cooperatives*. Available from the ICA for $40 to associates and $70 to non-associates. Price includes one hour of consulting.

   A detailed guide for setting up a worker cooperative.

Daniel Larson, Darrol Stanley, and James Warren. "ESOP Valuations of Closely Held Company Stock." *Financial Planner,* January 1981, pp. 2–6.

Ronald Ludwig and Jared Kaplan. *ESOPs*. Washington, D.C.: Bureau of National Affairs, Tax Management subsidiary. $40.

   A detailed explanation of ESOPs, containing technical explanations of legal issues, required legal forms, and a list of ESOP regulations and statutes.

National Center for Employee Ownership (NCEO). *An Employee Buyout Handbook*. Members—$12.50; Non-members—$25.00.

A detailed, step-by-step explanation of the steps necessary to evaluate whether an employee buyout is worth pursuing, including a variety of financial questions and guidelines.

NCEO. *A Model Employee Stock Ownership Plan.* Members—$75.00; Nonmembers—$100.00.

A 100-page compilation of the legal language for an ESOP, a plain English explanation of each provision, a suggested model for an employee handbook, a list of consultants, and other material. Contains several different options for tailoring plans to specific needs.

Robert Sellers. "Banks as Employee Stock Ownership Plan Sponsors and Lenders." Washington, D.C.: American Bankers Association, 1983. $25.00.

Introduction to the role of banks in ESOPs.

CASE STUDIES

Peter Barnes. "Confessions of a Socialist Entrepreneur." Available from the NCEO (members only) for $3.00.

The best article on what it actually is like to organize and run an employee-owned business, from the founder of the Solar Center.

Katrina Berman. *Worker Owned Plywood Companies.* Pullman, WA: Washington State University, 1967.

A pioneering study of worker plywood cooperatives.

"ESOPs: A Capital Idea." *INC.*, April 1982, pp. 36–46.

One of the best articles on how ESOPs are actually used.

Richard Long. "Job Attitudes and Organizational Performance Under Employee Ownership." *Academy of Management Journal,* December 1980, v. 23, no. 4, 726–737.

Examines effects of employee ownership on job attitudes in three firms and finds that positive impact is greatest when amount owned is highest and participation strongest.

Marc Miller. "Workers' Owned." *Southern Exposure*, v. 8, Winter 1980, pp. 12–21.

Case study of coop formed by low-income people in North Carolina.

Jonathan Rowe. "Weirton Steel: Buying Out the Bosses." *Washington Monthly,* January 1984, pp. 34–38.

Good discussion of the Weirton buyout.

John Simmons and William Mares. *Working Together.* New York: Alfred Knopf, 1983. $15.95.

Excellent account of over 50 companies using employee ownership or quality of worklife programs.

William F. Whyte, Tove Helland Hammer, Reed Nelson, Chris Meek and Robert Stern. *Worker Participation and Ownership.* Ithaca, NY: Cornell University, 1983.
> An outstanding look at several employee buyout cases and the Jamestown Area Labor-Management Committee program.

Linda Wintner. *Employee Buyouts: An Alternative to Plant Closings.* New York: The Conference Board, 1983. $25.
> A detailed look at several employee buyouts.

GENERAL STUDIES

Michael Conte and Arnold Tannenbaum. *Employee Ownership.* Ann Arbor: Survey Research Center, Univ. of Michigan, 1980. $8.00.
> A comprehensive study of the effects of employee ownership on profitability which finds that employee ownership firms are 1.5 times as profitable as conventional firms.

Karl Frieden. *Productivity and Workplace Democracy.* Washington, D.C.: National Center for Economic Alternatives, 1980.
> Summarizes the literature in this field.

Robert Jackall and Henry Levin, eds. *Worker Cooperatives in America.* Berkeley: University of California Press, 1985.
> A reader on worker cooperatives that brings together in one volume most of the best writings on the subject.

Louis Kelso and Mortimer Adler. *The Capitalist Manifesto.* New York: Random House, 1958.
> The basic book explaining Kelso's philosophy of broadened ownership.

Louis Kelso and Patricia Hetter. *Two-Factor Theory: The Economics of Reality.* New York: Random House, 1967.
> A briefer explanation of Kelso's theory.

Douglas Kruse. *Employee Ownership and Attitudes: Two Case Studies.* Norwood, PA: Norwood Editions, 1984. $15.95.
> Discusses two detailed case studies and the general philosophy of employee ownership.

Norman Kurland. "Beyond ESOPs: The Kelso-Adler Theory of Economic Justice." Available from the NCEO for $3.50 (members only).
> A complete bibliography on the philosophical writings on the theory of ESOPs and broadened ownership, briefly annotated.

Thomas Marsh and Dale McAllister. "ESOPs Tables: A Survey of Companies with Employee Stock Ownership Plans." *Journal of Corporation Law,* v. 6, no. 3, Spring 1981.

A survey of 229 companies with 10 or more employees. The best study available on the structure, performance, and characteristics of ESOP firms. It concludes with the finding that these companies are much more productive than their conventional counterparts.

NCEO. *Employee Ownership: A Bibliography.* Members—$8.00; Non-members —$13.00. 77 pp., partly annotated.

NCEO. *An Employee Ownership Reader.* Members—$10.00; Non-members— $15.00.

A comprehensive introduction to employee ownership, containing practical articles on ESOPs and cooperatives, case studies, suggestions on organizational development and legal structure, and more.

Deborah Groban Olson. "Some Union Experiences with Issues Raised by Worker Ownership in the U.S.: ESOPs, TRASOPs, Co-ops, Stock Plans and Board Representation." *Wisconsin Law Review,* December 1982.

An excellent review of unions' concerns and possibilities on these issues.

Corey Rosen and Katherine Klein. "Job-Creating Performance of Employee Ownership Companies." *Monthly Labor Review,* August 1983.

Reports a study of majority employee owned companies that showed that they created three times more net new jobs per year than comparable conventional firms.

Ira Wagner. "Report to the New York Stock Exchange on the Performance of Publicly Held Companies with Employee Ownership Plans." Arlington, VA: NCEO, 1984. Members—$10.00; Non-members—$12.50.

Report of a study of 13 publicly held companies at least 10% employee owned, which finds that they outperform their conventional counterparts.

FILMS

Bill Moyers Journal. "It's Not Working." WNET, 1980, 25 minutes, 16 mm, color. Rental $40. Available from California Newsreel, 630 Natoma St., San Francisco, CA 94103.

Examines closing of Youngstown steel mill and workers' efforts to buy it.

"The Mondragon Experiment." 58 mins., BBC. Available from California Newsreel, Rental $75.

An outstanding film on the Mondragon cooperatives, the largest and most successful worker-owned business network in the world.

CLIPPING SERVICE

The NCEO maintains a complete file of newspaper and other print media clippings from over 9,000 U.S. publications. Clipping service subscribers receive a bimonthly compilation of the clips. Members—$85; Non-members—$110.

Appendix III
Major Federal and State Laws

FEDERAL LAWS

1. *Regional Rail Reorganization Act of 1973*: This was the first statute to mention "ESOPs." It required a feasibility study of the use of an ESOP for the reorganization of the Northeast freight rail system into Conrail. The study eventually recommended against the idea.

2. *Employee Retirement and Income Security Act of 1974 (ERISA)*: This law created a specific statutory framework for ESOPs and carefully exempted them from certain requirements applicable to other plans (such as pension and profit sharing). The act thereby provided ESOPs with the unique authority among employee benefit plans to borrow money. It also required ESOPs to invest primarily in employer securities, whereas other employee benefit plans cannot invest more than 10% of their assets in employer securities unless they can demonstrate that to do so is fiduciarily sound. ESOPs were defined as "qualified employee benefit plans," meaning that contributions to them are tax deductible (within limits) and that they must abide by the allocation, vesting, and other rules ERISA applies to qualified benefit plans.

3. *Trade Act of 1974*: This act created an authority within the Department of Commerce to make certain kinds of assistance available for areas suffering adverse effects from foreign trade. The act contained provisions providing a preference for assisted firms using ESOPs, but they were never effectively implemented.

4. *Tax Reduction Act of 1975*: This act created the "TRASOP," the Tax Reduction Act Stock Ownership Plan. Under it, a company could get an additional 1% credit over and above the 10% Investment Tax Credit if an amount equal to at least 1% of the qualifying investment were contributed to an ESOP meeting the special rules of this act (including immediate vesting and allocation according to salary).

5. *Tax Reform Act of 1976*: This act extended the life of TRASOPs through 1980 and added a provision that allowed the employer an additional ½% credit if an employee contribution equal to ½% of the qualifying investment were matched by the

employer. The act contained an unusual congressional directive to the IRS to rewrite rules it had drafted earlier that Congress considered unfair to ESOPs.

6. *Revenue Act of 1978*: TRASOPs were extended to 1984 (this was later changed) and allocation and other rules for TRASOPs were tightened. The act also required leveraged ESOPs to offer employees a put option (the right to demand that the company repurchase an employee's shares at fair market value) where the stock was not publicly traded. A full pass-through of voting rights on all allocated shares was made mandatory for publicly traded companies, while closely held firms were required to pass through voting rights on issues which required more than a majority vote. These voting right rules applied to all ESOPs and, in closely held companies, to all qualified employee benefit plans investing more than 10% of their plan's assets in employer securities. Finally, the act created the General Stock Ownership Corporation, a special kind of statewide corporation in which all state residents could automatically become shareholders in state economic ventures. The idea was intended for Alaska, but never used.

7. *U.S. Railway Association Authorizations of 1979*: This act authorized an additional $2 million in loans to the Delaware and Hudson Railroad, provided the company set up an ESOP.

8. *Technical Corrections Act of 1979*: This act made a number of technical corrections to laws governing TRASOPs.

9. *ESOP Improvements Act of 1980*: This act further extended the TRASOP credit and made a variety of technical corrections to ESOP law. The act also made various technical changes in rules for employee contributions to TRASOPs.

10. *Small Business Employee Ownership Act*: Prior to this act, the SBA would not guarantee loans to ESOPs, and their rules for loans in other employee ownership situations were very restrictive. This act provided statutory authority for the SBA to make loan guarantees to ESOPs and made their rules for loans to employee ownership situations more liberal.

11. *Chrysler Loan Guarantee Act of 1980*: As part of the government's loan guarantee to Chrysler, the company was required to set up an ESOP and contribute $162.5 million worth of company stock to it by 1984.

12. *Economic Recovery Tax Act of 1981*: This act contained several important provisions. First, it phased out TRASOPs and replaced them with the "PAYSOP," payroll based stock ownership plan. Under the PAYSOP, a company could receive a tax credit equal to ½% of payroll for contributions to a PAYSOP of at least that amount in 1983 and 1984, increasing to .75% in 1985–7. Generally, PAYSOPs must follow the same rules that applied to TRASOPs, but with somewhat stricter allocation rules. Second, the act raised the limits on how much can be deducted for contributions to a leveraged ESOP. Under previous law, these were limited to 15% of payroll; under the new law they were raised to 25% of payroll to cover the principal part of the repayment and an unlimited amount for the interest portion.

Third, the act allowed companies that are substantially employee owned to require that departing employees take cash for the fair market value of their stock, rather than the stock itself, when receiving their ESOP distribution. Finally, the act broadened the put option requirement to include non-leveraged ESOPs.

13. *Tax Equity and Fiscal Responsibility Act of 1982*: This act tightened provisions for all employee benefit plans in an effort to address abuses occurring in some plans. "Top-heavy" plans, plans in which 60% of the benefits go to officers, highly compensated employees, and top shareholders, were required to set up faster vesting schedules and follow other rules designed to get more benefits to other employees. New limits were imposed on how much a company can deduct when it has more than one qualified employee benefit plan, and the dollar limit on annual additions to a participant's account was lowered from $47,475 to $30,000, adjustable for inflation after 1985.

14. *Trade Adjustment Assistance Act*: This act reauthorized the program, which can provide loans, loan guarantees, and technical assistance to firms adversely affected by foreign trade. The amendments provide that preference will be given to companies which channel at least 25% of the assistance they receive through an ESOP.

15. *Deficit Reduction Act of 1984*: This act contains the most significant incentives for employee ownership. They include:

a) A provision allowing an owner of an independent business to defer taxation on the gains made by a sale of stock to an ESOP or worker cooperative by reinvesting the gains within 12 months in the stock or stocks of other companies. When that new stock is sold, capital gains taxes would be due. At least 30% of the ownership of the firm must be held by the ESOP or cooperative after the transaction for the provision to be effective;

b) A provision allowing commercial lending institutions to deduct 50% of the interest income they receive from a loan to a company for the purpose of acquiring stock through an ESOP (the loan can be directly to the ESOP, or to the company if the company contributes an amount of stock equal to the principal portion of the loan to the ESOP);

c) A provision allowing an ESOP company to deduct dividends paid directly to ESOP participants; and

d) A provision allowing an ESOP or workers' cooperative to assume the estate tax liability of the estate of a business in return for a stock contribution from the estate worth at least as much as the tax liability.

STATE LAWS

General State Laws

Delaware and Maryland have passed laws declaring it the policy of the state to promote employee ownership, and for state agencies to issue reports on what they have done to comply. See the "Delaware Employee Ownership Act," 63–35, 1981 and the "Maryland Broadened Ownership Act," SB 131, 1979.

State Cooperative Statute Laws

Connecticut, Maine, and Massachusetts have each passed identical legislation establishing a state worker cooperative incorporation statute. The laws, modelled after the Massachusetts "Employee Cooperative Corporations Act," (chapter 104, Massachusetts General Laws, 1982), make it clear that companies can incorporate as worker cooperatives, use an internal account system similar to profit-sharing, be based on the membership of workers, follow one-member, one-vote rules, and use the word cooperative in their corporate name.

Laws Providing Financial and Technical Assistance Support

California, Illinois, Michigan, New Jersey, New York, and Pennsylvania have each passed laws providing loans and/or loan guarantees for worker buyout efforts, funds for technical assistance in buyout efforts, and programs for general outreach on employee ownership (not limited to buyouts).

California's law empowers the Department of Economic and Business Development to provide technical assistance and bond-backed financing for buyout efforts. Buyouts must result in companies that will be majority employee owned. Employees attempting a buyout can continue to receive unemployment insurance even though they are not actively seeking another job.

The Illinois law provides authority for the Department of Commerce to assist buyouts. Bond-backed financing can be used for low-interest loans with a limit of $250,000 or 25% of purchase price limit (whichever is lower). The company must have at least 60% of its voting stock owned by employees. The Department can also conduct outreach programs and provide technical assistance for buyout efforts.

Michigan has passed two laws in this area. The first, passed in 1979, provides the Department of Labor with authority to provide technical assistance for buyout efforts; the second, passed in 1981, provides the Michigan Economic Development Authority with authority to make bond-backed funding available for economic conversion projects, including employee buyouts. Loans generally cannot exceed $100,000,000 per deal, and must create or retain at least 100 jobs. Employees must end up with at least 60% of the voting stock.

"New Jersey's Employee Stock Ownership Plan Act" of 1984 provided the Department of Commerce with authority to assist employee buyouts through technical assistance and loans, loan guarantees, and direct interest subsidies. Requests must come through municipal governments, and employees must end up with 100% of the stock. No specific funds were appropriated for the program. The Department was also authorized to do research, hold conferences, and issue publications on employee ownership.

New York's "Employee Ownership Assistance Act" of 1983 provides the Department of Commerce with authority to promote the idea of employee ownership generally and to provide technical assistance for employee buyout efforts. The Job Development Authority can also issue bonds to provide loans for employee buyout efforts, with limits of 40% of project costs or $10,000,000, whichever is lower. Employees must end up with a majority of the voting stock.

Pennsylvania's "Employee Ownership Assistance Program," passed in 1984, is the most ambitious of these laws. $15 million is allocated over three years. $3 million is available for technical assistance for buyouts and $12 million for loans. The technical assistance portion is limited to 50% of the cost of a feasibility study, and is in the form of a loan. If the study is negative, the loan does not have to be repaid. Project loans are limited to 25% of project costs or $1.5 million, whichever is lower. At least two-thirds of the employees must make an equity investment worth 10% of the purchase price. Employees must end up with a majority of the company's voting stock.

Wisconsin's "Employee Ownership Act," passed in 1983, gives the Wisconsin Department of Development authority to provide technical assistance for employee buyouts and other employee ownership efforts and to conduct educational and research programs to help promote employee ownership. A "council on employee-owned businesses" was created as part of the act to oversee its implementation, and will consist of members from labor, business, government, academia, and the public. No specific funds were set aside for the program, and it does not disburse funds to support employee ownership efforts.

Other State Laws

Assembly Bill 2271 (untitled, 1982) in California amended state securities laws to exempt ESOPs from requirements which would have, in effect, made leveraged ESOPs almost impossible. Maryland HB 237 in 1979 also exempted ESOPs from state securities laws.

The New Hampshire Community Development Finance Authority Act of 1983 created a system of tax credits to fund a state economic development agency to assist community development corporations and worker-owned cooperatives. The program can provide both technical assistance and financing.

SB 659 (1983, untitled) provides that under West Virginia tax laws, contributions to repay a loan through an ESOP are fully deductible.

Notes

CHAPTER 1

1. Michael Conte and Arnold Tannenbaum, *Employee Ownership* (Ann Arbor: University of Michigan Survey Research Center, 1980), p. 3.
2. Thomas Marsh and Dale McAllister, "ESOPs Tables," *Journal of Corporation Law* 6, no. 3 (Spring 1981), pp. 613–617.
3. Corey Rosen and Katherine Klein, "Job-Creating Performance of Employee Owned Companies," *Monthly Labor Review* 106, no. 8 (August 1981), pp. 15–19.
4. Ira Wagner, "Report to the New York Stock Exchange on the Performance of Publicly Traded Companies with Employee Ownership Plans," unpublished paper (Arlington, VA: National Center for Employee Ownership, September 1984).
5. McKinsey and Company, *The Winning Performance of America's Mid-Sized Companies* (Washington, D.C.: McKinsey and Company, 1983), p. 20.
6. Robert Levering, Milton Moskowitz, and Michael Katz, *The 100 Best Companies in America to Work For* (Reading, MA: The Addison-Wesley Company, 1984).
7. Arnold Tannenbaum, Harold Cook, and Jack Lohmann, "Research Report: The Relationship of Employee Ownership to the Technological Adaptiveness and Performance of Companies," unpublished paper (Ann Arbor: University of Michigan Survey Research Center, 1984), pp. 1–2.
8. *Broadening the Ownership of New Capital: ESOPs and Other Alternatives*, A Staff Study Prepared for the use of the Joint Economic Committee of the U.S. Congress, June 17, 1976, p. 7.
9. Lester Thurow, "The Leverage of Our Wealthiest 400," *New York Times*, October 11, 1984, Op. Ed. page.
10. Statement of Senator Russell Long, U.S. Senate, *Congressional Record*, July 28, 1981.
11. Unpublished letter from Ronald Reagan to the *New Orleans Times Picayune*, October 1980.

CHAPTER 2

1. Richard Patard, "Employee Stock Ownership Plans in the 1920's," unpublished paper (Arlington, VA: National Center for Employee Ownership, 1982).
2. See for instance Louis Kelso, *The Capitalist Manifesto* (New York: Random House, 1958).
3. Marsh and McAllister, "ESOPs Tables," pp. 521–623.
4. Rosen and Klein, "Job-Creating Performance."
5. Levering, Moskowitz, and Katz, *The 100 Best Companies in America to Work For.*
6. Remarks of Ray Scannell, Third Annual Conference on Employee Ownership and Participation, American University, April 7, 1984.
7. Arthur Young and Co., "The Use of Incentive Stock Option Programs in Emerging or Fast Growth Companies," report to the National Venture Capital Association, February 1985 (unpublished).
8. *Employee Ownership,* v. 3, #4, Dec. 1984, p. 6.
9. Remarks of William Foote Whyte at annual meeting of the Industrial Relations Research Association, December 1984, Dallas, Texas.
10. "The Tax Magic That's Making Employee Stock Plans Multiply," *Business Week,* October 15, 1984, pp. 158–9.
11. Ibid.
12. Katrina Berman, "The Worker Owned Plywood Cooperatives," in Joyce Rothschild-Whitt and Frank Lindenfeld, eds., *Workplace Democracy and Social Change* (Boston: Porter-Sargent, 1982), pp. 161–166.
13. Mutual Aid Center, *Prospects for Workers' Cooperatives in Europe* (London: The Commission of the European Communities, December 1981).
14. Rosen and Klein, "Job-Creating Performance."
15. Marsh and McAllister, "ESOPs Tables."
16. Joseph Blasi and William Foote Whyte, "Employee Ownership and the Future of Unions," paper presented at the December 1984 conference of the Industrial Relations Research Association, Dallas, Texas.

CHAPTER 3

1. Marsh and McAllister, "ESOPs Tables," p. 596.
2. Ibid., p. 593.
3. Corey Rosen, "Employee Ownership in the Fortune 500," unpublished paper (Arlington, VA: National Center for Employee Ownership, 1981).
4. Marsh and McAllister, "ESOP's Tables," p. 586.
5. ESOP Association, *ESOP Survey, 1983* (Washington, D.C.: ESOP Association, 1983); Marsh and McAllister, "ESOPs Tables," p. 602; Rosen and Klein, "Job-Generating Performance."
6. ESOP Association, *ESOP Survey, 1983,* passim.

7. This is an estimate based on an analysis of the surveys mentioned above and case files maintained by the Center.

8. Tannenbaum, Cook, and Lohmann, "Research Report," p. 2.

9. Bruce Stokes, *Worker Participation, Productivity and the Quality of Working Life* (Washington, D.C.: Worldwatch Institute, 1978); Karl Frieden, *Workplace Democracy and Productivity* (Washington, D.C.: National Center for Economic Alternatives, 1980); Paul Blumberg, *Industrial Democracy: The Sociology of Participation* (New York: Shocken Books, 1968).

10. A good review of these criticisms can be found in Ivar Berg, *Managers and Work Reform* (New York: Free Press, 1978).

11. Remarks of Glen Watts at Second Annual Federal Mediation and Conciliation Service Conference on Labor/Management Cooperation, Washington, D.C., June 1984.

12. For a good review of these theories, see Derek Jones and Jan Svenjar, *Participatory and Self-Managed Firms* (Lexington, MA: Lexington Books, 1983).

13. Berman, "The Worker Owned Plywood Cooperatives."

14. Conte and Tannenbaum, *Employee Ownership*, p. 3.

15. Marsh and McAllister, "ESOPs Tables," pp. 612–616.

16. Ibid., p. 611.

17. Rosen and Klein, "Job-Creating Performance," pp. 15–19.

18. These results have been obtained as of this writing but have not yet been published.

19. Wagner, "Report to the New York Stock Exchange on the Performance of Publicly Held Employee Ownership Companies," pp. 6–7.

20. For a review, see Derek Jones and Jan Svenjar, "The Economic Performance of Participatory and Self-Managed Firms: A Historical Perspective and a Review," in Jones and Svenjar, eds., *Participatory and Self-Managed Firms.*

21. Tannenbaum et al., "Research Report," pp. 21–22.

22. See, for instance, William Foote Whyte, Tove Helland Hammer, Christopher Meek, et al., *Worker Participation and Ownership* (Ithaca, NY: ILR Press, 1983), pp. 118–120; Christopher Gunn, *Workers' Self-Management in the United States* (Ithaca, NY: Cornell University Press, 1984), pp. 34–54; Tove Hammer and Robert Stern, "Employee Ownership: Implications for the Organizational Distribution of Power," *Academy of Management Journal* 23 (March 1980), pp. 78–100; Richard Long, "Job Attitudes and Organizational Performance," *Academy of Management Journal* 23 (December 1980), pp. 726–737.

23. Raymond Russell, Art Hochner, and Stuart Perry, "Participation, Influence and Worker Ownership," *Industrial Relations* 18 (1979), pp. 330–340.

24. Edward Greenberg, "Participation in Industrial Decision-Making and Work Satisfaction: The Case of Producer Cooperatives," *Social Science Quarterly* 60, no. 4 (March 1980); Susan Rhodes and Richard Steers, "Conventional vs. Worker-Owned Organizations," *Human Relations* 34, no. 12 (1981), pp. 1013–1036.

25. Long, "Job Attitudes."
26. Hammer and Stern, "Employee Ownership."
27. Edward E. Lawler III and Lyman W. Porter, "Perceptions Regarding Management Compensation," *Industrial Relations* 3 (1963), pp. 41–49.
28. J. Richard Hackman and Edward E. Lawler III, "Employee Reactions to Job Characteristics," *Journal of Applied Psychology Monograph* 55 (1971), pp. 259–286; J. Richard Hackman and Gregory R. Oldham, "Motivation Through the Design of Work: Test of a Theory," *Organizational Behavior and Human Performance* 16 (1976), pp. 250–279.
29. S. Kerr and C.A. Schriesheim, "Consideration, Initiating Structure, and Organizational Criteria—An Update of Korman's 1966 Review," *Personnel Psychology* 27 (1974), pp. 555–568; G.A. Yukl, "Toward a Behavioral Theory of Leadership," *Organizational Behavior and Human Performance* 6 (1972), pp. 119–130.
30. V.H. Vroom and P.W. Yetton, *Leadership and Decision-Making* (Pittsburgh, PA: University of Pittsburgh Press, 1973).
31. Albert Cherns, "Can Behavioral Science Help Design Organizations?" *Organizational Dynamics* (Spring 1977), pp. 44–64.

CHAPTER 4

1. Conte and Tannenbaum, *Employee Ownership*; Richard J. Long, "The Relative Effects of Share Ownership vs. Control on Job Attitudes in an Employee-Owned Company," *Human Relations* 31 (1978), pp. 753–763; Long, "Job Attitudes"; Hammer and Stern, "Employee Ownership."
2. This measure was adapted from J.E. Kwoka, Jr., "The Conception of Work: A Conceptual Framework," *Social Science Quarterly* 57 (1976), pp. 632–643.
3. Tannenbaum, Cook, and Lohmann, "Research Report."
4. R.T. Mowday, R.M. Steers, and Lyman W. Porter, "The Measurement of Organizational Commitment," *Journal of Vocational Behavior* 14 (1979), pp. 224–247.
5. Cortland Cammann, M. Fichman, G. Douglas Jenkins, Jr., and J.R. Klesh, "Assessing the Attitudes and Perceptions of Organizational Members," in Stanley Seashore, ed., *Assessing Organizational Change* (New York: John Wiley and Sons, 1983).
6. Ibid.
7. Kwoka, "The Conception of Work."
8. William Glick, "Problems in Cross-Level Inferences," in Karlene H. Roberts and L. Burnstein, eds., *Issues in Aggregation* (San Francisco: Jossey-Bass, 1980); G. Keppel, *Design and Analysis, A Researcher's Handbook, 2nd Edition* (New Jersey: Prentice Hall, 1982); Denise M. Rousseau, "Issues of Level in Organizational Research: Multi-Level and Cross-Level Perspectives," in L.L. Cummings and Barry Staw, *Research in Organizational Behavior, Volume 7* (Greenwich, CT: JAI Press, 1984).

9. William H. Glick and Karlene H. Roberts, "Hypothesized Interdependence, Assumed Interdependence," *Academy of Management Review* 9, no. 4 (1984), p. 724.

CHAPTER 6

1. At the individual level of analysis, the correlation of Employee-Perceived Influence and ESOP Satisfaction is .37; Employee-Perceived Influence and Organizational Commitment is .41; Employee-Perceived Influence and Job Satisfaction is .34; and Employee-Perceived Influence and Turnover Intention is − .26. All of these are significant at the .0001 level.

2. We chose to use Management-Perceived Worker Influence instead of Employee-Perceived Worker Influence in these analyses for several reasons. First, the strong relationship of the outcome variables and Employee-Perceived Worker Influence is, in part, a reflection of common method variance. That is, these scales were measured with fairly similarly worded items, on the same survey, and were completed by the same employee.

   Second, the strong relationship of the outcome variables and Employee-Perceived Worker Influence is also, in part, a reflection of the fact that a person's attitudes tend to coincide or "hang together." For example, if a person feels very satisfied with his or her work, isn't he or she likely to say that he or she has sufficient influence in company decision-making? Conversely, if a person is very unsatisfied, he or she obviously lacks sufficient power and influence to change his or her situation.

   Third, to be consistent with our basic analyses, we would need to analyze the relationship of Employee-Perceived Worker Influence and the outcome variables at the company level. Thus, we would be correlating mean scores. However, the correlation of mean scores may be a very poor representation of the actual correlation of the individual-level data. Further, the correlation of the mean scores is unpredictable; it may overestimate, underestimate, or fairly represent the individual-level data. There is no set pattern. This problem is called the ecological fallacy. We mentioned it briefly in chapter 4. Two examples from our data may be helpful: At the company level of analysis, the correlation of Employee-Perceived Worker Influence and ESOP Satisfaction is .49 (adjusted R^2 = .22). At the individual level of analysis, the correlation is .37 (adjusted R^2 = .14). The correlation of Employee-Perceived Worker Influence and Turnover Intention, at the company level of analysis, is − .26 (adjusted R^2 = .04). At the individual level of analysis, the correlation is − .33 (adjusted R^2 = .11). (For additional details, see the footnote above.)

   For all these reasons, Management-Perceived Worker Influence is a more appropriate measure of Worker Influence. While we know from table 6–7 that Management-Perceived Worker Influence and Employee-Perceived Worker Influence are very strongly related, Mangement-Perceived Worker Influence is—in this case—the more objective measure. The relationship of Management-Perceived Worker Influence and the employee outcomes cannot possibly be due to within-individual perceptual biases or to ecological fallacy effects.

CHAPTER 7

1. Telephone interview between John Simmons and Rich Biernacki, June 1981.
2. Ibid.
3. "When the Workers Own the Factory," *New Jersey Monthly,* August 1982, p. 35.
4. James May, *Unions and Employee Ownership: A Symposium* (Washington, D.C.: The National Center for Employee Ownership, 1982), p. 29.
5. Ibid.
6. Ibid.
7. "Revival at Dying GM Factory," *The New York Times,* October 26, 1981.
8. "UAW rank-file vote buyout of Clark plant," *The Star-Ledger,* October 30, 1981, p. 1.
9. "Buyout Hyatt Clark Ind., Inc." Harvard Business School case study (unpublished paper), 1983, pp. 8 and 12.
10. *New Jersey Monthly,* August 1982, p. 36.
11. "Hyatt after 2 years of employee ownership," *The Daily Journal,* October 31, 1983, p. 1.
12. "A Modern ESOP's Fables," *Newsweek,* December 31, 1984.
13. "General Motors retracts threat to buy roller bearings elsewhere," *The Star Ledger,* December 18, 1984.
14. "Profit-Sharing: Lowe's Largesse," *Newsweek,* March 31, 1975.
15. "The Money Tree," *San Francisco Chronicle,* July 15, 1983.
16. Remarks of Robert L. Strickland at the annual conference of The ESOP Association, Washington, D.C., 1984.
17. "Lowe's is Shooting for a Bigger League," *Building Supply News,* January 1983.
18. The Lowe's Companies Profit-Sharing Annual Report, 1972.
19. Remarks of Robert L. Strickland at the Second Annual ESOP Symposium, Georgetown University Law Center, Washington, D.C., September 25, 1980.
20. "Buchan's million dollar prophesy comes true," *National Home Center News,* December 17, 1984.
21. "Will Success Spoil Jerry Gorde?," *Inc. Magazine,* February 1984.
22. Ibid.
23. Ibid.
24. Ibid.
25. Ibid.
26. Ibid.
27. "Management by Walking Away," *Inc. Magazine,* October 1983.
28. Quad/Graphics Annual Report, 1983.
29. "Management by Walking Away."
30. Quad/Graphics fact sheet, 1984.

31. "Management by Walking Away."
32. "Family History Repeats Itself," *The Graphic Arts Monthly,* September 1977.
33. "Management by Walking Away."
34. Quad/Graphics fact sheet, 1984.
35. "Management by Walking Away."
36. Ibid.
37. Ibid.
38. *Quad News,* October 1984.
39. Ibid.
40. "Management by Walking Away."
41. *Quad News*, October 1984.
42. Any uncited material was obtained directly through the research project.

CHAPTER 8

1. Peter Barnes, "Reflections of a Socialist Entrepreneur," unpublished paper, 1983.
2. Ibid.
3. Ibid.
4. Ibid.
5. Ibid.
6. Any uncited material was obtained directly through the research project.

CHAPTER 9

1. This term is borrowed from William Foote Whyte, who used it first.
2. Sar Levitan and Clifford Johnson, *Second Thoughts on Work* (Kalamazoo, MI: W.E. Upjohn Institute, 1982), pp. 55–6.
3. Albert Gallatin, for instance, said that "the democratic principle upon which this nation was founded should not be restricted to the political process but should be applied to the industrial operations as well." Quoted in Ronald Mason, *Participatory and Workplace Democracy* (Carbondale: So. Illinois University Press, 1982), p. 149.
4. Mason makes this point in *Participatory and Workplace Democracy.*
5. Thomas Peters and Robert Waterman, *In Search of Excellence* (New York: Warner Books, 1983).
6. This view has been best developed by David Ellerman of the Industrial Cooperative Association in his pamphlet "What is a Workers' Cooperative?" (Somerville, MA: ICA, 1981).
7. See, for instance, Keith Bradley and Alan Gelb, *Worker Capitalism: The New Industrial Relations* (Cambridge, MA: MIT Press, 1984).

Index

About the Authors

Corey Rosen is the executive director and co-founder of the National Center for Employee Ownership, a private non-profit membership, research, and information organization located in Arlington, Virginia. He received his B.A. from Wesleyan University and his Ph.D. in politics from Cornell. He taught politics at Ripon College and worked as a professional staff member in the U.S. Senate before co-founding the Center in 1981. He has written over 40 articles on employee ownership and lectures widely on the subject.

Katherine J. Klein is assistant professor of industrial and organizational psychology in the Department of Psychology at the University of Maryland at College Park. She received her B.A. from Yale University in 1978 and her Ph.D. from the University of Texas at Austin in 1984. From March 1982 through March 1985, she served as research coordinator for the National Center for Employee Ownership. She has continuing research interests in employee ownership, worker participation, labor-management relations, and computerized manufacturing automation. In addition, she is interested in the impact of work on workers' self-concept and psychological well-being.

Karen Young helped co-found the National Center for Employee Ownership in 1981. She is managing director and editor of the bimonthly newsletter. Prior to that she served on the staff of the U.S. Senate Small Business Committee. She has also worked as a researcher on the Law of the Sea Project at the University of Rochester's Research Center. She has served as president of the Virginia Citizen's

Consumer Council where she helped organize the proclamation of Consumer Awareness Day by the governor and its passage by the General Assembly in Virginia. She holds a B.A. in English from George Mason University in Virginia and an M.A. in organizational behavior from George Washington University, Washington, D.C.